I0114702

V.I. Lenin

FIGHT AGAINST STALINISM
&
IMPERIALISM: THE HIGHEST STAGE OF CAPITALISM

FIGHT AGAINST STALINISM
&
IMPERIALISM: THE HIGHEST STAGE OF CAPITALISM

V.I. Lenin

Reprinted by Frederick Ellis
8000 E. Girard, Suite 507
Denver CO 80231
ISBN 978-0-9793363-7-9

FIGHT AGAINST STALINISM

Contents

On Lenin's Testament

Lenin's Testament

The Bureaucracy

The Monopoly of Foreign Trade

The Nationalities Question

ON LENIN'S TESTAMENT

On Lenin's Testament
By Leon Trotsky

The postwar epoch has brought into wide currency the psychological biography, the masters of which art often pull their subject up out of society by the roots. The fundamental driving force of history is presented as the abstraction, personality. The behavior of the "political animal," as Aristotle brilliantly defined mankind, is resolved into personal passions and instincts.

The statement that personality is abstract may seem absurd. Are not the superpersonal forces of history really the abstract things? And what can be more concrete than a living man? However, we insist upon our statement. If you remove from a personality, even the most richly endowed, the content which is introduced into it by the milieu, the nation, the epoch, the class, the group, the family, there remains an empty automaton, a psycho-physical robot, an object of natural, but not of social or "humane," science.

The causes of this abandonment of history and society must, as always, be sought in history and society. Two decades of wars, revolutions, and crises have given a bad shake-up to that sovereign, human personality. To have weight in the scales of contemporary history, a thing must be measured in millions. For this, the offended personality seeks revenge. Unable to cope with society on the rampage, it turns its back upon society. Unable to explain itself by means of historic processes, it tries to explain history from within itself. Thus the Indian philosophers built universal systems by contemplating their own navels.

The school of pure psychology

The influence of Freud upon the new biographical school is undeniable, but superficial. In essence these parlor psychologists are inclining to a belletristic irresponsibility. They employ not so much the method as the terminology of Freud, and not so much for analysis as for literary adornment.

In his recent work Emil Ludwig, the most popular representative of this genre, has taken a new step along the chosen path: he has replaced the study of the hero's life and activity with dialogue. Behind the answers of the statesman to questions put to him, behind his intonations and grimaces, the writer discovers his real motives. Conversation becomes almost a confession. In its technique Ludwig's new approach to the hero suggests Freud's approach to his patient: it is a matter of bringing the personality to the surface with its own cooperation. But with all this external similarity, how different it is in essence! The fruitfulness of Freud's work is attained at the price of a heroic break with all kinds of conventions. The great psychoanalyst is ruthless. At work he is like a surgeon, almost like a butcher with rolled-up sleeves. Anything you want, but there is not one hundredth of one percent of diplomacy in his technique. Freud bothers least of all about the prestige of his patient, or about considerations of good form, or any other kind of false note or frill. And it is for this reason that he can carry on his dialogue only face-to-face, without secretary or stenographer, behind padded doors.

Not so Ludwig. He enters into a conversation with Mussolini, or with Stalin, in order to present the world with an authentic portrait of their souls. Yet the whole conversation follows a program previously agreed upon. Every word is taken down by a stenographer. The eminent patient knows quite well what can be useful to him in this process and what harmful. The writer is sufficiently experienced to distinguish rhetorical tricks and sufficiently polite not to notice them. The dialogue developing under these circumstances, if it does indeed resemble a confession, resembles one put on for the talking pictures.

Emil Ludwig has every reason to declare: "I understand nothing of politics." This is supposed to mean: "I stand above politics." In reality it is a mere formula of personal neutrality—or to borrow from Freud, it is that "mental censor" which makes easier for the psychologist his political function. In the same way diplomats do not interfere with the inner life of the country to whose government they are accredited, but this does not prevent them on occasion from supporting plots and financing acts of terrorism.

One and the same person in different conditions develops different sides of his personality. How many Aristotles are herding swine, and how many swineherds wear a crown on their heads! But Ludwig can lightly resolve even the contradiction between

Bolshevism and fascism into a mere matter of individual psychology. Even the most penetrating psychologist could not with impunity adopt such a tendentious "neutrality." Casting loose from the social conditioning of human consciousness, Ludwig enters into a realm of mere subjective caprice. The "soul" has not three dimensions, and it therefore lacks the refractory quality common to all other substances. The writer loses his taste for the study of facts and documents. What is the use of this colorless evidence when it can be replaced with bright guesses?

In his work on Stalin, as in his book about Mussolini, Ludwig remains "outside politics." This does not in the least prevent his works from becoming a political weapon. Whose weapon? In the one case Mussolini's, in the other that of Stalin and his group. Nature abhors a vacuum. If Ludwig does not occupy himself with politics, this is not saying that politics does not occupy itself with Ludwig.

Upon the publication of my autobiography some three years ago, the official Soviet historian Pokrovsky, now dead, wrote: "We must answer this book immediately, put our young scholars to work refuting all that can be refuted, etc." But it is a striking fact that no one, absolutely no one, responded. Nothing was analyzed, nothing was refuted. There was nothing to refute, and nobody could be found capable of writing a book which would find readers.

A frontal attack proving impossible, it became necessary to resort to a flanking movement. Ludwig, of course, is not a historian of the Stalin school. He is an independent psychological portraitist. But a writer foreign to all politics may prove the most convenient means for putting into circulation ideas which can find no other support but a popular name. Let us see how this works out in actual fact.

"Six words"

Citing the testimony of Karl Radek, Emil Ludwig borrows from him the following episode:

> After the death of Lenin we sat together, nineteen members of the Central Committee, tensely waiting to learn what our lost leader would say to us from his grave. Lenin's widow gave us his letter. Stalin read it. No one stirred during the reading. When it came to Trotsky the words occurred: "His non-Bolshevik past is not accidental." At that point Trotsky interrupted the reading and asked:

"What does it say there?" The sentence was repeated. Those were the only words spoken in that solemn moment.

And then in the character of analyst, and not narrator, Ludwig makes the following remark on his own account: "A terrible moment, when Trotsky's heart must have stopped beating; this phrase of six words essentially determined the course of his life." How simple it seems to find a key to the riddles of history! These unctuous lines of Ludwig would doubtless have uncovered to me myself the very secret of my destiny if . . . if this Radek-Ludwig story did not happen to be false from beginning to end, false in small things and great, in what matters and in what matters not.

To begin with, the testament was written by Lenin not two years before his death as our author affirms, but one year. It was dated January 4, 1923; Lenin died on January 21, 1924. His political life had broken off completely in March 1923. Ludwig speaks as though the testament had never been published in full. As a matter of fact it has been reproduced dozens of times in all languages of the world press. The first official reading of the testament in the Kremlin occurred, not at a session of the Central Committee, as Ludwig writes, but in the Council of Elders at the Thirteenth Congress of the party on May 22, 1924. It was not Stalin who read the testament, but Kamenev in his then position as permanent president of the central party bodies. And finally—most important—I did not interrupt the reading with an emotional exclamation because of the absence of any motive whatever for such an act. Those words which Ludwig wrote down at the dictation of Radek are not in the text of the testament. They are an outright invention. Difficult as it may be to believe, this is the fact.

If Ludwig were not so careless about the factual basis of his psychological patterns, he might without difficulty have got possession of an exact text of the testament, established the necessary facts and dates, and thus avoided those wretched mistakes with which his work about the Kremlin and the Bolsheviks is unfortunately brimful.

The so-called testament was written at two periods, separated by an interval of ten days: December 25, 1922, and January 4, 1923. At first only two persons knew of the document: the stenographer, M. Volodicheva, who wrote it from dictation, and Lenin's wife, N. Krupskaya.[1] As long as there remained a glimmer of hope for Lenin's recovery, Krupskaya left the document under lock and key. After Lenin's death, not long before the Thirteenth Congress, she handed the testament to the Secretariat of the Central Committee in order that through the party congress it should be brought to the attention of the party for whom it was destined.

At that time the party apparatus was semiofficially in the hands of the troika (Zinoviev, Kamenev, Stalin)—as a matter of fact, already in the hands of Stalin. The troika decisively expressed themselves against reading the testament at the congress—the motive not at all difficult to understand. Krupskaya insisted upon her wish. At this stage the dispute was going on behind the scenes. The question was transferred to a meeting of the Elders at the Congress—that is, the leaders of the provincial delegations. It was here that the oppositional members of the Central Committee first learned about the testament, I among them. After a decision had been adopted that nobody should make notes, Kamenev began to read the text aloud. The mood of the listeners was indeed tense in the highest degree. But so far as I can restore the picture from memory, I should say that those who already knew the contents of the document were incomparably the most anxious. The troika introduced, through one of its henchmen, a resolution previously agreed upon with the provincial leaders: the document should be read to each delegation separately in executive session; no one should dare to make notes; at the plenary session the testament must not be referred to. With the gentle insistence characteristic of her, Krupskaya argued that this was a direct violation of the will of Lenin, to whom you could not deny the right to bring his last advice to the attention of the party. But the members of the Council of Elders, bound by factional discipline, remained obdurate; the resolution of the troika was adopted by an overwhelming majority.

In order to grasp the significance of those mystical and mythical "six words" which are supposed to have decided my fate, it is necessary to recall certain preceding and accompanying circumstances. Already in the period of sharp disputes on the subject of the October Revolution, certain "Old Bolsheviks" from the right wing had more than once pointed out with vexation that Trotsky after all had not formerly been a Bolshevik. Lenin always stood up against these voices. Trotsky long ago understood that a union with the Mensheviks was impossible, he said, for example, on November 14, 1917—"and since then there has been no better Bolshevik."[2] On Lenin's lips those words meant something.

Two years later, while explaining in a letter to the foreign Communists the conditions under which Bolshevism had developed, how there had been disagreements and splits, Lenin pointed out that "at the decisive moment, at the moment when it seized the power and created the Soviet Republic, Bolshevism was united *and drew to itself all the best elements in the currents of socialist thought that were nearest to it.*"[3] No current closer to Bolshevism than that which I represented up to 1917 existed either in Russia or in the West. My union with Lenin had been predetermined by the logic of ideas and the logic of events. At the decisive moment Bolshevism drew into its ranks "all the best elements" in the tendencies "that were nearest to it." Such was Lenin's appraisal of the situation. I have no reason to dispute him.

At the time of our two months' argument on the trade union question (winter of 1920-21), Stalin and Zinoviev had again attempted to put into circulation references to the non-Bolshevik past of Trotsky. In answer to this, the less restrained leaders of the opposite camp had reminded Zinoviev of his conduct during the period of the October insurrection. Thinking over from all sides on his deathbed how relations would crystallize in the party without him, Lenin could not but foresee that Stalin and Zinoviev would try to use my non-Bolshevik past in order to mobilize the Old Bolsheviks against me. The testament tries, incidentally, to forestall this danger, too. Here is what it says immediately after its characterization of Stalin and Trotsky: "I will not further characterize the other members of the Central Committee as to their personal qualities. I will only remind you that the October episode of Zinoviev and Kamenev was not, of course, accidental, but that it ought as little to be used against them personally as the non-Bolshevism of Trotsky."

This remark that the October episode "was not accidental" pursues a perfectly definite goal: to warn the party that in critical circumstances Zinoviev and Kamenev may again reveal their lack of firmness. This warning stands, however, in no relation with the remark about Trotsky. In regard to him it is merely recommended not to use his non-Bolshevik past as an argument *ad hominem.* I therefore had no motive for putting the question which Radek attributes to me. Ludwig's guess that my heart "stopped beating" also falls to the ground. Least of all did the testament set out to make a guiding role in the party work difficult for me. As we shall see below, it pursued an exactly opposite aim.

"The mutual relations of Stalin and Trotsky"

The central position in the testament, which fills two typewritten pages, is devoted to a characterization of the mutual relations of Stalin and Trotsky, "the two most able leaders of the present Central Committee." Having remarked upon the "exceptional abilities" of Trotsky ("the most able man in the present Central Committee"), Lenin immediately points out his adverse traits: "far-reaching self-confidence" and "a disposition to be too much attracted by the purely administrative side of affairs." However serious the faults indicated may be in themselves, they do not—I remark in passing—bear any relation to "underestimating the peasants" or "lacking faith in the inner forces of the revolution" or any other of the inventions of the epigones in recent years.

On the other side Lenin writes: "Stalin, having become general secretary, has concentrated an enormous power in his hands; and I am not sure that he always knows how to use this power with sufficient caution."

It is not a question here of the political influence of Stalin, which at that period was insignificant, but of the administrative power which he had concentrated in his hands, "having become general secretary." This is a very exact and carefully weighed formula; we shall return to it later.

The testament insists upon an increase of the number of members of the Central Committee to fifty, even to one hundred, in order that with this compact pressure it may restrain the centrifugal tendencies in the Political Bureau. This organizational proposal has still the appearance of a neutral guarantee against personal conflicts. But only ten days later it seemed to Lenin inadequate, and he added a supplementary proposal which also gave to the whole document its final physiognomy: ". . . I propose to the comrades to find a way to remove Stalin from that position and appoint to it another man who in all other respects[4] differs from Stalin only in superiority—namely, more patient, more loyal, more polite and more attentive to comrades, less capricious, etc."

During the days when the testament was dictated, Lenin was still trying to give to his critical appraisal of Stalin as restrained an expression as possible. In the coming weeks his tone would become sharper and sharper right up to the last hour when his voice ceased forever. But even in the testament, enough is said to motivate the demand for a change of general secretary: along with rudeness and capriciousness, Stalin is accused of *lack of loyalty*. At this point the characterization becomes a heavy indictment.

As will appear later, the testament could not have been a surprise to Stalin. But this did not soften the blow. Upon his first acquaintance with the document, in the Secretariat, in the circle of his closest associates, Stalin let fly a phrase which gave quite unconcealed expression to his real feelings toward the author of the testament. The conditions under which this phrase spread to wide circles, and above all the inimitable quality of the reaction itself, is in my eyes an unqualified guarantee of the authenticity of the episode. Unfortunately this winged phrase cannot be quoted in print.

The concluding sentence of the testament shows unequivocally on which side, in Lenin's opinion, the danger lay. To remove Stalin—just him and him only—meant to cut him off from the apparatus, to withdraw from him the possibility of pressing on the long arm of the lever, to deprive him of all that power which he had concentrated in his hands in this office. Who, then, should be named general secretary? Someone who, having the positive qualities of Stalin, should be more patient, more loyal, less capricious. This was the phrase which struck home most sharply to Stalin. Lenin obviously did not consider him irreplaceable since he proposed that we seek a more suitable person for his post. In tendering his resignation, as a matter of form, the general secretary capriciously kept repeating: "Well, I really am rude. . . . Ilyich suggested that you find another who would differ from me *only* in greater politeness. Well, try to find him." "Never mind," answered the voice of one of Stalin's then friends. "We are not afraid of rudeness. Our whole party is rude, proletarian." A drawing-room conception of politeness is here indirectly attributed to Lenin. As to the accusation of inadequate loyalty, neither Stalin nor his friends had a word to say. It is perhaps not without interest that the supporting voice came from A.P. Smirnov, then people's commissar of agriculture, but now under the ban as a Right Oppositionist. Politics knows no gratitude.

Radek, who was then still a member of the Central Committee, sat beside me during the reading of the testament. Yielding with abandon to the influence of the moment and lacking inner discipline, Radek took instant fire from the testament and leaned to me with the words, "Now they won't dare go against you." I answered him, "On the contrary, they will have to go the limit, and moreover as quickly as possible." The very next days of that Thirteenth Congress demonstrated that my judgment was the more sober. The troika were compelled to forestall the possible effect of the testament by placing the party as soon as possible before a fait accompli. The very reading of the document to the local delegations with "outsiders" not admitted, was converted into a downright struggle against me. The leaders of the delegations in their reading would swallow some words, emphasize others, and offer commentaries to the effect that the letter had been written by a man seriously ill and under the influence of trickery and intrigue. The machine was already in complete control. The mere fact that the troika was able to transgress the will of Lenin, refusing to read his letter at the congress, sufficiently characterizes the composition of the congress and its atmosphere. The testament did not weaken or put a stop to the inner struggle, but on the contrary lent it a disastrous tempo.

Lenin's attitude toward Stalin

Politics is persistent. It can press into its service even those who demonstratively turn their backs to it. Ludwig writes: "Stalin followed Lenin fervently up to his death." If this phrase expressed merely the mighty influence of Lenin upon his pupils, including Stalin, there could be no argument. But Ludwig means something more. He wants to suggest an exceptional closeness to the teacher of this particular pupil. As an especially precious testimony Ludwig cites upon this point the words of Stalin himself: "I am only a pupil of Lenin, and my aim is to be his worthy pupil." It is too bad when a professional psychologist operates uncritically with a trite phrase, the conventional modesty of which contains not one atom of intimate content. Ludwig becomes here a mere transmitter of the official legend manufactured during these recent years. I doubt if he has the remotest idea of the contradictions into which his indifference to facts has brought him. If Stalin actually was following Lenin up to his death, how then explain the fact that the last document dictated by Lenin, on the eve of his second stroke, was a curt letter to Stalin, a few lines in all, *breaking off all personal and comradely relations?* This single event of its kind in the life of Lenin, a sharp break with one of his close associates, must have had very serious psychological causes, and would be, to say the least, incomprehensible in relation to a pupil who "fervently" followed his teacher up to the end. Yet we hear not a word about this from Ludwig.

When Lenin's letter breaking with Stalin became widely known among the leaders of the party, the troika having by that time fallen to pieces, Stalin and his close friends found no other way out but to revive that same old story about the incompetent condition of Lenin. As a matter of fact the testament, as also the letter breaking off relations, was written in those months (December 1922 to the beginning of March 1923) during which Lenin in a series of programmatic articles gave the party the most mature fruits of his thinking. That break with Stalin did not drop out of a clear sky. It flowed from a long series of preceding conflicts upon matters of principle and upon practical matters alike, and it sets forth the whole bitterness of these conflicts in a tragic light.

Lenin undoubtedly valued highly certain of Stalin's traits: his firmness of character, tenacity, stubbornness, even ruthlessness, and craftiness—qualities necessary in a war and consequently in its general staff. But Lenin was far from thinking that these gifts, even on an extraordinary scale, were sufficient for the leadership of the party and the state. Lenin saw in Stalin a revolutionist, but not a statesman in the grand style. Theory had too high an importance for Lenin in a political struggle. Nobody considered Stalin a theoretician, and he himself up to 1924 never made any pretense to this vocation. On the contrary, his weak theoretical grounding was too well known in a small circle. Stalin is not acquainted with the West; he does not know any foreign language. He was never brought into the discussion of problems of the international workers' movement. And finally Stalin was not—this is less important, but not without significance—either a writer or an orator in the strict sense of the word. His articles, in spite of all the author's caution, are loaded not only with theoretical blunders and naivetes, but also with crude sins against the Russian language. In the eyes of Lenin, Stalin's value was wholly in the sphere of party administration and machine maneuvering. But even here Lenin made substantial reservations, and these increased during the last period.

Lenin despised idealistic moralizings. But this did not prevent him from being a rigorist of revolutionary morals—of those rules of conduct, that is, which he considered necessary for the success of the revolution and the creation of the new society. In Lenin's rigorism, which flowed freely and naturally from his character, there was not a drop of pedantry or bigotry or stiffness. He knew people too well and took them as they were. He would combine the faults of some with the virtues of others, and sometimes also with their faults, and never cease to watch keenly what came of it. He knew also that times change, and we with them. The party had risen with one jump from the underground to the height of power. This created for each of the old revolutionists a startlingly sharp change in personal situation and in relations with others. What Lenin discovered in Stalin under these new conditions he cautiously but clearly remarked in his testament: a lack of loyalty and an inclination to the abuse of power. Ludwig missed these hints. It is in them, however, that one can find the key to the relations between Lenin and Stalin in the last period.

Lenin was not only a theoretician and technician of the revolutionary dictatorship, but also a vigilant guardian of its moral foundations. Every hint at the use of power for personal interests kindled threatening fires in his eyes. "How is that any better than bourgeois parliamentarism?" he would ask to express more effectively his choking indignation. And he would not infrequently add on the subject of parliamentarism one of his rich definitions. Stalin meanwhile was more and more broadly and indiscriminately using the possibilities of the revolutionary dictatorship for the recruiting of people personally obligated and devoted to him. In his position as general secretary he became the dispenser of favor and fortune. Here the foundation was laid for an inevitable conflict. *Lenin gradually lost his moral trust in Stalin.* If you understand that basic fact, then all the particular episodes of the last period take their places accordingly, and give a real and not a false picture of the attitude of Lenin to Stalin.

Sverdlov and Stalin as types of organizers

In order to accord the testament its proper place in the development of the party, it is here necessary to make a digression. Up to the spring of 1919 the chief organizer of the party had been Sverdlov. He did not have the name of general secretary, a name which was then not yet invented, but he was that in reality. Sverdlov died at the age of 34 in March 1919 from the so-called Spanish fever. In the spread of the civil war and the epidemic, mowing people down right and left, the party hardly realized the weight of this loss. In two funeral speeches Lenin gave an appraisal of Sverdlov which throws a reflected but very clear light also upon his later relations with Stalin. "In the course of our revolution, in its victories," Lenin said, "it fell to Sverdlov to express more fully and more wholly than anybody else the very essence of the proletarian revolution." Sverdlov was "before all and above all an organizer." From a modest underground worker, neither theoretician nor writer, there grew up in a short time "an organizer who acquired irreproachable authority, an organizer of the whole Soviet power in Russia, and an organizer of the work of the party unique in his understanding." Lenin had no taste for the exaggerations of anniversary or funeral panegyrics. His appraisal of Sverdlov was at the same time a characterization of the task of the organizer: "Only thanks to the fact that we had such an organizer as Sverdlov were we able in war times to work as though we had *not one single conflict worth speaking of.*"

So it was in fact. In conversations with Lenin in those days we remarked more than once, and with ever renewed satisfaction, one of the chief conditions of our success: the unity and solidarity of the governing group. In spite of the dreadful pressure of events and difficulties, the novelty of the problems, and sharp practical disagreements occasionally bursting out, the work proceeded with extraordinary smoothness and friendliness, and without interruptions. With a brief word we would recall episodes of the old revolutions. "No, it is better with us." "This alone guarantees our victory." The solidarity of the center had been prepared by the whole history of Bolshevism and was kept up by the unquestioned authority of the leaders—and above all of Lenin. But in the inner mechanics of this unexampled unanimity the chief technician had been Sverdlov. The secret of his art was simple: to be guided by the interests of the cause and that only. No one of the party workers had any fear of intrigues creeping down from the party staff. The basis of this authority of Sverdlov was *loyalty.*

Having tested out mentally all the party leaders, Lenin in his funeral speech drew the practical conclusion: "Such a man we can never replace, if by replacement we mean the possibility of finding one comrade combining such qualities. . . . The work which he did alone can now be accomplished only by a whole group of men who, following in his footsteps, will carry on his service."[5] These words were not rhetorical, but a strictly practical proposal. And the proposal was carried out. Instead of a single secretary, there was appointed a collegium of three persons.

From these words of Lenin it is evident, even to those unacquainted with the history of the party, that during the life of Sverdlov, Stalin played no leading role in the party machinery—either at the time of the October Revolution or in the period of laying the foundations and walls of the Soviet state. Stalin was also not included in the first secretariat which replaced Sverdlov.

When at the Tenth Congress, two years after the death of Sverdlov, Zinoviev and others, not without a hidden thought of the struggle against me, supported the candidacy of Stalin for general secretary—that is, placed him de jure in the position which Sverdlov had occupied de facto—Lenin spoke in a small circle against this plan, expressing his fear that "this cook will prepare only peppery dishes." That phrase alone, taken in connection with the character of Sverdlov, shows us the differences between the two types of organizers: the one tireless in smoothing over conflicts, easing the work of the collegium, and the other a specialist in peppery dishes—not even afraid to spice them with actual poison. If Lenin did not in March 1921 carry his opposition to the limit—that is, did not appeal openly to the congress against the candidacy of Stalin—it was because the post of secretary, even though "general," had in the conditions then prevailing, with the power and influence concentrated in the Political Bureau, a strictly subordinate significance. Perhaps also Lenin, like many others, did not adequately realize the danger in time.

Toward the end of 1921, Lenin's health broke sharply. On December 7, in taking his departure upon the insistence of his physician, Lenin, little given to complaining, wrote to the members of the Political Bureau: "I am leaving today. In spite of my reduced quota of work and increased quota of rest, these last days the insomnia has increased devilishly. I am afraid I cannot speak either at the party congress or the Soviet congress."[6]

For five months he languishes, half removed by doctors and friends from his work, in continual alarm over the course of governmental and party affairs, in continual struggle with his lingering disease. In May he has the first stroke. For two months Lenin is unable to speak or write or move. In July he begins slowly to recover. Remaining in the country, he enters by degrees into active correspondence. In October he returns to the Kremlin and officially takes up his work.

"There is no evil without good," he writes privately in the draft of a future speech. "I have been sitting quiet for a half year and looking on 'from the sidelines.' "[7] Lenin means to say: I formerly sat too steadily at my post and failed to observe many things; the long interruption has now permitted me to see much with fresh eyes. What disturbed him most, unquestionably, was the monstrous growth of bureaucratic power, the focal point of which had become the Organization Bureau of the Central Committee.

The necessity of removing the boss who was specializing in peppery dishes became clear to Lenin immediately after his return to work. But this personnel question had become notably complicated. Lenin could not fail to see how extensively his absence had been made use of by Stalin for a one-sided selection of men—often in direct conflict with the interests of the cause. The general secretary was now relying upon a numerous faction, bound together by ties which, if not always intellectual, were at least firm. A change of the heads of the party machine had already become impossible without the preparation of a serious political attack. At this time occurred the "conspiratorial" conversation between Lenin and me in regard to a combined struggle against Soviet and party bureaucratism, and his proposal of a "bloc" against the Organization Bureau—the fundamental stronghold of Stalin at that time. The fact of this conversation as well as its content soon found their reflection in documents, and they constitute an episode of the party history undeniable and not denied by anyone.

However, in only a few weeks there came a new decline in Lenin's health. Not only continual work, but also executive conversations with the comrades were again forbidden by his physicians. He had to think out further measures of struggle alone within four walls. To control the backstage activities of the secretariat, Lenin worked out some general measures of an organizational character. Thus arose the plan of creating a highly authoritative party center in the form of a Control Commission composed of reliable and experienced members of the party, completely independent from the hierarchical viewpoint—that is, neither officials nor administrators—and at the same time endowed with the right to call to account for violations of legality, of party and Soviet democracy, and for lack of revolutionary morality, all officials without exception, not only of the party, including members of the Central Committee, but also, through mediation of the Workers' and Peasants' Inspection, the high officials of the state.

On January 23, through Krupskaya, Lenin sent for publication in *Pravda* an article[8] on the subject of his proposed reorganization of the central institutions. Fearing at once a traitorous blow from his disease and a no less traitorous response from the Secretariat, Lenin demanded that his article be printed in *Pravda* immediately; this implied a direct appeal to the party. Stalin refused Krupskaya this request on the ground of the necessity of discussing the question in the Political Bureau. Formally this meant merely a day's postponement. But the very procedure of referring it to the Political Bureau boded no good. At Lenin's direction Krupskaya turned to me for cooperation. I demanded an immediate meeting of the Political Bureau. Lenin's fears were completely confirmed: all the members and alternates present at the meeting, Stalin, Molotov, Kuibyshev, Rykov, Kalinin, and Bukharin, were not only against the reform proposed by Lenin, but also against printing his article. To console the sick man, whom any sharp emotional excitement threatened with disaster, Kuibyshev, the future head of the Central Control Commission, proposed that they print a special issue of *Pravda* containing Lenin's article, but consisting of only one copy. It was thus "fervently" that these people followed their teacher. I rejected with indignation the proposal to hoodwink Lenin, spoke essentially in favor of the reform proposed by him, and demanded the immediate publication of his article. I was supported by Kamenev who had come in an hour late. The attitude of the majority was at last broken down by the argument that Lenin in any case would put his article in circulation; it would be copied on typewriters and read with redoubled attention, and it would be thus all the more pointedly directed against the Political Bureau. The article appeared in *Pravda* the next morning, January 25. This episode also found its reflection in due season in official documents, upon the basis of which it is here described.

I consider it necessary in general to emphasize the fact that since I do not belong to the school of pure psychology, and since I am accustomed to trust firmly established facts rather than their emotional reflection in memory, the whole present exposition, with the exception of specially indicated episodes, is set forth by me on the basis of documents in my archives and with a careful verification of dates, testimony, and factual circumstances in general.

The disagreements between Lenin and Stalin

Organizational policy was not the only arena of Lenin's struggle against Stalin. The November plenum of the Central Committee (1922),[9] sitting without Lenin and without me, introduced unexpectedly a radical change in the system of foreign trade, undermining the very foundation of the state monopoly. In a conversation with Krassin, then people's commissar of foreign trade, I spoke of this resolution of the Central Committee approximately as follows: "They have not yet knocked the bottom out of the barrel, but they have bored several holes in it." Lenin heard of this. On December 13 he wrote me: "I earnestly urge you to take upon yourself at the coming plenum the defense of our common view as to the unconditional necessity of preserving and enforcing the monopoly. . . . The previous plenum took a decision in this matter wholly in conflict with monopoly of foreign trade."

Refusing any concessions upon this question, Lenin insisted that I appeal to the Central Committee and the congress. The blow was directed primarily against Stalin, responsible as general secretary for the presentation of questions at the plenums of the Central Committee. That time, however, the thing did not go to the point of open struggle. Sensing the danger, Stalin yielded without a struggle, and his friends with him. At the December plenum the November decision was revoked. "It seems we captured the position without firing a shot, by mere movements of maneuver," Lenin wrote me jokingly on December 21.

The disagreement in the sphere of national policy was still sharper. In the autumn of 1922 we were preparing the transformation of the Soviet state into a federated union of national republics. Lenin considered it necessary to go as far as possible to meet the demands and claims of those nationalists who had long lived under oppression and were still far from recovering from its consequences. Stalin, on the other hand, who in his position as people's commissar for nationalities directed the preparatory work, was conducting in this sphere a policy of bureaucratic centralism. Lenin, convalescing in a village near Moscow, carried on a polemic with Stalin in letters addressed to the Political Bureau. In his first remarks on Stalin's project for the federated union, Lenin was extremely gentle and restrained. He was still hoping in those days—toward the end of September 1922—to adjust the question through the Political Bureau and without open conflict. Stalin's answers, on the other hand, contained a noticeable irritation. He thrust back at Lenin the reproach of "hurriedness," and with it an accusation of "national liberalism"—that is, indulgence to the nationalism of the outlanders. This correspondence, although extremely interesting politically, is still concealed from the party.

The bureaucratic national policy had already at that time provoked a keen opposition in Georgia, uniting the flower of Georgian Bolshevism against Stalin and his right-hand man, Ordzhonikidze. Through Krupskaya, Lenin got into private contact with the leaders of the Georgian opposition (Mdivani, Makharadze, etc.) against the faction of Stalin, Ordzhonikidze, and Dzerzhinsky. The struggle in the borderlands was too keen, and Stalin had bound himself too closely with definite groupings, to yield in silence as he had on the question of the monopoly of foreign trade. In the next few weeks Lenin became convinced that it would be necessary to appeal to the party. At the end of December, he dictated a voluminous letter on the national question, which was to take the place of his speech at the party congress if illness prevented him from appearing.

Lenin employed against Stalin an accusation of administrative impulsiveness and spitefulness against an alleged nationalism. "Spitefulness in general," he wrote weightily, "plays the worst possible role in politics." The struggle against the just, even though at first exaggerated, demands of the nations formerly oppressed, Lenin qualified as a manifestation of Great Russian bureaucratism. He for the first time named his opponents by name: "It is, of course, necessary to hold Stalin and Dzerzhinsky responsible for all this out-and-out Great Russian nationalistic campaign." That the Great Russian, Lenin, accuses the Georgian, Dzhugashvili,[10] and the Pole, Dzerzhinsky, of Great Russian nationalism, may seem paradoxical; but the question here is not one of national feelings and partialities, but of two systems of politics whose differences reveal themselves in all spheres, the national question among them. In mercilessly condemning the methods of the Stalin faction, Rakovsky wrote some years later: "To the national question, as to all other questions, the bureaucracy makes its approach from the point of view of convenience of administration and regulation."[11] Nothing better could be said.

Stalin's verbal concessions did not quiet Lenin in the least, but on the contrary sharpened his suspicions. "Stalin will make a rotten compromise," Lenin warned me through his secretary, "in order then to deceive." And that was just Stalin's course. He was ready to accept at the coming congress any theoretical formulation of the national policy provided it did not weaken his factional support in the center and in the borderlands. To be sure, Stalin had plenty of ground for fearing that Lenin saw through his plans completely. But on the other hand, the condition of the sick man was continually growing worse. Stalin coolly included this not unimportant factor in his calculations. The practical policy of the General Secretariat became the more decisive, the worse became Lenin's health. Stalin tried to isolate the dangerous supervisor from all information which might give him a weapon against the Secretariat and its allies. This policy of blockade naturally was directed against the people closest to Lenin. Krupskaya did what she could to protect the sick man from contact with the hostile machinations of the Secretariat. But Lenin knew how to guess a whole situation from accidental symptoms. He was clearly aware of the activities of Stalin, his motives and calculations. It is not difficult to imagine what reactions they provoked in his mind. We should remember that at that moment there already lay on Lenin's writing table, besides the testament insisting upon the removal of Stalin, also the documents on the national question which Lenin's secretaries Fotieva and Glyasser, sensitively reflecting the mood of their chief, were describing as "a bombshell against Stalin."

A half year of sharpening struggle

Lenin developed his idea of the role of the Central Control Commission as a protector of party law and unity in connection with the question of reorganizing the Workers' and Peasants' Inspection (Rabkrin), whose head for several preceding years had been Stalin. On March 4, 1923, *Pravda* published an article famous in the history of the party, "Better Fewer, but Better."[12] This work was written at several different times. Lenin did not like to, and could not, dictate. He had a hard time writing the article. On March 2 he finally listened to it with satisfaction: "At last it seems all right." This article included the reform of the guiding party institutions on a broad political perspective, both national and international. Upon this side of the question, however, we cannot pause here. Highly important for our theme, however, is the estimate which Lenin gave of the Workers' and Peasants' Inspection. Here are Lenin's words: "Let us speak frankly. The People's Commissariat of Rabkrin does not enjoy at the present moment a shadow of authority. Everybody knows that a worse organized institution than our Commissariat of Rabkrin does not exist, and that in the present circumstances you cannot expect a thing of that commissariat."

This extraordinarily biting allusion in print by the head of the government to one of the most important state institutions was a direct and unmitigated blow against Stalin as the organizer and head of this inspectorate. The reason for this should now be clear. The inspectorate was to serve chiefly as an antidote to bureaucratic distortions of the revolutionary dictatorship. This responsible function could be fulfilled successfully upon condition of complete loyalty in its leadership, but it was just this loyalty which Stalin lacked. He had converted the inspectorate like the party Secretariat into an implement of machine intrigues, of protection for "his men" and persecution of his opponents. In the article "Better Fewer, but Better" Lenin openly pointed out that his proposed reform of the inspectorate, at whose head Tsyurupa had not long ago been placed, must inevitably meet the resistance of "all our bureaucracy, both the Soviet and the party bureaucracy." In parenthesis Lenin adds significantly, "We have bureaucratism not only in the Soviet institutions but also in the party." This was a perfectly deliberate blow at Stalin as general secretary.

Thus it would be no exaggeration to say that the last half year of Lenin's political life, between his convalescence and his second illness, was filled with a sharpening struggle against Stalin. Let us recall once more the principal dates. In September 1922, Lenin opened fire against the national policy of Stalin. In the first part of December, he attacked Stalin on the question of the monopoly of foreign trade. On December 25, he wrote the first part of his testament. On December 30, he wrote his letter on the national question (the "bombshell"). On January 4, 1923, he added a postscript to his testament on the necessity of removing Stalin from his position as general secretary. On January 23, he drew up against Stalin a heavy battery: the project of a Control Commission. In an article on March 2, he dealt Stalin a double blow, both as organizer of the inspectorate and as general secretary. On March 5, he wrote me on the subject of his memorandum on the national question: "If you would agree to undertake its defense, I could be at rest." On that same day[13] he for the first time openly joined forces with the irreconcilable Georgian enemies of Stalin, informing them in a special note that he was backing their cause "with all my heart" and was preparing for them documents against Stalin, Ordzhonikidze, and Dzerzhinsky. "With all my heart"—this expression was not a frequent one with Lenin.

"This question [the national question] has worried him extremely," testifies his secretary, Fotieva, "and he was preparing to speak on it at the party congress."[14] But a month before the congress Lenin finally broke down, and without even having given instructions in regard to the article. A weight rolled from Stalin's shoulders. At the caucus of the Council of Elders at the Twelfth Congress he already made bold to speak, in the style characteristic of him, of Lenin's letter as the document of a sick man under the influence of "womenfolk." (That is, Krupskaya and the two secretaries.) Under pretext of the necessity of finding out the actual will of Lenin, it was decided to put the letter under lock and key. There it remains to this day.

The dramatic episodes enumerated above, vivid enough in themselves, do not in the remotest degree convey the fervor with which Lenin was living through the party events of the last months of his active life. In letters and articles he laid upon himself the usual very severe censorship. Lenin understood well enough from his first stroke the nature of his illness. After he returned to work in October 1922, the capillary vessels of his brain did not cease to remind him of themselves by a hardly noticeable, but ominous and more and more frequent nudge, obviously threatening a relapse. Lenin soberly estimated his own situation in spite of the quieting assurances of his physicians. At the beginning of March, when he was compelled again to withdraw from work, at least from meetings, interviews, and telephone conversations, he carried away into his sick room a number of troubling observations and dreads. The bureaucratic apparatus had become an independent factor in big politics with Stalin's secret factional staff in the Secretariat of the Central Committee. In the national sphere, where Lenin demanded special sensitiveness, the fangs of imperial centralism were revealing themselves more and more openly. The ideas and principles of the revolution were bending to the interests of combinations behind the scenes. The authority of the dictatorship was more and more often serving as a cover for the dictates of functionaries.

Lenin keenly sensed the approach of a political crisis and feared that the apparatus would strangle the party. The policies of Stalin became for Lenin in the last period of his life the incarnation of a rising monster of bureaucratism. The sick man must more than once have shuddered at the thought that he had not succeeded in carrying out that reform of the apparatus about which he had talked with me before his second illness. A terrible danger, it seemed to him, threatened the work of his whole life.

And Stalin? Having gone too far to retreat, spurred on by his own faction, fearing that concentrated attack whose threads all issued from the sickbed of his dread enemy, Stalin was already going headlong, was openly recruiting partisans by the distribution of party and Soviet positions, was terrorizing those who appealed to Lenin through Krupskaya, and was more and more persistently issuing rumors that Lenin was already not responsible for his actions. Such was the atmosphere from which rose Lenin's letter breaking with Stalin absolutely. No, it did not drop from a clear sky. It meant merely that the cup of endurance had run over. Not only chronologically, but politically and morally, it drew a last line under the attitude of Lenin to Stalin.

Is it not surprising that Ludwig, gratefully repeating the official story about the pupil faithful to his teacher "up to his very death," says not a word of this final letter or indeed of all the other circumstances which do not accord with the present Kremlin legends? Ludwig ought at least to know the fact of the letter, if only from my autobiography, with which he was once acquainted, for he gave it a favorable review. Maybe Ludwig had doubts of the authenticity of my testimony. But neither the existence of the letter nor its contents were ever disputed by anybody. Moreover, they are confirmed in stenographic minutes of the Central Committee. At the July plenum in 1926, Zinoviev said: "At the beginning of the year 1923, Vladimir Ilyich, in a personal letter to Comrade Stalin, broke off all comradely relations with him" (Stenographic Minutes of the Plenum, No. 4, page 32). And other speakers, among them M.I. Ulyanova, Lenin's sister, spoke of the letter as of a fact generally known in the circles of the Central Committee. In those days it could not even enter Stalin's head to oppose this testimony. Indeed, he has not ventured to do that so far as I know, in a direct form, even subsequently.[15]

It is true that the official historians have in recent years made literally gigantic efforts to wipe out of the memory of man this whole chapter of history. And so far as the Communist youth are concerned, these efforts have achieved certain results. But investigators exist, it would seem, exactly for the purpose of destroying legends and confirming the real facts in their rights. Or is this not true of psychologists?

The hypothesis of the "duumvirate"

We have indicated above the signposts of the final struggle between Lenin and Stalin. At all these stages Lenin sought my support and found it. From the speeches, articles, and letters of Lenin you could without difficulty adduce dozens of testimonies to the fact that, after our temporary disagreement on the question of the trade unions,[16] throughout 1921 and 1922 and the beginning of 1923, Lenin did not lose one chance to emphasize in open forum his solidarity with me, to quote this or that statement from me, to support this or that step which I had taken. We must understand that his motives were not personal, but political. What may have alarmed him and grieved him in the last months, indeed, was my not-active-enough support of his fighting measures against Stalin. Yes, such is the paradox of the situation! Lenin, fearing in the future a split on the line of Stalin and Trotsky, demanded of me a more energetic struggle against Stalin. The contradiction here, however, is only superficial. It was in the interests of the stability of the party leadership in the future, that Lenin now wished to condemn Stalin sharply and disarm him. What restrained me was the fear that any sharp conflict in the ruling group at that time, when Lenin was struggling with death, might be understood by the party as a casting of lots for Lenin's mantle. I will not raise the question here as to whether my restraint in that case was right or not, nor the broader question as to whether it would have been possible at that time to ward off the advancing danger with organizational reforms and personal shiftings. But how far were all the actual positions of the actors from the picture which is given us by this popular German writer who so lightly picks the keys to all enigmas!

We heard from him that the testament "decided the fate of Trotsky"—that is, evidently served as a cause of Trotsky's losing power. According to another version of Ludwig, expounded alongside of this with not even an attempt to reconcile them, Lenin desired "a duumvirate of Trotsky and Stalin." This latter thought, also, doubtless suggested by Radek, gives excellent proof that even now, even in the close circle around Stalin, even in the tendentious manipulation of a foreign writer invited in for a conversation, nobody dared assert that Lenin saw his successor in Stalin. In order not to come into too crude conflict with the text of the testimony and a whole series of other documents, it is necessary to put forward ex post facto this idea of a duumvirate.

But how reconcile this story with Lenin's advice: remove the general secretary? That would have meant to deprive Stalin of all the weapons of his influence. You do not treat in this way the candidate for duumvir. No, and moreover this second hypothesis of Radek-Ludwig, although more cautious, finds no support in the text of the testament. The aim of the document was defined by its author—to guarantee the stability of the Central Committee. Lenin sought the road to this goal not in the artificial combination of a duumvirate, but in strengthening the collective control over the activity of the leaders. How in doing this he conceived the relative influence of individual members of the collective leadership—as to this the reader is free to draw his own conclusions on the basis of the above quotations from the testament. But he should not lose sight of the fact that the testament was not the last word of Lenin and that his attitude to Stalin became more severe the more closely he felt the denouement approaching.

Ludwig would not have made so capital a mistake in his appraisal of the meaning and spirit of the testament if he had interested himself a little bit in its further fate. Concealed by Stalin and his group from the party, the testament was reprinted and republished only by Oppositionists—of course, secretly. Hundreds of my friends and partisans were arrested and exiled for copying and distributing those two little pages. On November 7, 1927—the tenth anniversary of the October Revolution—the Moscow Oppositionists took part in the anniversary demonstration with a placard: "Fulfill the Testament of Lenin." Specially chosen troops of Stalinists broke into the line of march and snatched away the criminal placard. Two years later, at the moment of my banishment abroad, a story was even created of an insurrection in preparation by the "Trotskyists" on November 7, 1927. The summons to "fulfill the testament of Lenin" was interpreted by the Stalinist faction as a summons to insurrection! And even now the testament is forbidden publication by any section of the Communist International. The Left Opposition, on the contrary, is republishing the testament upon every appropriate occasion in all countries. Politically these facts exhaust the question.

Radek as a source of information

Still, where did that fantastic tale come from about how I leapt from my seat during the reading of the testament, or rather of the "six words" which are not in the testament, with the question: "What does it say there?" Of this I can only offer a hypothetical explanation. How correct it may be, let the reader judge.

Radek belongs to the tribe of professional wits and storytellers. By this I do not mean that he does not possess other qualities. Suffice it to say that at the Seventh Congress of the party on March 8, 1918, Lenin, who was in general very restrained in personal comments, considered it possible to say: "I return to Comrade Radek, and here I want to remark that he has accidentally succeeded in uttering a serious remark. . . ." And once again later on: "This time it did happen that we got a perfectly serious remark from Radek. . . ."[17]

People who speak seriously only by way of exception have an organic tendency to improve reality, for in its raw form reality is not always appropriate to their stories. My personal experience has taught me to adopt a very cautious attitude to Radek's testimonies. His custom is not to recount events, but to take them as the occasion for a witty discourse. Since every art, including the anecdotal, aspires toward a synthesis, Radek is inclined to unite together various facts or the brighter features of various episodes, even though they took place at different times and places. There is no malice in this. It is the manner of his calling.

And so it happened, apparently, this time. Radek, according to all the evidence, has combined a session of the Council of Elders at the Thirteenth Congress with a session of the plenum of the Central Committee of 1926, in spite of the fact that an interval of more than two years lay between the two. At that plenum also, secret manuscripts were read, among them the testament. This time Stalin did actually read them, and not Kamenev, who was then already sitting beside me in the Opposition benches. The reading was provoked by the fact that during those days copies of the testament, Lenin's letter on the national question, and other documents kept under lock and key were already circulating rather broadly in the party. The party apparatus was getting nervous and wanted to find out what it was that Lenin actually said. "The Opposition knows and we don't know," they were saying. After prolonged resistance Stalin found himself compelled to read the forbidden documents at a session of the Central Committee—thus automatically bringing them into the stenographic record, printed in secret notebooks for the heads of the party apparatus.

This time also, there were no exclamations during the reading of the testament, for the document was long ago too well known to the members of the Central Committee. But I did actually interrupt Stalin during the the reading of the correspondence on the national question. The episode in itself is not so important, but maybe it will be of use to the psychologists for certain inferences.

Lenin was extremely economical in his literary means and methods. He carried on his business correspondence with close colleagues in telegraphic language. The form of address was always the last name of the addressee with the letter "T"(*Tovarishch:* comrade), and the signature was "Lenin." Complicated explanations were replaced by a double or triple underlining of separate words, extra exclamation points, etc. We all well knew the peculiarities of Lenin's manner, and therefore even a slight departure from his laconic custom attracted attention.

In sending his letter on the national question Lenin wrote me on March 5:

> Esteemed Comrade Trotsky:
>
> I earnestly ask you to undertake the defense of the Georgian affair at the Central Committee of the party. That affair is now under "prosecution" at the hands of Stalin and Dzerzhinsky and I cannot rely on their impartiality. Indeed, quite the contrary! If you would agree to undertake its defense, I could be at rest. If for some reason you do not agree, send me back all the papers. I will consider that a sign of your disagreement.
>
> With the very best comradely greetings,
>
> Lenin
>
> March 5, 1923

Both the content and the tone of this slight note, dictated by Lenin during the last day of his political life, were no less painful to Stalin than the testament. A lack of "impartiality"—does not this imply, indeed, that same lack of loyalty? The last thing to be felt in this note is any confidence in Stalin—"indeed, quite the contrary"—the thing emphasized is confidence in me. A confirmation of the tacit union between Lenin and me against Stalin and his faction was at hand. Stalin controlled himself badly during the reading. When he arrived at the signature he hesitated: "With the very best comradely greetings"—that was too demonstrative from Lenin's pen. Stalin read: "With communist greetings." That sounded more dry and official. At that moment I did rise in my seat and ask: "What is written there?" Stalin was obliged, not without embarrassment, to read the authentic text of Lenin. Someone of his close friends shouted at me that I was quibbling over details although I had only sought to verify a text. That slight incident made an impression. There was talk about it among the heads of the party. Radek, who at that time was no longer a member of the Central Committee, learned of it at the plenum from others and perhaps from me. Five years later when he was already with Stalin and no longer with me, his flexible memory evidently helped him to compose this synthetic episode which stimulated Ludwig to so effective and so mistaken an inference.

Although Lenin, as we have seen, found no reason to declare in his testament that my non-Bolshevik past was "not accidental," still I am ready to adopt that formula on my own authority. In the spiritual world the law of causation is as inflexible as in the physical world. In that general sense my political orbit was, of course, "not accidental," but the fact that I became a Bolshevik was also not accidental. The question how seriously and permanently I came over to Bolshevism is not to be decided either by a bare chronological record or by the guesses of literary psychology. A theoretical and political analysis is necessary. This, of course, is too big a theme and lies wholly outside the frame of the present article. For our purpose it suffices that Lenin, in describing the conduct of Zinoviev and Kamenev in 1917 as "not accidental," was not making a philosophical reference to the laws of determinism, but a political warning for the future. It is exactly for this reason that Radek found it necessary, through Ludwig, to transfer this warning from Zinoviev and Kamenev to me.

The legend of "Trotskyism"

Let us recall the chief signposts of this question. From 1917 to 1924, not a word was spoken of the contrast between Trotskyism and Leninism. In this period occurred the October Revolution, the civil war, the construction of the Soviet state, the creation of the Red Army, the working out of the party program, the establishment of the Communist International, the formation of its cadres, and the drawing up of its fundamental documents. After the withdrawal of Lenin from his work in the nucleus of the Central Committee, serious disagreements developed. In 1924 the specter of "Trotskyism"—after careful preparation behind the scenes—was brought forth on the stage. The entire inner struggle of the party was henceforth carried on within the frame of a contrast between Trotskyism and Leninism. In other words, the disagreements created by new circumstances and new tasks between me and the epigones were presented as a continuation of my old disagreements with Lenin. A vast literature was created upon this theme. The sharpshooters were always Zinoviev and Kamenev. In their character of old and very close colleagues of Lenin they stood at the head of "the Bolshevik Old Guard" against Trotskyism. But under the pressure of deep social processes this group itself fell apart. Zinoviev and Kamenev found themselves obliged to acknowledge that the so-called "Trotskyists" had been right upon fundamental questions. New thousands of Old Bolshevists adhered to "Trotskyism."

At the July 1926 plenum, Zinoviev announced that his struggle against me had been the greatest mistake of his life—"*more dangerous* than the mistake of 1917." Ordzhonikidze was not entirely wrong in calling to him from his seat: "Then why did you dupe the entire party?" (See the already quoted stenographic minutes.) To this weighty rejoinder Zinoviev officially found no answer. But he gave an unofficial explanation at a conference of the Opposition in October 1926. "You must understand," he said in my presence, to his closest friends, some Leningrad workers who honestly believed in the legend of Trotskyism, "you must understand that it was a struggle for power. The trick was to string together the old disagreements with new issues. For this purpose 'Trotskyism' was invented. . . ."

During their two-year stay in the Opposition, Zinoviev and Kamenev managed to expose completely the backstage mechanics of the preceding period when they with Stalin had created the legend of "Trotskyism" by conspiratorial methods. A year later, when it became finally clear that the Opposition would be compelled to swim long and stubbornly against the current, Zinoviev and Kamenev threw themselves on the mercy of the victor. As a first condition of their party rehabilitation it was demanded that they rehabilitate the legend of Trotskyism. They agreed. At that time I decided to reinforce their own previous declarations on this matter through a series of authoritative testimonials.[18] It was Radek, no other than Karl Radek, who gave the following written testimony:

> I was present at the conversation with Kamenev when L.B. [Kamenev] said he would openly declare at the Plenum of the Central Committee how they, that is, Kamenev and Zinoviev, together with Stalin, decided to utilize the old disagreements between L.D. [Trotsky] and Lenin so as to keep Comrade Trotsky from the leadership of the party after Lenin's death. Moreover, I have heard repeated from the lips of Zinoviev and Kamenev the tale of how they had "invented" Trotskyism as a topical slogan.
>
> K. Radek
>
> December 25, 1927

Similar written testimonies were given by Preobrazhensky, Pyatakov, Rakovsky, and Eltsin. Pyatakov, the present director of the State Bank, summed up Zinoviev's testimony in the following words: "'Trotskyism' had been invented in order to replace the real differences of opinion with fictitious differences, that is, to utilize past differences which had no bearing upon the present but which were resurrected artificially for the definite purpose mentioned above."

This is clear enough, is it not? And V. Eltsin, a representative of the younger generation, wrote: "None of the supporters of the 1925 group (the Zinovievists) who were present raised any objections to this. Everyone received this information of Zinoviev as a generally known fact."

The above-cited testimony of Radek was submitted by him on December 25, 1927. A few weeks later he was already in exile, and a few months later, on the meridian of Tomsk, he became convinced of the correctness of Stalin's position, a thing which had not been revealed to him earlier in Moscow. But from Radek also the powers demanded, as a condition sine qua non, an acknowledgment of the reality of this same legend of "Trotskyism." After Radek agreed to this, he had nothing left to do but repeat the old formulas of Zinoviev which the latter had himself exposed in 1926, only to return to them again in 1928. Radek has gone further. In a conversation with a credulous foreigner he has amended the testament of Lenin in order to find in it support for this epigonist legend of "Trotskyism."

From this short historic review, resting exclusively upon documentary data, many conclusions may be drawn. One is that a revolution is an austere process and does not spare its human vertebrae.

The course of subsequent events in the Kremlin and in the Soviet Union was determined not by a single document, even though it were the testament of Lenin, but by historical causes of a far deeper order. A political reaction after the enormous effort of the years of the insurrection and the civil war was inevitable. The concept of reaction must here be strictly distinguished from the concept of counterrevolution. Reaction does not necessarily imply a social overturn—that is, a transfer of power from one class to another. Even tsarism had its periods of progressive reform and its periods of reaction. The mood and orientation of the ruling class changes according to circumstances. This is true also of the working class. The pressure of the petty bourgeoisie upon the proletariat, tired from the tumult, entailed a revival of petty-bourgeois tendencies in the proletariat itself and a first deep reaction on the crest of which the present bureaucratic apparatus headed by Stalin rose to power.

Those qualities which Lenin valued in Stalin—stubbornness of character and craftiness—remained, of course, even then. But they found a new field of action and a new point of application. Those features which in the past had represented a minus in Stalin's personality—narrowness of outlook, lack of creative imagination, empiricism—now gained an effective significance important in the highest degree. They permitted Stalin to become the semiconscious instrument of the Soviet bureaucracy, and they impelled the bureaucracy to see in Stalin its inspired leader. This ten-year struggle among the heads of the Bolshevik Party has indubitably proved that under the conditions of this new stage of the revolution, Stalin has been developing to the limit those very traits of his political character against which Lenin in the last period of his life waged irreconcilable war. But this question, standing even now at the focus of Soviet politics, would carry us far beyond the limits of our historic theme.

Many years have passed since the events we have related. If even ten years ago there were factors in action far more powerful than the counsel of Lenin, it would now be utterly naive to appeal to the testament as an effective political document. The international struggle between the two groups which have grown out of Bolshevism long ago outgrew the question of the fate of individuals. Lenin's letter, known under the name of his testament, has henceforward chiefly a historic interest. But history, we may venture to think, has also its rights, which moreover do not always conflict with the interests of politics. The most elementary of scientific demands—correctly to establish facts and to verify rumors by document—may at least be recommended alike to politician and historian. And this demand might well be extended even to the psychologist.

December 31, 1932

LENIN'S TESTAMENT

Letter to the congress

I.

I would urge strongly that at this congress a number of changes be made in our political structure.

I want to tell you of the considerations to which I attach most importance.

At the head of the list I set an increase in the number of Central Committee members to a few dozen or even a hundred. It is my opinion that without this reform our Central Committee would be in great danger if the course of events were not quite favorable for us (and that is something we cannot count on).

Then, I intend to propose that the congress should on certain conditions invest the decisions of the State Planning Commission with legislative force, meeting in this respect the wishes of Comrade Trotsky—to a certain extent and on certain conditions.

As for the first point, i.e., increasing the number of CC members, I think it must be done in order to raise the prestige of the Central Committee, to do a thorough job of improving our administrative machinery, and to prevent conflicts between small sections of the CC from acquiring excessive importance for the future of the party.

It seems to me that our party has every right to demand from the working class fifty to one hundred CC members, and that it could get them from it without unduly taxing the resources of that class.

Such a reform would considerably increase the stability of our party and ease its struggle in the encirclement of hostile states, which, in my opinion, is likely to and must become much more acute in the next few years. I think that the stability of our party would gain a thousandfold by such a measure.

Lenin

December 23, 1922
Taken down by M.V.

II.

Continuation of the notes.
December 24, 1922

By stability of the Central Committee, of which I spoke above, I mean measures against a split, as far as such measures can at all be taken. For, of course, the white guard in *Russkaya Mysl* (it seems to have been S.S. Oldenburg) was right when, first, in the white guards' game against Soviet Russia he banked on a split in our party, and when secondly, he banked on grave differences in our party to cause that split.

Our party relies on two classes and therefore its instability would be possible and its downfall inevitable if there were no agreement between those two classes. In that event this or that measure, and generally all talk about the stability of our CC, would be futile. No measures of any kind could prevent a split in such a case. But I hope that this is too remote a future and too improbable an event to talk about.

I have in mind stability as a guarantee against a split in the immediate future, and I intend to deal here with a few ideas concerning personal qualities.

I think that from this standpoint the prime factors in the question of stability are such members of the CC as Stalin and Trotsky. I think relations between them make up the greater part of the danger of a split, which could be avoided, and this purpose, in my opinion, would be served, among other things, by increasing the number of CC members to fifty or one hundred.

Comrade Stalin, having become general secretary, has unlimited authority concentrated in his hands, and I am not sure whether he will always be capable of using that authority with sufficient caution. Comrade Trotsky, on the other hand, as his struggle against the CC on the question of the People's Commissariat for Communications has already proved,[1] is distinguished not only by outstanding ability. He is personally perhaps the most capable man in the present CC, but he has displayed excessive self-assurance and shown excessive preoccupation with the purely administrative side of the work.

These two qualities of the two outstanding leaders of the present CC can inadvertently lead to a split, and if our party does not take steps to avert this, the split may come unexpectedly.

I shall not give any further appraisals of the personal qualities of other members of the CC. I shall just recall that the October episode with Zinoviev and Kamenev[2] was, of course, no accident, but neither can the blame for it be laid upon them personally, any more than non-Bolshevism can upon Trotsky.

Speaking of the young CC members, I wish to say a few words about Bukharin and Pyatakov. They are, in my opinion, the most outstanding figures (among the youngest ones), and the following must be borne in mind about them: Bukharin is not only a most valuable and major theorist of the party; he is also rightly considered the favorite of the whole party, but his theoretical views can be classified as fully Marxist only with great reserve, for there is something scholastic about him (he has never made a study of dialectics and, I think, never fully understood it).

December 25. As for Pyatakov, he is unquestionably a man of outstanding will and outstanding ability, but shows too much zeal for administrating and the administrative side of the work to be relied upon in a serious political matter.

Both of these remarks, of course, are made only for the present, on the assumption that both these outstanding and devoted party workers fail to find an occasion to enhance their knowledge and amend their one-sideness.

Lenin

December 25, 1922
Taken down by M.V.

Addition to the letter of December 24,1922

Stalin is too rude and this defect, although quite tolerable in our midst and in dealings among us Communists, becomes intolerable in a general secretary. That is why I suggest that the comrades think about a way of removing Stalin from that post and appointing another man in his stead who in all other respects differs from Comrade Stalin in having only one advantage, namely, that of being more tolerant, more loyal, more polite, and more considerate to the comrades, less capricious, etc. This circumstance may appear to be a negligible detail. But I think that from the standpoint of safeguards against a split and from the standpoint of what I wrote above about the relationship between Stalin and Trotsky it is not a detail, or it is a detail which can assume decisive importance.

Lenin

Taken down by L.F.
January 4, 1923

III.

Continuation of the notes.
December 26, 1922

The increase in the number of CC members to fifty or even one hundred must, in my opinion, serve a double or even a treble purpose: the more members there are in the CC, the more men will be trained in CC work and the less danger there will be of a split due to some indiscretion. The enlistment of many workers to the CC will help the workers to improve our administrative machinery, which is pretty bad. We inherited it, in effect, from the old regime, for it was absolutely impossible to reorganize it in such a short time, especially in conditions of war, famine, etc. That is why those "critics" who point to the defects of our administrative machinery out of mockery or malice may be calmly answered that they do not in the least understand the conditions of the revolution today. It is altogether impossible in five years to reorganize the machinery adequately, especially under the conditions in which our revolution took place. It is enough that in five years we have created a new type of state in which the workers are leading the peasants against the bourgeoisie; and in a hostile international environment this in itself is a gigantic achievement. But knowledge of this must on no account blind us to the fact that, in effect, we took over the old machinery of state from the tsar and the bourgeoisie and that now, with the onset of peace and the satisfaction of the minimum requirements against famine, all our work must be directed towards improving the administrative machinery.

I think that a few dozen workers, being members of the CC, can deal better than anybody else with checking, improving, and remodeling our state apparatus. The Workers' and Peasants' Inspection, on whom this function devolved at the beginning, proved unable to cope with it and can be used only as an "appendage" or, on certain conditions, as an assistant to these members of the CC. In my opinion, the workers admitted to the Central Committee should come preferably not from among those who have had long service in Soviet bodies (in this part of my letter the term workers everywhere includes peasants), because those workers have already acquired the very traditions and the very prejudices which it is desirable to combat.

The working-class members of the CC must be mainly workers of a lower stratum than those promoted in the last five years to work in Soviet bodies; they must be people closer to being rank-and-file workers and peasants, who, however, do not fall into the category of direct or indirect exploiters. I think that by attending all sittings of the CC and all sittings of the Political Bureau, and by reading all the documents of the CC, such workers can form a staff of devoted supporters of the Soviet system, able, first, to give stability to the CC itself, and second, to work effectively on the renewal and improvement of the state apparatus.

Lenin

Taken down by L. F.
December 26, 1922

In increasing the number of its members, the CC, I think, must also and perhaps mainly devote attention to checking and improving our administrative machinery, which is no good at all. For this we must enlist the services of highly qualified specialists, and the task of supplying those specialists must devolve upon the Workers' and Peasants' Inspection.

How are we to combine these checking specialists, people with adequate knowledge, and the new members of the CC? This problem must be resolved in practice.

It seems to me that the Workers' and Peasants' Inspection (as a result of its development and of our perplexity about its development) has led all in all to what we now observe, namely, to an intermediate position between a special people's commissariat and a special function of the members of the CC; between an institution that inspects anything and everything and an aggregate of not very numerous but first-class inspectors, who must be well paid (this is especially indispensable in our age when everything must be paid for and inspectors are directly employed by the institutions that pay them better).

If the number of CC members is increased in the appropriate way, and they go through a course of state management year after year with the help of highly qualified specialists and of members of the Workers' and Peasants' Inspection who are highly authoritative in every branch—then, I think, we shall successfully solve this problem which we have not managed to do for such a long time.

To sum up, one hundred members of the CC at the most and not more than four to five hundred assistants, members of the Workers' and Peasants' Inspection, engaged in inspecting under their direction.

Lenin

December 29, 1922
Taken down by M.V.

[Lenin, *Collected Works*, 4th ed. (Moscow: Progress Publishers, 1960-70), vol. 33, pp. 593-97, 603-04. Unless otherwise indicated, all the Lenin selections are from this edition. Spelling, capitalization, and punctuation have been slightly revised.]

To Comrade Stalin

Top secret
Personal

Copy to Comrades Kamenev and Zinoviev
Dear Comrade Stalin:

You have been so rude as to summon my wife to the telephone and use bad language. Although she had told you that she was prepared to forget this, the fact nevertheless became known through her to Zinoviev and Kamenev. I have no intention of forgetting so easily what has been done against me, and it goes without saying that what has been done against my wife I consider having been done against me as well. I ask you, therefore, to think it over whether you are prepared to withdraw what you have said and to make your apologies or whether you prefer that relations between us should be broken off.

Respectfully yours,
Lenin

March 5, 1923

THE BUREAUCRACY

Political Report to the Eleventh Party Congress

The state capitalism discussed in all books on economics is that which exists under the capitalist system where the state brings under its direct control certain capitalist enterprises. But ours is a proletarian state; it rests on the proletariat; it gives the proletariat all political privileges; and through the medium of the proletariat it attracts to itself the lower ranks of the peasantry (you remember that we began this work through the Poor Peasants' Committees).[1] That is why very many people are misled by the term state capitalism.[2] To avoid this we must remember the fundamental thing that state capitalism in the form we have here is not dealt with in any theory, or in any books, for the simple reason that all the usual concepts connected with this term are associated with bourgeois rule in capitalist society. Our society is one which has left the rails of capitalism but has not yet got on to new rails. The state in this society is not ruled by the bourgeoisie, but by the proletariat. We refuse to understand that when we say "state" we mean ourselves, the proletariat, the vanguard of the working class. State capitalism is capitalism which we shall be able to restrain, and the limits of which we shall be able to fix. This state capitalism is connected with the state, and the state is the workers, the advanced section of the workers, the vanguard. We are the state.

State capitalism is capitalism that we must confine within certain bounds; but we have not yet learned to confine it within those bounds. That is the whole point. And it rests with us to determine what this state capitalism is to be. We have sufficient, quite sufficient political power; we also have sufficient economic resources at our command, but the vanguard of the working class which has been brought to the forefront to directly supervise, to determine the boundaries, to demarcate, to subordinate and not be subordinated itself, lacks sufficient ability for it. All that is needed here is ability, and that is what we do not have.

Never before in history has there been a situation in which the proletariat, the revolutionary vanguard, possessed sufficient political power and had state capitalism existing alongside it. The whole question turns on our understanding that this is the capitalism that we can and must permit, that we can and must confine within certain bounds; for this capitalism is essential for the broad masses of the peasantry and for private capital, which must trade in such a way as to satisfy the needs of the peasantry. We must organize things in such a way as to make possible the customary operation of capitalist economy and capitalist exchange, because this is essential for the people. Without it, existence is impossible. All the rest is not an absolutely vital matter to this camp. They can resign themselves to all that. You Communists, you workers, you, the politically enlightened section of the proletariat, which undertook to administer the state, must be able to arrange it so that the state, which you have taken into your hands, shall function the way you want it to. Well, we have lived through a year, the state is in our hands; but has it operated the New Economic Policy in the way we wanted in this past year? No. But we refuse to admit that it did not operate in the way we wanted. How did it operate? The machine refused to obey the hand that guided it. It was like a car that was going not in the direction the driver desired, but in the direction someone else desired; as if it were being driven by some mysterious, lawless hand, God knows whose, perhaps of a profiteer, or of a private capitalist, or of both. Be that as it may, the car is not going quite in the direction the man at the wheel imagines, and often it goes in an altogether different direction. This is the main thing that must be remembered in regard to state capitalism. In this main field we must start learning from the very beginning, and only when we have thoroughly understood and appreciated this can we be sure that we shall learn. . . .

. . . The main economic power is in our hands. All the vital large enterprises, the railways, etc., are in our hands. The number of leased enterprises, although considerable in places, is on the whole insignificant; altogether it is infinitesimal compared with the rest. The economic power in the hands of the proletarian state of Russia is quite adequate to ensure the transition to communism. What then is lacking? Obviously, what is lacking is culture among the stratum of the Communists who perform administrative functions. If we take Moscow with its 4,700 Communists in responsible positions, and if we take that huge bureaucratic machine, that gigantic heap, we must ask: who is directing whom? I doubt very much whether it can truthfully be said that the Communists are directing that heap. To tell the truth, they are not directing, they are being directed. Something analogous happened here to what we were told in our history lessons when we were children: sometimes one nation conquers another, the nation that conquers is the conqueror and the nation that is vanquished is the conquered nation. This is simple and intelligible to all. But what happens to the culture of these nations? Here things are not so simple. If the conquering nation is more cultured than the vanquished nation, the former imposes its culture upon the latter; but if the opposite is the case, the vanquished nation imposes its culture upon the conqueror. Has not something like this happened in the capital of the RSFSR? Have the 4,700 Communists (nearly a whole army division, and all of them the very best) come under the influence of an alien culture? True, there may be the impression that the vanquished have a high level of culture. But that is not the case at all. Their culture is miserable, insignificant, but it is still at a higher level than ours. Miserable and low as it is, it is higher than that of our responsible Communist administrators, for the latter lack administrative ability. Communists who are put at the head of departments—and sometimes artful saboteurs deliberately put them in these positions in order to use them as a shield—are often fooled. This is a very unpleasant admission to make, or, at any rate, not a very pleasant one; but I think we must admit it, for at present this is the salient problem. I think that this is the political lesson of the past year; and it is around this that the struggle will rage in 1922.

Will the responsible Communists of the RSFSR and of the Russian Communist Party realize that they cannot administer; that they only imagine they are directing, but are actually being directed? If they realize this they will learn, of course; for this business can be learned. But one must study hard to learn it, and our people are not doing this. They scatter orders and decrees right and left, but the result is quite different from what they want.

The competition and rivalry that we have placed on the order of the day by proclaiming NEP is a serious business. It appears to be going on in all government offices; but as a matter of fact it is one more form of the struggle between two irreconcilably hostile classes. It is another form of the struggle between the bourgeoisie and the proletariat. It is a struggle that has not yet been brought to a head, and culturally it has not yet been resolved even in the central government departments in Moscow. Very often the bourgeois officials know the business better than our best Communists, who are invested with authority and have every opportunity, but who cannot make the slightest use of their rights and authority. . . .

. . . In connection with NEP some people are beginning to fuss around, proposing to reorganize our government departments and to form new ones. All this is pernicious twaddle. In the present situation the key feature is people, the proper choice of people. A revolutionary who is accustomed to struggle against petty reformists and uplift educators finds it hard to understand this. Soberly weighed up, the political conclusion to be drawn from the present situation is that we have advanced so far that we cannot hold all the positions; and we need not hold them all.

Internationally our position has improved vastly these last few years. The Soviet type of state is our achievement; it is a step forward in human progress; and the information the Communist International receives from every country every day corroborates this. Nobody has the slightest doubt about that. From the point of view of practical work, however, the position is that unless the Communists render the masses of the peasants practical assistance they will lose their support. Passing laws, passing better decrees, etc., is not now the main object of our attention. There was a time when the passing of decrees was a form of propaganda. People used to laugh at us and say that the Bolsheviks do not realize that their decrees are not being carried out; the entire white-guard press was full of jeers on that score. But at that period this passing of decrees was quite justified. We Bolsheviks had just taken power, and we said to the peasant, to the worker: "Here is a decree; this is how we would like to have the state administered. Try it!" From the very outset we gave the ordinary workers and peasants an idea of our policy in the form of decrees. The result was the enormous confidence we enjoyed and now enjoy among the masses of the people. This was an essential period at the beginning of the revolution; without it we should not have risen on the crest of the revolutionary wave; we should have wallowed in its trough. Without it we should not have won the confidence of all the workers and peasants who wanted to build their lives on new lines. But this period has passed, and we refuse to understand this. Now the peasants and workers will laugh at us if we order this or that government department to be formed or reorganized. The ordinary workers and peasants will display no interest in this now, and they will be right because this is not the central task today. This is not the sort of thing with which we Communists should now go to the people. Although we who are engaged in government departments are always overwhelmed with so many petty affairs, this is not the link that we must grasp, this is not the key feature. The key feature is that we have not got the right men in the right places; that responsible Communists who acquitted themselves magnificently during the revolution have been given commercial and industrial functions about which they know nothing; and they prevent us from seeing the truth, for rogues and rascals hide magnificently behind their backs. The trouble is that we have no such thing as practical control of how things have been done. This is a prosaic job, a small job; these are petty affairs. But after the greatest political change in history, bearing in mind that for a time we shall have to live in the midst of the capitalist system, the key feature now is not politics in the narrow sense of the word (what we read in the newspapers is just political fireworks; there is nothing socialist in it at all), the key feature is not resolutions, not departments, and not reorganization. As long as these things are necessary we shall do them, but don't go to the people with them. Choose the proper men and introduce practical control. That is what the people will appreciate. . . .

[Lenin, *Collected Works,* vol. 33, pp. 278-80; 288-89; 303-04.]

Comments on Lenin's Proposal Concerning the Work of Deputies

1) The problems posed are so general that this is the equivalent of posing no problems at all. The deputies are supposed to strive to make everything go well in all areas and in every respect—this is what the draft resolution comes down to. The various points, at least in outward *appearance,* give instructions on how to achieve a state of affairs where all goes well in every area, even down to the proper editing of *Ekonomicheskaya Zhizn* [Economic Life].

2) The apparatus designated for carrying out these general tasks is Rabkrin. However, by its essence Rabkrin is not suited for this and cannot become so. We must not shut our eyes to the fact that those who work in Rabkrin are mainly officials who have come to grief in various other fields. From this, among other things, results the extraordinary growth of intrigue in the organs of Rabkrin, which has long been proverbial throughout the entire country. There is no basis whatever for thinking that this apparatus (not the small group at its head, but the organization as a whole) can be strengthened and restored to health, for the good workers will in the future continue to be assigned to essential work and not to jobs as inspectors. Hence, the plan to raise up the Soviet state apparatus using Rabkrin as a lever is clearly a fantasy.

3) Similarly, I just do not believe in the possibility of cultivating administrators and economic officials from the ranks of nonparty workers and peasants through Rabkrin. For this, a system of schools and courses is necessary, in particular courses connected with specific branches of economic and state activity.

4) I am very much afraid that the relationship between the deputies can become a source of difficulties. Here the dictaphone will not help. Once there are two deputies, there must be perfect regularity in their relationship.

5) The main thing is that, as before, I cannot picture the kind of organ which can in practice manage economic work on a day-to-day basis. If it is a bad thing that the Central Statistical Administration is an academic institution, then it is a hundred times worse, and frankly disastrous, that Gosplan is an academic institution. As early as the beginning of last year it was clear that a unifying economic organ exercising practical control did not exist. The present reorganization of Gosplan in *outward*

appearance advances Gosplan to what I proposed last year, but only in outward appearance. Essentially, the fractionating of responsibility still exists, and it is completely uncertain who in practice controls the orders for fuel, transport, raw materials, money. In case of interdepartmental conflict, these questions are placed before STO [the Council of Labor and Defense] or the Politburo and resolved slapdash and at the very moment when the water is reaching our throats. There should be an institution with an economic calendar for the coming year hanging on its wall, an institution that makes projections, and in the light of these projections, coordinates. Gosplan should be such an institution. I think that the chairmanship of Gosplan would be a far more realistic task for one of the deputies than anything discussed in the resolution.

[April 19, 1922] L. Trotsky

Additional on my note of yesterday on the work of deputies:

1) The creation of a good apparatus can only be achieved by means of consistent, uninterrupted, day-to-day efforts, pressure, instructions, correction, etc. In any case, this work cannot be done from the outside through a special department that looks in from time to time and notes everything that is necessary. This is a utopia. Such a department has never existed anywhere in the world and, given the logic of things, it cannot exist.

With our New Economic Policy it would be a good thing to have *state control* through which can be posed a limited, but well-defined task requiring knowledge of Soviet laws and accounting practice. The more Rabkrin concentrates on and specializes in this task, the more help it will prove to be in putting our entire Soviet apparatus in good order, and primarily in putting our budget in good order, and consequently our finances too.

2) "Verification of execution," which the draft resolution speaks of as the principal practical task, does not in actual fact appear to be the principal task, at least not in the sense that we spoke of it in 1918, 1919, and 1920. At that time instructions were simply not carried out (through carelessness, ineptness, forgetfulness, indiscipline). Now this is only the case in the most "humanitarian" departments. Formally speaking, instructions are carried out. But nothing comes of this, for in the process of being carried out, the orders in practice come to nothing, on the one hand from material shortages, on the other out of ignorance, ineptness,

etc.—goodwill granted. A swoop from without, even a well-considered one, will only show once again that things are going badly. We must teach the copy-typists to make better copies (without errors), the telephone operators not to garble numbers, the bookkeepers to enter expenses and income punctually and accurately, etc., etc. We must initiate evening review courses for office, departmental, production, and trade officials, etc. How else? There is nobody to replace them. Consequently, we must raise their standards without distracting them from their work. This is a difficult road, but there is no other.

3) There must be some system in the work. In the meantime, *the example of lack of system*—and this is the most important and the most dangerous thing—*comes from above.* All economic questions are decided in a haphazard fashion and always later than they should be. There is no controlling economic organ to work without interruption, look ahead, and be answerable for its work. Everyone sees this and senses this (to a considerable extent, the present crisis[3] was due to causes that could have been foreseen). Hence we have proposals, at times fantastic and inexpedient, but responding to a profound need. Preobrazhensky proposes a CC Econburo. Krasin—a comrade of a totally different stamp—already proposed the same thing: a CC Supreme Econcommission. And it must be said that even a CC Econburo would be a step forward in comparison to the present state of affairs, where the CC establishes an Economics Commission, a Budget Commission, a Gold Commission, etc., etc. All of this is the result of the lack of a forward-looking, controlling, economic organ. As conceived, Gosplan should have been such an organ. In its composition, methods of work, and ideological direction, it has not, cannot, and will not be such.

It is necessary to make Gosplan a tool for putting the economy in order, and for this we must put a stop to the continual disorganization of the economy through improvisation and lack of foresight with regard to this central question. Nothing can be accomplished in the field of economy with propagandistic and retributive measures if the economy is yanked in all directions without system and without plan.

L. Trotsky

[*The Trotsky Papers*, ed. by Jan Meijer (The Hague: Mouton, 1971), vol. 2, pp. 730-34. Translated from Russian by the editor.]

Granting Legislative Functions to the State Planning Commission

This idea was suggested by Comrade Trotsky, it seems, quite a long time ago. I was against it at the time, because I thought that there would then be a fundamental lack of coordination in the system of our legislative institutions. But after closer consideration of the matter, I find that in substance there is a sound idea in it, namely: the State Planning Commission stands somewhat apart from our legislative institutions, although, as a body of experienced people, experts, representatives of science and technology, it is actually in a better position to form a correct judgment of affairs.

However, we have so far proceeded from the principle that the State Planning Commission must provide the state with critically analyzed material and the state institutions must decide state matters. I think that in the present situation, when affairs of state have become unusually complicated, when it is necessary time and again to settle questions of which some require the expert opinion of the members of the State Planning Commission on some points but not on others—I think that we must now take a step towards extending the competence of the State Planning Commission.

I imagine that step to be such that the decisions of the State Planning Commission could not be rejected by ordinary procedure in Soviet bodies, but would need a special procedure to be reconsidered. For example, the question should be submitted to a session of the All-Russia Central Executive Committee, prepared for reconsideration according to a special instruction, involving the drawing up, under special rules, of memoranda to examine whether the State Planning Commission decision is subject to reversal. Lastly, special time limits should be set for the reconsideration of State Planning Commission decisions, etc.

In this respect I think we can and must accede to the wishes of Comrade Trotsky, but not in the sense that specifically any one of our political leaders, or the chairman of the Supreme Economic Council, etc., should be chairman of the State Planning Commission. I think that personal matters are at present too closely interwoven with the question of principle. I think that the attacks which are now made against the chairman of the State Planning

Commission, Comrade Krzhizhanovsky and Comrade Pyatakov, his deputy, and which proceed along two lines, so that, on the one hand, we hear charges of extreme leniency, lack of independent judgment and lack of backbone, and, on the other, charges of excessive coarseness, drill-sergeant methods, lack of solid scientific background, etc.—I think these attacks express two sides of the question, exaggerating them to the extreme, and that in actual fact we need a skillful combination in the State Planning Commission of two types of character, of which one may be exemplified by Comrade Pyatakov and the other by Comrade Krzhizhanovsky.

I think that the State Planning Commission must be headed by a man who, on the one hand, has scientific education, namely, either technical or agronomic, with decades of experience in practical work in the field of technology or of agronomics. I think this man must possess not so much the qualities of an administrator as broad experience and the ability to enlist the services of other men.

Lenin

December 27, 1922
Taken down by M.V.

Continuation of the letter
on the legislative nature of
State Planning Commission
decisions.
December 28, 1922

I have noticed that some of our comrades who are able to exercise a decisive influence on the direction of state affairs exaggerate the administrative side, which, of course, is necessary in its time and place, but which should not be confused with the scientific side, with a grasp of the broad facts, the ability to recruit men, etc.

In every state institution, especially in the State Planning Commission, the combination of these two qualities is essential; and when Comrade Krzhizhanovsky told me that he had enlisted the services of Comrade Pyatakov for the Commission and had come to terms with him about the work, I, in consenting to this, on the one hand, entertained certain doubts and, on the other, sometimes hoped that we would thus get the combination of the two types of statesmen. To see whether those hopes are justified, we must now wait and consider the matter on the strength of somewhat longer experience, but in principle, I think, there can be no doubt that such a combination of temperaments and types (of men and qualities) is absolutely necessary for the correct functioning of state institutions. I think that here it is just as harmful to exaggerate "administrating" as it is to exaggerate anything at all. The chief of a state institution must possess a high degree of personal appeal and sufficiently solid scientific and technical knowledge to be able to check people's work. That much is basic. Without it the work cannot be done properly. On the other hand, it is very important that he should be capable of administering and should have a worthy assistant, or assistants, in the matter. The combination of these two qualities in one person will hardly be found, and it is hardly necessary.

Lenin

Taken down by L.F.
December 28, 1922

Continuation of the
notes on the State
Planning Commission.
December 29,1922

The State Planning Commission is apparently developing in all respects into a commission of experts. Such an institution cannot be headed by anybody except a man with great experience and an all-round scientific education in technology. The administrative element must in essence be subsidiary. A certain independence and autonomy of the State Planning Commission is essential for the prestige of this scientific institution and depends on one thing, namely, the conscientiousness of its workers and their conscientious desire to turn our plan of economic and social development into reality.

This last quality may, of course, be found now only as an exception, for the overwhelming majority of scientists, who naturally make up the commission, are inevitably infected with bourgeois ideas and bourgeois prejudices. The check on them from this standpoint must be the job of several persons who can form the presidium of the commission. These must be Communists to keep a day-to-day check on the extent of the bourgeois scientists' devotion to our cause displayed in the whole course of the work and see that they abandon bourgeois prejudices and gradually adopt the socialist standpoint. This work along the twin lines of scientific checking and pure administration should be the ideal of those who run the State Planning Commission in our republic.

Lenin

Taken down by M.V.
December 29, 1922

Is it rational to divide the work of the State Planning Commission into separate jobs? Should we not, on the contrary, try to build up a group of permanent specialists who would be systematically checked by the presidium of the commission and could solve the whole range of problems within its ambit? I think that the latter would be the more reasonable and that we must try to cut down the number of temporary and urgent tasks.

Lenin

December 29, 1922
Taken down by M.V.

[Lenin, *Collected Works*, vol. 36, pp. 598-602.]

Trotsky: January 15, 1923
Letter to the Politburo (excerpt)

Comrade Stalin, advancing the proposal to appoint me deputy chairman (a proposal that was never placed before the Politburo or the plenum and never discussed in them) proposes "placing" Vesenkha [the Supreme Council of the National Economy] "under my special care." Putting the question in this way . . . is fundamentally incorrect. The special care of the Vesenkha should reside with the chairman of Vesenkha. The role of special "administrator" will only divide responsibility and introduce uncertainty and confusion in this area where clarity and certainty are valuable and important above all. We need correct, practical coordination of the work of the economic departments, and not in the least—two-stage management of each of them individually. . . .

Without a unifying plan and unified management, no economic work is possible. This plan should not be academic, but practical. Separating the plan from the supervision of its execution is impossible. Our planning body is Gosplan, the other bodies (STO [Council of Labor and Defense], Sovnarkom [Council of People's Commissars], Finkomitet [Financial Committee], the collegium of deputies, CC) are obliged either to rely on Gosplan or else to improvise and set up innumerable commissions. The only way out of this situation is to take Gosplan in hand, i.e., to place responsible officials on its staff for regular day-to-day work, combining them with specialists in the proper proportions. It is necessary for higher institutions to receive from Gosplan high quality material, well worked out, verified, and moreover, it goes without saying, in keeping with the Soviet, Communist point of view.

With such a properly functioning Gosplan, only large-scale questions of a principled nature will go back to the higher bodies, ones which require legislative decisions or new direction in principle.

To use an analogy, I would say that Gosplan will play the role of general staff, and STO the role of Military Revolutionary Council.

[*Trotsky Papers*, vol. 2, pp. 820-22. Translated by the editor.]

How We Should Reorganize the Workers' and Peasants' Inspection

(Recommendation to the Twelfth Party Congress)

It is beyond question that the Workers' and Peasants' Inspection is an enormous difficulty for us and that so far this difficulty has not been overcome. I think that the comrades who try to overcome the difficulty by denying that the Workers' and Peasants' Inspection is useful and necessary are wrong. But I do not deny that the problem presented by our state apparatus and the task of improving it is very difficult, that it is far from being solved, and is an extremely urgent one.

With the exception of the People's Commissariat of Foreign Affairs, our state apparatus is to a considerable extent a survival of the past and has undergone hardly any serious change. It has only been slightly touched up on the surface, but in all other respects it is a most typical relic of our old state machine. And so, to find a method of really renovating it, I think we ought to turn for experience to our civil war.

How did we act in the more critical moments of the civil war? We concentrated our best party forces in the Red Army; we mobilized the best of our workers; we looked for new forces at the deepest roots of our dictatorship.

I am convinced that we must go to the same source to find the means of reorganizing the Workers' and Peasants' Inspection. I recommend that our Twelfth Party Congress adopt the following plan of reorganization, based on some enlargement of our Central Control Commission.

The plenary meetings of the Central Committee of our party are already revealing a tendency to develop into a kind of supreme party conference. They take place, on the average, not more than once in two months, while the routine work is conducted, as we know, on behalf of the Central Committee by our Political Bureau, our Organization Bureau, our Secretariat, and so forth. I think we ought to follow the road we have thus taken to the end and definitely transform the plenary meetings of the Central Committee into supreme party conferences convened once in two months jointly with the Central Control Commission. The Central Control Commission should be amalgamated with the main body of the reorganized Workers' and Peasants' Inspection on the following lines.

I propose that the congress should elect seventy-five to one hundred new members to the Central Control Commission. They should be workers and peasants and should go through the same party screening as ordinary members of the Central Committee because they are to enjoy the same rights as the members of the Central Committee.

On the other hand, the staff of the Workers' and Peasants' Inspection should be reduced to three or four hundred persons, specially screened for conscientiousness and knowledge of our state apparatus. They must also undergo a special test as regards their knowledge of the principles of scientific organization of labor in general, and of administrative work, office work and so forth, in particular.

In my opinion, such an amalgamation of the Workers' and Peasants' Inspection with the Central Control Commission will be beneficial to both these institutions. On the one hand, the Workers' and Peasants' Inspection will thus obtain such high authority that it will certainly not be inferior to the People's Commissariat of Foreign Affairs. On the other hand, our Central Committee, together with the Central Control Commission, will definitely take the road of becoming a supreme party conference, which in fact it has already taken, and along which it should proceed to the end so as to be able to fulfill its functions properly in two respects: in respect to *its own* methodical, expedient, and systematic organization and work and in respect to maintaining contacts with the broad masses through the medium of the best of our workers and peasants.

I foresee an objection that, directly or indirectly, may come from those spheres which make our state apparatus antiquated, i.e., from those who urge that its present utterly impossible, indecently prerevolutionary form be preserved (incidentally, we now have an opportunity which rarely occurs in history of ascertaining the period necessary for bringing about radical social changes; we now see clearly *what* can be done in five years and what requires much more time).

The objection I foresee is that the change I propose will lead to nothing but chaos. The members of the Central Control Commission will wander around all the institutions, not knowing where, why, or to whom to apply, causing disorganization everywhere and distracting employees from their routine work, etc., etc.

I think that the malicious source of this objection is so obvious that it does not warrant a reply. It goes without saying that the presidium of the Central Control Commission, the people's commissar of the Workers' and Peasants' Inspection and his collegium (and also, in the proper cases, the Secretariat of our Central Committee) will have to put in years of persistent effort to get the commissariat properly organized, and to get it to function smoothly in conjunction with the Central Control Commission. In my opinion, the people's commissar of the Workers' and Peasants' Inspection, as well as the whole collegium, can (and should) remain and guide the work of the entire Workers' and Peasants' Inspection, including the work of all the members of the Central Control Commission who will be "placed under his command." The three or four hundred employees of the Workers' and Peasants' Inspection that are to remain, according to my plan, should, on the one hand, perform purely secretarial functions for the other members of the Workers' and Peasants' Inspection and for the supplementary members of the Central Control Commission; and, on the other hand, they should be highly skilled, specially screened, particularly reliable, and highly paid, so that they may be relieved of their present truly unhappy (to say the least) position of Workers' and Peasants' Inspection officials.

I am sure that the reduction of the staff to the number I have indicated will greatly enhance the efficiency of the Workers' and Peasants' Inspection personnel and the quality of all its work, enabling the people's commissar and the members of the collegium to concentrate their efforts entirely on organizing work and on systematically and steadily improving its efficiency, which is so absolutely essential for our workers' and peasants' government and for our Soviet system.

On the other hand, I also think that the people's commissar of the Workers' and Peasants' Inspection should work on partly amalgamating and partly coordinating those higher institutions for the organization of labor (the Central Institute of Labor, the Institute for the Scientific Organization of Labor, etc.), of which there are now no fewer than twelve in our republic. Excessive uniformity and a consequent desire to amalgamate will be harmful. On the contrary, what is needed here is a reasonable and expedient mean between amalgamating all these institutions and properly delimiting them, allowing for a certain independence for each of them.

Our own Central Committee will undoubtedly gain no less from this reorganization than the Workers' and Peasants' Inspection. It will gain because its contacts with the masses will be greater and because the regularity and effectiveness of its work will improve. It will then be possible (and necessary) to institute a stricter and more responsible procedure of preparing for the meetings of the Political Bureau, which should be attended by a definite number of members of the Central Control Commission determined either for a definite period or by some organizational plan.

In distributing work to the members of the Central Control Commission, the people's commissar of the Workers' and Peasants' Inspection, in conjunction with the Presidium of the Central Control Commission, should impose on them the duty either of attending the meetings of the Political Bureau for the purpose of examining all the documents appertaining to matters that come before it in one way or another; or of devoting their working time to theoretical study, to the study of scientific methods of organizing labor; or of taking a practical part in the work of supervising and improving our machinery of state, from the higher state institutions to the lower local bodies, etc.

I also think that in addition to the political advantages accruing from the fact that the members of the Central Committee and the Central Control Commission will, as a consequence of this reform, be much better informed and better prepared for the meetings of the Political Bureau (all the documents relevant to the business to be discussed at these meetings should be sent to all the members of the Central Committee and the Central Control Commission not later than the day before the meeting of the Political Bureau, except in absolutely urgent cases, for which special methods of informing the members of the Central Committee and the Central Control Commission and of settling these matters must be devised), there will also be the advantage that the influence of purely personal and incidental factors in our Central Committee will diminish, and this will reduce the danger of a split.

Our Central Committee has grown into a strictly centralized and highly authoritative group, but the conditions under which this group is working are not commensurate with its authority. The reform I recommend should help to remove this defect, and the members of the Central Control Commission, whose duty it will be to attend all meetings of the Political Bureau in a definite number, will have to form a compact group which should not allow anybody's authority without exception, neither that of the general secretary nor of any other member of the Central Committee, to prevent them from putting questions, verifying documents, and, in general, from keeping themselves fully informed of all things and from exercising the strictest control over the proper conduct of affairs.

Of course, in our Soviet republic, the social order is based on the collaboration of two classes: the workers and peasants, in which the "Nepmen," i.e., the bourgeoisie, are now permitted to participate on certain terms. If serious class disagreements arise between these classes, a split will be inevitable. But the grounds for such a split are not inevitable in our social system, and it is the principal task of our Central Committee and Central Control Commission, as well as of our party as a whole, to watch very closely over such circumstances as may cause a split and to forestall them, for in the final analysis the fate of our republic will depend on whether the peasant masses will stand by the working class, loyal to their alliance, or whether they will permit the "Nepmen," i.e., the new bourgeoisie, to drive a wedge between them and the working class, to split them off from the working class. The more clearly we see this alternative, the more clearly all our workers and peasants understand it, the greater are the chances that we shall avoid a split, which would be fatal for the Soviet republic.

January 23, 1923

[Lenin, *Collected Works*, vol. 33, pp. 481-86.]

Better Fewer, But Better

In the matter of improving our state apparatus, the Workers' and Peasants' Inspection should not, in my opinion, strive either after quantity or hurry. We have so far been able to devote so little thought and attention to the efficiency of our state apparatus that it would now be quite legitimate if we took special care to secure its thorough organization, and concentrated in the Workers' and Peasants' Inspection a staff of workers really abreast of the times, i.e., not inferior to the best West European standards. For a socialist republic this condition is, of course, too modest. But our experience of the first five years has fairly crammed our heads with mistrust and skepticism. These qualities assert themselves involuntarily when, for example, we hear people dilating at too great length and too flippantly on "proletarian" culture. For a start, we should be satisfied with real bourgeois culture; for a start, we should be glad to dispense with the cruder types of prebourgeois culture, i.e., bureaucratic culture or serf culture, etc. In matters of culture, haste and sweeping measures are most harmful. Many of our young writers and Communists should get this well into their heads.

Thus, in the matter of our state apparatus we should now draw the conclusion from our past experience that it would be better to proceed more slowly.

Our state apparatus is so deplorable, not to say wretched, that we must first think very carefully how to combat its defects, bearing in mind that these defects are rooted in the past, which, although it has been overthrown, has not yet been overcome, has not yet reached the stage of a culture that has receded into the distant past. I say culture deliberately, because in these matters we can only regard as achieved what has become part and parcel of our culture, of our social life, our habits. We might say that the good in our social system has not been properly studied, understood, and taken to heart; it has been hastily grasped at; it has not been verified or tested, corroborated by experience, and not made durable, etc. Of course, it could not be otherwise in a revolutionary epoch, when development proceeded at such breakneck speed that in a matter of five years we passed from tsarism to the Soviet system.

It is time we did something about it. We must show sound skepticism for too rapid progress, for boastfulness, etc. We must give thought to testing the steps forward we proclaim every hour, take every minute and then prove every second that they are flimsy, superficial and misunderstood. The most harmful thing here would be haste. The most harmful thing would be to rely on the assumption that we know at least something, or that we have any considerable number of elements necessary for the building of a really new state apparatus, one really worthy to be called socialist, Soviet, etc.

No, we are ridiculously deficient of such an apparatus, and even of the elements of it, and we must remember that we should not stint time on building it and that it will take many, many years.

What elements have we for building this apparatus? Only two. First, the workers who are absorbed in the struggle for socialism. These elements are not sufficiently educated. They would like to build a better apparatus for us, but they do not know how. They cannot build one. They have not yet developed the culture required for this; and it is culture that is required. Nothing will be achieved in this by doing things in a rush, by assault, by vim or vigor, or in general, by any of the best human qualities. Secondly, we have elements of knowledge, education, and training, but they are ridiculously inadequate compared with all other countries.

Here we must not forget that we are too prone to compensate (or imagine that we can compensate) our lack of knowledge by zeal, haste, etc.

In order to renovate our state apparatus we must at all costs set out, first, to learn, secondly, to learn, and thirdly, to learn, and then see to it that learning shall not remain a dead letter, or a fashionable catchphrase (and we should admit in all frankness that this happens very often with us), that learning shall really become part of our very being, that it shall actually and fully become a constituent element of our social life. In short, we must not make the demands that are made by bourgeois Western Europe, but demands that are fit and proper for a country which has set out to develop into a socialist country.

The conclusions to be drawn from the above are the following: we must make the Workers' and Peasants' Inspection a really exemplary institution, an instrument to improve our state apparatus.

In order that it may attain the desired high level, we must follow the rule: "Measure your cloth seven times before you cut."

For this purpose, we must utilize the very best of what there is in our social system and utilize it with the greatest caution, thoughtfulness, and knowledge to build up the new people's commissariat.

For this purpose, the best elements that we have in our social system—such as, first, the advanced workers, and second, the really enlightened elements for whom we can vouch that they will not take the word for the deed and will not utter a single word that goes against their conscience—should not shrink from admitting any difficulty and should not shrink from any struggle in order to achieve the object they have seriously set themselves.

We have been bustling for five years trying to improve our state apparatus, but it has been mere bustle, which has proved useless in these five years, or even futile, or even harmful. This bustle created the impression that we were doing something, but in effect it was only clogging up our institutions and our brains.

It is high time things were changed.

We must follow the rule: Better fewer, but better. We must follow the rule: Better get good human material in two or even three years than work in haste without hope of getting any at all.

I know that it will be hard to keep to this rule and apply it under our conditions. I know that the opposite rule will force its way through a thousand loopholes. I know that enormous resistance will have to be put up, that devilish persistence will be required, that in the first few years at least, work in this field will be hellishly hard. Nevertheless, I am convinced that only by such effort shall we be able to achieve our aim; and that only by achieving this aim shall we create a republic that is really worthy of the name of Soviet, socialist, and so on and so forth.

Many readers probably thought that the figures I quoted by way of illustration in my first article[4] were too small. I am sure that many calculations may be made to prove that they are. But I think that we must put one thing above all such and other calculations, i.e., our desire to obtain really exemplary quality.

I think that the time has at last come when we must work in real earnest to improve our state apparatus and in this there can scarcely be anything more harmful than haste. That is why I would sound a strong warning against inflating the figures. In my opinion, we should, on the contrary, be especially sparing with figures in this matter. Let us say frankly that the People's Commissariat of the Workers' and Peasants' Inspection does not at present enjoy the slightest authority. Everybody knows that no other institutions are worse organized than those of our Workers' and Peasants' Inspection, and that under present conditions nothing can be expected from this people's commissariat. We must have this firmly fixed in our minds if we really want to create within a few years an institution that will, first, be an exemplary institution, secondly, win everybody's absolute confidence, and, thirdly, prove to all and sundry that we have really justified the work of such a highly placed institution as the Central Control Commission. In my opinion, we must immediately and irrevocably reject all general figures for the size of office staffs. We must select employees for the Workers' and Peasants' Inspection with particular care and only on the basis of the strictest test. Indeed, what is the use of establishing a people's commissariat which carries on anyhow, which does not enjoy the slightest confidence, and whose word carries scarcely any weight? I think that our main object in launching the work of reconstruction that we now have in mind is to avoid all this.

The workers whom we are enlisting as members of the Central Control Commission must be irreproachable Communists, and I think that a great deal has yet to be done to teach them the methods and objects of their work. Furthermore, there must be a definite number of secretaries to assist in this work, who must be put to a triple test before they are appointed to their posts. Lastly, the officials whom in exceptional cases we shall accept directly as employees of the Workers' and Peasants' Inspection must conform to the following requirements:

First, they must be recommended by several Communists.

Second, they must pass a test for knowledge of our state apparatus.

Third, they must pass a test in the fundamentals of the theory of our state apparatus, in the fundamentals of management, office routine, etc.

Fourth, they must work in such close harmony with the members of the Central Control Commission and with their own secretariat that we could vouch for the work of the whole apparatus.

I know that these requirements are extraordinarily strict, and I am very much afraid that the majority of the "practical" workers in the Workers' and Peasants' Inspection will say that these requirements are impracticable, or will scoff at them. But I ask any of the present chiefs of the Workers' and Peasants' Inspection, or anyone associated with that body, whether they can honestly tell me the practical purpose of a people's commissariat like the Workers' and Peasants' Inspection. I think this question will help them recover their sense of proportion. Either it is not worthwhile having another of the numerous reorganizations that we have had of this hopeless affair, the Workers' and Peasants' Inspection, or we must really set to work, by slow, difficult, and unusual methods, and by testing these methods over and over again, to create something really exemplary, something that will win the respect of all and sundry for its merits, and not only because of its rank and title.

If we do not arm ourselves with patience, if we do not devote several years to this task, we had better not tackle it at all.

In my opinion we ought to select a minimum number of the higher labor research institutes, etc., which we have baked so hastily, see whether they are organized properly, and allow them to continue working, but only in a way that conforms to the high standards of modern science and gives us all its benefits. If we do that it will not be utopian to hope that within a few years we shall have an institution that will be able to perform its functions, to work systematically and steadily on improving our state apparatus, an institution backed by the trust of the working class, of the Russian Communist Party and the whole population of our republic.

The spadework for this could be begun at once. If the People's Commissariat of the Workers' and Peasants' Inspection accepted the present plan of reorganization, it could now take preparatory steps and work methodically until the task is completed, without haste, and not hesitating to alter what has already been done.

Any halfhearted solution would be extremely harmful in this matter. A measure for the size of the staff of the Workers' and Peasants' Inspection based on any other consideration would in fact be based on the old bureaucratic considerations, on old prejudices, on what has already been condemned, universally ridiculed, etc.

In substance, the matter is as follows:

Either we prove now that we have really learned something about state organization (we ought to have learned something in five years), or we prove that we are not sufficiently mature for it. If the latter is the case, we had better not tackle the task.

I think that with the available human material it will not be immodest to assume that we have learned enough to be able systematically to rebuild at least one people's commissariat. True, this one people's commissariat will have to be the model for our entire state apparatus.

We ought at once to announce a contest in the compilation of two or more textbooks on the organization of labor in general, and on management in particular. We can take as a basis the book already published by Yermansky, although it should be said in parentheses that he obviously sympathizes with Menshevism and is unfit to compile textbooks for the Soviet system. We can also take as a basis the recent book by Kerzhentsev, and some of the other partial textbooks available may be useful too.

We ought to send several qualified and conscientious people to Germany, or to Britain, to collect literature and to study this question. I mention Britain in case it is found impossible to send people to the USA or Canada.

We ought to appoint a commission to draw up the preliminary program of examinations for prospective employees of the Workers' and Peasants' Inspection; ditto for candidates to the Central Control Commission.

These and similar measures will not, of course, cause any difficulties for the people's commissar or the collegium of the Workers' and Peasants' Inspection, or for the Presidium of the Central Control Commission.

Simultaneously, a preparatory commission should be appointed to select candidates for membership of the Central Control Commission. I hope that we shall now be able to find more than enough candidates for this post among the experienced workers in all departments, as well as among the students of our Soviet higher schools. It would hardly be right to exclude one or another category beforehand. Probably preference will have to be given to a mixed composition for this institution, which should combine many qualities and dissimilar merits. Consequently, the task of drawing up the list of candidates will entail a considerable amount of work. For example, it would be least desirable for the staff of the new people's commissariat to consist of people of one type, only of officials, say, or for it to exclude people of the propagandist type, or people whose principal quality is sociability or the ability to penetrate into circles that are not altogether customary for officials in this field, etc.

* * *

I think I shall be able to express my idea best if I compare my plan with that of academic institutions. Under the guidance of their Presidium, the members of the Central Control Commission should systematically examine all the papers and documents of the Political Bureau. Moreover, they should divide their time correctly between various jobs in investigating the routine in our institutions, from the very small and privately owned offices to the highest state institutions. And lastly, their functions should include the study of theory, i.e., the theory of organization of the work they intend to devote themselves to, and practical work under the guidance either of older comrades or of teachers in the higher institutes for the organization of labor.

I do not think, however, that they will be able to confine themselves to this sort of academic work. In addition, they will have to prepare themselves for work which I would not hesitate to call training to catch, I will not say rogues, but something like that, and working out special ruses to screen their movements, their approach, etc.

If such proposals were made in West European government institutions they would rouse frightful resentment, a feeling of moral indignation, etc.; but I trust that we have not become so bureaucratic as to be capable of that. NEP has not yet succeeded in gaining such respect as to cause any of us to be shocked at the idea that somebody may be caught. Our Soviet republic is of such recent construction, and there are such heaps of the old lumber still lying around, that it would hardly occur to anyone to be shocked at the idea that we should delve into them by means of ruses, by means of investigations sometimes directed to rather remote sources or in a roundabout way. And even if it did occur to anyone to be shocked by this, we may be sure that such a person would make himself a laughingstock.

Let us hope that our new Workers' and Peasants' Inspection will abandon what the French call *pruderie*, which we may call ridiculous primness, or ridiculous swank, and which plays entirely into the hands of our Soviet and party bureaucracy. Let it be said in parentheses that we have bureaucrats in our party offices as well as in Soviet offices.

When I said above that we must study and study hard in institutes for the higher organization of labor, etc., I did not by any means imply "studying" in the schoolroom way, nor did I confine myself to the idea of studying only in the schoolroom way. I hope that not a single genuine revolutionary will suspect me of refusing in this case to understand "studies" to include resorting to some semihumorous trick, cunning device, piece of trickery, or something of that sort. I know that in the staid and earnest states of Western Europe such an idea would horrify people and that not a single decent official would even entertain it. I hope, however, that we have not yet become as bureaucratic as all that and that in our midst the discussion of this idea will give rise to nothing more than amusement.

Indeed, why not combine pleasure with utility? Why not resort to some humorous or semihumorous trick to expose something ridiculous, something harmful, something semiridiculous, semiharmful, etc.?

It seems to me that our Workers' and Peasants' Inspection will gain a great deal if it undertakes to examine these ideas, and that the list of cases in which our Central Control Commission and its colleagues in the Workers' and Peasants' Inspection achieved a few of their most brilliant victories will be enriched by not a few exploits of our future Workers' and Peasants' Inspection and Central Control Commission members in places not quite mentionable in prim and staid textbooks.

* * *

How can a party institution be amalgamated with a Soviet institution? Is there not something improper in this suggestion?

I do not ask these questions on my own behalf, but on behalf of those I hinted at above when I said that we have bureaucrats in our party institutions as well as in the Soviet institutions.

But why, indeed, should we not amalgamate the two if this is in the interests of our work? Do we not all see that such an amalgamation has been very beneficial in the case of the People's Commissariat of Foreign Affairs, where it was brought about at the very beginning? Does not the Political Bureau discuss from the party point of view many questions, both minor and important, concerning the "moves" we should make in reply to the "moves" of foreign powers in order to forestall their, say, cunning, if we are not to use a less respectable term? Is not this flexible amalgamation of a Soviet institution with a party institution a source of great strength in our politics? I think that what has proved its usefulness, what has been definitely adopted in our foreign politics and has become so customary that it no longer calls forth any doubt in this field, will be at least as appropriate (in fact, I think it will be much more appropriate) for our state apparatus as a whole. The functions of the Workers' and Peasants' Inspection cover our state apparatus as a whole, and its activities should affect all and every state institution without exception: local, central, commercial, purely administrative, educational, archival, theatrical, etc.—in short, all without any exception.

Why then should not an institution, whose activities have such wide scope, and which moreover requires such extraordinary flexibility of forms, be permitted to adopt this peculiar amalgamation of a party control institution with a Soviet control institution?

I see no obstacles to this. What is more, I think that such an amalgamation is the only guarantee of success in our work. I think that all doubts on this score arise in the dustiest corners of our government offices, and that they deserve to be treated with nothing but ridicule.

* * *

Another doubt: is it expedient to combine educational activities with official activities? I think that it is not only expedient, but necessary. Generally speaking, in spite of our revolutionary attitude towards the West European form of state, we have allowed ourselves to become infected with a number of its most harmful and ridiculous prejudices; to some extent we have been deliberately infected with them by our dear bureaucrats, who counted on being able again and again to fish in the muddy waters of these prejudices. And they did fish in these muddy waters to so great an extent that only the blind among us failed to see how extensively this fishing was practiced.

In all spheres of social, economic, and political relationships we are "frightfully" revolutionary. But as regards precedence, the observance of the forms and rites of office management, our "revolutionariness" often gives way to the mustiest routine. On more than one occasion, we have witnessed the very interesting phenomenon of a great leap forward in social life being accompanied by amazing timidity whenever the slightest changes are proposed.

This is natural, for the boldest steps forward were taken in a field which was long reserved for theoretical study, which was promoted mainly, and even almost exclusively, in theory. The Russian, when away from work, found solace from bleak bureaucratic realities in unusually bold theoretical constructions, and that is why in our country these unusually bold theoretical constructions assumed an unusually lopsided character. Theoretical audacity in general constructions went hand in hand with amazing timidity as regards certain very minor reforms in office routine. Some great universal agrarian revolution was worked out with an audacity unexampled in any other country, and at the same time the imagination failed when it came to working out a tenth-rate reform in office routine; the imagination, or patience, was lacking to apply to this reform the general propositions that produced such brilliant results when applied to general problems.

That is why in our present life reckless audacity goes hand in hand, to an astonishing degree, with timidity of thought even when it comes to very minor changes.

I think that this has happened in all really great revolutions, for really great revolutions grow out of the contradictions between the old, between what is directed towards developing the old, and the very abstract striving for the new, which must be so new as not to contain the tiniest particle of the old.

And the more abrupt the revolution, the longer will many of these contradictions last.

* * *

The general feature of our present life is the following: we have destroyed capitalist industry and have done our best to raze to the ground the medieval institutions and landed proprietorship, and thus created a small and very small peasantry, which is following the lead of the proletariat because it believes in the results of its revolutionary work. It is not easy for us, however, to keep going until the socialist revolution is victorious in more developed countries merely with the aid of this confidence because economic necessity, especially under NEP, keeps the productivity of labor of the small and very small peasants at an extremely low level. Moreover, the international situation, too, threw Russia back and, by and large, reduced the labor productivity of the people to a level considerably below prewar. The West European capitalist powers, partly deliberately and partly unconsciously, did everything they could to throw us back, to utilize the elements of the civil war in Russia in order to spread as much ruin in the country as possible. It was precisely this way out of the imperialist war that seemed to have many advantages. They argued somewhat as follows: "If we fail to overthrow the revolutionary system in Russia, we shall, at all events, hinder its progress towards socialism." And from their point of view they could argue in no other way. In the end, their problem was half solved. They failed to overthrow the new system created by the revolution, but they did prevent it from at once taking the step forward that would have justified the forecasts of the socialists, that would have enabled the latter to develop the productive forces with enormous speed, to develop all the potentialities which, taken together, would have produced socialism; socialists would thus have proved to all and sundry that socialism contains within itself gigantic forces and that mankind had now entered into a new stage of development of extraordinarily brilliant prospects.

The system of international relationships which has now taken shape is one in which a European state, Germany, is enslaved by the victor countries. Furthermore, owing to their victory, a number of states, the oldest states in the West, are in a position to make some insignificant concessions to their oppressed classes—concessions which, insignificant though they are, nevertheless retard the revolutionary movement in those countries and create some semblance of "class truce."

At the same time, as a result of the last imperialist war, a number of countries of the East, India, China, etc., have been completely jolted out of the rut. Their development has definitely shifted to general European capitalist lines. The general European ferment has begun to affect them, and it is now clear to the whole world that they have been drawn into a process of development that must lead to a crisis in the whole of world capitalism.

Thus, at the present time we are confronted with the question—shall we be able to hold on with our small and very small peasant production, and in our present state of ruin, until the West European capitalist countries consummate their development towards socialism? But they are consummating it not as we formerly expected. They are not consummating it through the gradual "maturing" of socialism, but through the exploitation of some countries by others, through the exploitation of the first of the countries vanquished in the imperialist war combined with the exploitation of the whole of the East. On the other hand, precisely as a result of the first imperialist war, the East has been definitely drawn into the general maelstrom of the world revolutionary movement.

What tactics does this situation prescribe for our country? Obviously the following. We must display extreme caution so as to preserve our workers' government and to retain our small and very small peasantry under its leadership and authority. We have the advantage that the whole world is now passing to a movement that must give rise to a world socialist revolution. But we are laboring under the disadvantage that the imperialists have succeeded in splitting the world into two camps; and this split is made more complicated by the fact that it is extremely difficult for Germany, which is really a land of advanced, cultured, capitalist development, to rise to her feet. All the capitalist powers of what is called the West are pecking at her and preventing her from rising. On the other hand, the entire East, with its hundreds of millions of exploited working people, reduced to the last degree of human suffering, has been forced into a position where its physical and material strength cannot possibly be compared with the physical, material, and military strength of any of the much smaller West European states.

Can we save ourselves from the impending conflict with these imperialist countries? May we hope that the internal antagonisms and conflicts between the thriving imperialist countries of the West and the thriving imperialist countries of the East will give us a second respite as they did the first time, when the campaign of the West European counterrevolution in support of the Russian counterrevolution broke down owing to the antagonisms in the camp of the counterrevolutionaries of the West and the East, in the camp of the Eastern and Western exploiters, in the camp of Japan and the USA?

I think the reply to this question should be that the issue depends upon too many factors, and that the outcome of the struggle as a whole can be forecast only because in the long run capitalism itself is educating and training the vast majority of the population of the globe for the struggle.

In the last analysis, the outcome of the struggle will be determined by the fact that Russia, India, China, etc., account for the overwhelming majority of the population of the globe. And during the past few years it is this majority that has been drawn into the struggle for emancipation with extraordinary rapidity, so that in this respect there cannot be the slightest doubt what the final outcome of the world struggle will be. In this sense, the complete victory of socialism is fully and absolutely assured.

But what interests us is not the inevitability of this complete victory of socialism, but the tactics which we, the Russian Communist Party, we, the Russian Soviet government, should pursue to prevent the West European counterrevolutionary states from crushing us. To ensure our existence until the next military conflict between the counterrevolutionary imperialist West and the revolutionary and nationalist East, between the most civilized countries of the world and the orientally backward countries which, however, comprise the majority, this majority must become civilized. We, too, lack enough civilization to enable us to pass straight on to socialism, although we do have the political requisites for it. We should adopt the following tactics, or pursue the following policy, to save ourselves.

We must strive to build up a state in which the workers retain the leadership of the peasants, in which they retain the confidence of the peasants, and by exercising the greatest economy remove every trace of extravagance from our social relations.

We must reduce our state apparatus to the utmost degree of economy. We must banish from it all traces of extravagance, of which so much has been left over from tsarist Russia, from its bureaucratic capitalist state machine.

Will not this be a reign of peasant limitations?

No. If we see to it that the working class retains its leadership over the peasantry, we shall be able, by exercising the greatest possible thrift in the economic life of our state, to use every saving we make to develop our large-scale machine industry, to develop electrification, the hydraulic extraction of peat, to complete the Volkhov Power Project, etc.[5]

In this, and in this alone, lies our hope. Only when we have done this shall we, speaking figuratively, be able to change horses, to change from the peasant, muzhik horse of poverty, from the horse of an economy designed for a ruined peasant country, to the horse which the proletariat is seeking and must seek—the horse of large-scale machine industry, of electrification, of the Volkhov Power Station, etc.

That is how I link up in my mind the general plan of our work, of our policy, of our tactics, of our strategy, with the functions of the reorganized Workers' and Peasants' Inspection. This is what, in my opinion, justifies the exceptional care, the exceptional attention that we must devote to the Workers' and Peasants' Inspection in raising it to an exceptionally high level, in giving it a leadership with Central Committee rights, etc., etc.,

And this justification is that only by thoroughly purging our government machine, by reducing to the utmost everything that is not absolutely essential in it, shall we be certain of being able to keep going. Moreover, we shall be able to keep going not on the level of a small-peasant country, not on the level of universal limitation, but on a level steadily advancing to large-scale machine industry.

These are the lofty tasks that I dream of for our Workers' and Peasants' Inspection. That is why I am planning for it the amalgamation of the most authoritative party body with an "ordinary" people's commissariat.

March 2, 1923

[Lenin, *Collected Works*, vol. 33, pp. 487-502.]

The Tasks of the Twelfth Congress

Let us now proceed to a question of first-class importance, that of the relation between the party and the state machine. In that latest article of Comrade Lenin's [6] which I have mentioned more than once, Comrade Lenin writes about the state machine—and I must say straight out that nobody else would have ventured to utter such words—such words as one doesn't repeat so easily [*laughter*]. Vladimir Ilyich writes about our state machine that it is neither more nor less than very similar to the tsarist state machine, anointed, as they say, colored in the Soviet style, but if you examine it, it is the same old bureaucratic machine.

Isn't that nice to hear? It's a real Easter egg for international Menshevism [*laughter*]. It's very much "better" than industry working at a loss. But how are we to understand it? Here, of course, we have one of Lenin's especially emphatic formulations; in order the more firmly to get this into the party's head, to hammer it in as deeply as possible, he doesn't refrain from using drastic words which would earn anybody else a hole in the head. But this is not the sole explanation. We must go more thoroughly into the question. What is our state machine? Did it fall among us from out of the heavens? No, of course it didn't.

Who built it? It grew up on the basis of the soviets of workers', peasants', Red Army men's, and Cossacks' deputies. Who led these soviets? The Communist Party. What the party is we know well. What the soviets are we know well also, of course. We said and we say: The soviets are the best form of government in the interests of the working masses. Our party is the best of parties. It is the teacher of the other parties in the Communist International. That is generally recognized. And here we see coming into being out of the soviets, that is, the best representation of the working masses, under the leadership of the party which is the best party in the Communist International, a state machine of which it has been said that it is . . . little different from the old tsarist machine.

From this, perhaps, some simple-minded fellow, from the so-called Workers' Truth group,[7] let's say, will draw the conclusion:

Should we not take a hammer—just the hammer, without the sickle [*laughter*]—and carry out some mechanical operations on this machine? Such a conclusion would, however, be groundless, since we should then have to pick up the fragments and begin again. Why? Because this machine, which really is wretchedly bad, nevertheless did not drop onto our shoulders, but was created by us under the pressure of historical necessity out of the material which we had to hand. Who is responsible? We all are, and we shall answer for it.

Where has this "quality" of the state machine come from? From this circumstance, that we did not and do not know how to do very much, but we have been forced to do a lot, and often have enlisted people who know, or only half know, but don't want to do it even a quarter properly, and sometimes don't want to do it at all and do it minus a hundred percent. In the operations which we carry out you often cannot distinguish between calculation and magic, but in the state machine there are not a few people who consciously pass off magic as calculation. So here we have been constructing a state machine which begins with a young, selflessly devoted but quite inexperienced Communist, goes on through an indifferent office clerk, and ends with a gray-haired expert who sometimes, under irreproachable forms, engages in sabotage.

Well now, can we abolish this all at once? Can we do without this machine? Of course we can't. What must we do? Our task is to take this bad machine as it exists and set about transforming it systematically. Not anyhow or slapdash, but in a planned way, calculated to cover a long period. Up to now the state machine has been constructed on the principle of going from one case to the next. First we assembled material, then we reduced it. When an institution had become extremely overgrown, we cut it down. If we have learned anything in the last five years, Comrade Lenin notes in his article, then it is to estimate time, that is, to appreciate how comparatively little can be done in five years in the sense of replacing the old by the new. And how systematically we must therefore approach our great tasks.

Comrades, this is a very important idea. To take power is one thing, but to reeducate people, to train them in new methods of work, to teach even such a thing (a small thing, but presupposing a displacement of the entire psychology!), such a small thing, I say, as that a Soviet official ought to behave attentively and respectfully to an old, illiterate peasant woman who has come into a big, high-ceilinged hall and gazes around her and doesn't know before which inkstand to beat her forehead on the ground—and there sits our red-tapist, directing her with the tip of his finger to number so-and-do, and she hesitates, turning this way and that, in front of number so-and-so, utterly helpless, and leaves the office without achieving anything.

And if she could formulate her ideas, she would formulate them, I think, in Lenin's words, what things were like seven or eight years ago they are also like today; in the same way then she went into the office and in the same way she failed to get what she went for because they said things to her she couldn't understand in a language she couldn't understand, not trying to help her, but trying to get rid of her. This, of course, doesn't go on everywhere and all the time. But if it is only one-third true to life then there is a frightful abyss between the state machine and the working masses. I recently wrote an article about this "tip of a big problem," an article which was transmitted to your newspapers by telephone for reprinting, but, as, alas, Soviet technique is still poor, I only half recognized this article as it appeared here [*laughter*] but the point of this article was what I have just expressed.[8]

Comrades, what is the meaning of Comrade Lenin's plan, which has now already been adopted by an overwhelming majority in the party? This plan means an approach to a *planned* reconstruction of the state machine. The party created the state machine, yes, the party created it, and then it looked at what it had created. . . . Remember what the Bible says: God created, looked at his creation and said that it was good [*laughter*], but the party has created, looked and . . . has shaken its head [*laughter, prolonged applause*]. And now, after this silent shaking of the head along comes a man who has ventured to call what has been constructed by its name and to do this at the top of his voice.

But this is not the voice of despair—oh, no! The conclusion to be drawn from the situation is this, that whereas we have in five years created this clumsy, creaking machine which to a considerable degree is not "ours," we must now devote a minimum of five years to altering and reconstructing it so as to make it more like a machine about which there will be no occasion to express oneself so strongly. . . . That is why I pay attention to that phrase which Comrade Lenin puts in parentheses.[9] Yes, we have now for the first time learned to estimate the "capacity" of the time in which our efforts are confined. A lot of time is needed. And so it is not now just a question of making corrections—we shall, of course, make corrections from one case to case in the future as well—but our fundamental task is that of *systematic, planned reconstruction of the state machine.*

Through what agency? Through that which erected it, through the party. And for this party too we need a fresh, improved organ for sounding this machine, a probe which is not only moral but also political and practical—not on the plane of formal state inspection, which has already shown its complete bankruptcy, but on the plane of party penetration into the heart of the matter to carry out a selection process in the most important fields of work. Again, what this organ will be like at first, how this Central Control Commission will work in conjunction with the Workers' and Peasants' Inspection, is a matter for further experience, and serious-minded workers cannot entertain any illusions about the possibility of rapid changes.

But it would be quite base on our part to say that nothing can come of this planned approach to the problem, to report that "your ears won't grow any higher than your forehead," and so on. It is, of course, a very difficult task, but for just that reason it must be dealt with in a planned way, systematically, not on a case-to-case basis. Precisely for this reason there is needed an authoritative central party-and-Soviet organ which will be able to sound the state machine in a new way both from the angle of its general efficiency and from that of how it responds to a simple illiterate old woman; and all this, perhaps, will be given us by a combined organ of the Central Control Commission and the Workers' and Peasants' Inspection, working on the principle of selecting the best workers and systematically educating them in a combination of formal state-service practices with the methods of the Workers' and Peasants' Inspection—of what is best in it, that is, a small nucleus. This experiment must be made, and we are making it. . . .

Our work, comrades, is very slow, very partial, even though within the framework of a great plan. Our methods of work are "prosaic": balances and calculations, the food tax and the export of grain—all this we are doing step by step, brick by brick. . . . Isn't there a danger in all this of a sort of hairsplitting degeneration of the party? We cannot permit such a degeneration, any more than a breakup of the party's unity of action even to the slightest extent, for even if the present period is going to be prolonged "seriously and for a long time, yet it is not going on forever." And perhaps it won't even last for a long time.

A revolutionary outbreak on a big scale, such as the beginning of revolution in Europe, can occur sooner than many of us now think. And if there is one of Lenin's many teachings on strategy that we ought especially firmly to keep in memory, it is what he has called *the politics of sharp turns:* today on the barricades, tomorrow in the pigsty of the Third State Duma, today the call to world revolution, to the world October, tomorrow negotiations with Kuhlmann and Czernin, signature of the obscene peace of Brest-Litovsk.[10]

The situation changed, or we estimated it afresh in a new way—the western campaign, "We want Warsaw." The situation was estimated afresh—the peace of Riga, also a rather foul peace, as you know. And then—stubborn work, brick by brick, thereafter, reduction in establishments, checking—do we need five telephone operators or only three, if three are enough, don't dare to employ five, for the peasant will have to give several extra bushels of grain to pay for them—petty, everyday, hairsplitting work—and there, look, the flame of revolution blazes up from the Ruhr.[11] What, shall it catch us in a stage of degeneration? No, comrades, no.

We are not degenerating, we are changing our methods and procedures, but the revolutionary conservatism of the party remains higher than anything else for us. We are learning to draw up balance sheets and at the same time we are looking with sharp eyes to West and East, and events won't catch us by surprise. By purging ourselves, and enlarging our proletarian base we shall strengthen ourselves.

We go forward in agreement with the peasantry and the petty bourgeoisie, we allow the Nepmen; but in the party we will allow no Nepmanism or petty bourgeois, no—we shall burn it out of the party with sulphuric acid and redhot irons [*applause*], and at the Twelfth Congress, which will be the first congress held since October without Vladimir Ilyich and one of the few congresses in the history of our party held without him, we shall say to one another that among the basic precepts which we shall inscribe on our minds with a sharp chisel there will be this—don't get ossified, remember the art of sharp turns, maneuver but don't lose yourself, enter into agreements with temporary or long-term allies but don't let them wedge themselves into the party, remain yourselves, the vanguard of the world revolution. And if the signal sounds from the West—and it will sound—though we may be at that moment up to our necks in calculations, balance sheets, and NEP generally, we shall respond without wavering or delay: We are revolutionaries from head to foot, we have been and we shall remain such, we shall be revolutionaries to the end [*stormy applause, all rise and applaud*].

[*Leon Trotsky Speaks* (New York: Pathfinder, 1972), pp. 155-58; 72-73. Spelling, capitalization, and punctuation slightly revised.]

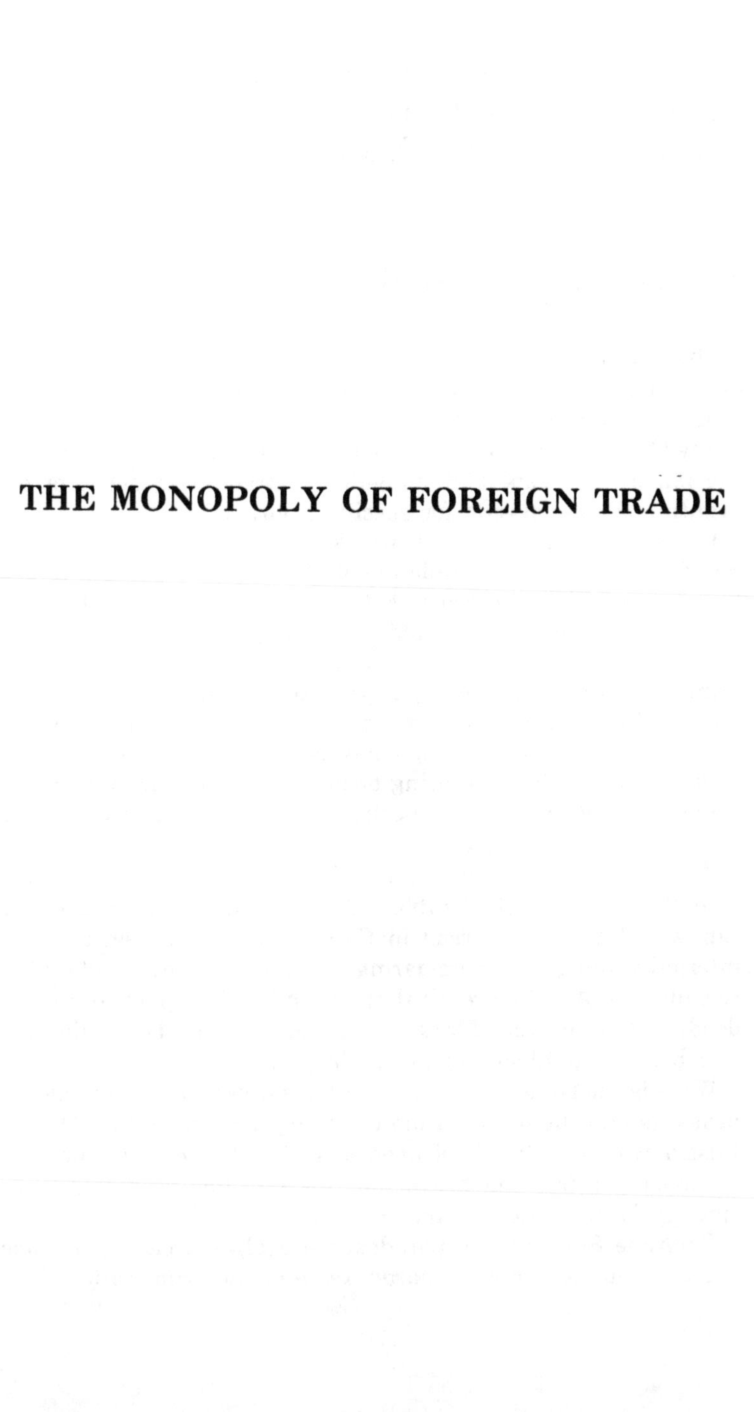

THE MONOPOLY OF FOREIGN TRADE

Letter to J.V. Stalin for Members of the CC, RCP(B) re the Foreign Trade Monopoly

To Comrade Stalin, Secretary of the CC

October 13, 1922

The decision of the plenary meeting of the CC of October 6 (Minutes no. 7, point 3) institutes what seems to be an unimportant, partial reform: "implement a number of separate decisions of the Council of Labor and Defense on temporary permission for the import and export of individual categories of goods or on granting the permission for specific frontiers."

In actual fact, however, this wrecks the foreign-trade monopoly. Small wonder that Comrade Sokolnikov has been trying to get this done and has succeeded. He has always been for it; he likes paradoxes and has always undertaken to prove that monopoly is not to our advantage. But it is surprising that people who in principle favor the monopoly have voted for this without asking for detailed information from any of the business executives.

What does the decision that has been adopted signify?

Purchasing offices are being opened for the import and export trade. The owner of such an office has the right to buy and sell *only* specially listed goods.

Where is the control over this? Where are the means of control?

In Russia flax costs 4 rubles 50 kopeks, in Britain it costs 14 rubles. All of us have read in *Capital* how capitalism changes internally and grows more daring when interest rates and profits rise quickly. All of us recall that capitalism is capable of taking deadly risks and that Marx recognized this long before the war and before capitalism began its "leaps".

What is the situation now? What force is capable of holding the peasants and the traders from extremely profitable deals? Cover Russia with a network of overseers? Catch the neighbor in a purchasing office and prove that his flax has been sold to be smuggled out of the country?

Comrade Sokolnikov's paradoxes are always clever, but one must distinguish between paradoxes and the grim truth.

No "legality" on such a question is at all possible in the Russian countryside. No comparison with smuggling in general ("All the same," they say, "smuggling is also flourishing in spite of the monopoly") is in any way correct; it is one thing to deal with the professional smuggler on the frontier and another with *all* the peasantry, who will *all* defend themselves and fight the authorities when they try to deprive them of the profit "belonging to them."

Before we have had an opportunity to test the monopoly system, which is only just beginning to bring us millions (and will give us tens of millions and more), we are introducing complete chaos; we are shaking loose the very supports that we have only just begun to strengthen.

We have begun to build up a system; the foreign-trade monopoly and the cooperatives are both only in the process of being built up. Some results will be forthcoming in a year or two. The profit from foreign trade runs into hundreds percent, and we are *beginning* to receive millions and tens of millions. We have *begun* to build up mixed companies[1]; we have begun to learn to receive *half* of their (monstrous) profits. We can already see signs of very substantial state profits. We are giving this up in the hope of duties which cannot yield any comparable profit; we are giving everything up and chasing a specter!

The question was brought up at the plenary meeting hastily. There was no serious discussion worth mentioning. We have no reason for haste. Our business executives are only just beginning to go into things. Is there anything like a correct approach to the matter when major questions of trade policy are decided in a slapdash manner, without collecting the pertinent material, without weighing the *pros* and *cons* with documents and figures? Tired people vote in a few minutes and that's the end of it. We have weighed less complicated political questions over and over again and frequently it took us several months to reach a decision.

I regret it very much that illness prevented me from attending the meeting on that day and that I am now compelled to seek an exception to the rule.

But I think that the question must be weighed and studied, that haste is harmful.

I propose that the decision on this question be deferred for two months, i.e., until the next plenary meeting; in the interim information and verified *documents* on the experience of our trade policy should be collected.

V. Ulyanov (Lenin)[2]

PS: In the conversation I had with Comrade Stalin yesterday (I did not attend the plenary meeting and tried to get my information from the comrades who were there), we spoke, incidentally, of the proposal temporarily to open the Petrograd and Novorossiisk ports. It seems to me that both examples show the extreme danger of such experiments even for a most restricted list of goods. The opening of the Petrograd port would intensify the smuggling of flax across the Finnish frontier to prodigious proportions. Instead of combating professional smugglers we shall have to combat *all the peasantry* of the flax-growing region. In this fight we shall almost assuredly be beaten, and beaten irreparably. The opening of the Novorossiisk port would quickly drain us of surplus grain. Is this a cautious policy at a time when our reserves for war are small? When a series of systematic measures to increase them have not yet had time to show results?

Then the following should be given consideration. The foreign trade monopoly has started a stream of gold into Russia. It is only just becoming possible to calculate; the first trip of such and such a merchant to Russia for six months has given him, say, hundreds percent of profit; he increases his price for this right from 25 to 50 percent in favor of the Commissariat of Foreign Trade. Furthermore, it has become possible for us to learn and to *increase* this profit. Everything will at once collapse, the whole work will stop, because if here and there various ports are opened for a time, *not a single merchant will pay a penny for this kind of "monopoly."* That is obvious. Before taking such a risk things have to be thought over and weighed several times. Besides there is the political risk of letting through not foreign merchants by name, which we check, but the entire petty bourgeoisie in general.

With the start of foreign trade we have begun to reckon on an influx of gold. I see no other settlement except for a liquor monopoly,[3] but here there are very serious moral considerations, and also some businesslike objections from Sokolnikov.

Lenin

PPS: I have just been informed (1:30 a.m.) that some business executives have applied for a postponement. I have not yet read this application, but I wholeheartedly support it. It is only a matter of two months.

Lenin

[Lenin, *Collected Works,* vol. 33, pp. 375-78.]

To L.D. Trotsky

Comrade Trotsky:

I am sending you Krestinsky's letter. Write me as soon as possible whether you agree; at the plenum, I am going to fight for the monopoly.

What about you?

Yours,
Lenin

PS: It would be best returned *soon.*

[December 12, 1922]

[Lenin, *Collected Works,* vol. 45, p. 601.]

December 12, 1922

To Comrade Lenin

V.I.:

Maintaining and *strengthening* the monopoly of foreign trade appears absolutely imperative. But at the present time, in practice, the opponents of foreign trade are not staging a frontal assault against it, but rather are employing intricate, flanking maneuvers. On the other hand, modification and improvement of the methods of the monopoly of foreign trade is absolutely imperative.

The danger may arise that under the guise of improving the methods of implementing the monopoly, measures may be slipped in that essentially undercut the monopoly.

Comrade Avanesov came by today and let me in on the basic conclusions of his commission. As I understood him, he does not want the trade monopoly to be implemented directly by the People's Commissariat of Foreign Trade, but rather by large-scale economic units (syndicates, concerns) under the control of Foreign Trade. Krestinsky, obviously in agreement with Stomonyakov, is proposing that important economic units (i.e., once again, obviously, syndicates and concerns, in part departments) have their permanent representatives at corresponding points and that these representatives should establish sections in the trade delegations. This plan has something in common with Avanesov's, however with this very important difference—Krestinsky is taking the trade delegations as the basis, as the direct trading (buying and selling) organs of the republic. Individual economic units will operate through sections of the trade delegations, while these sections are organized in agreement with the corresponding economic units. Avanesov, however, directly designates these representative bodies of the syndicates as basic trading organs, retaining controlling functions for the trade delegations.

Perhaps the development of these will lead to something. But for the moment, perhaps it would be safer to take the trade delegations as the basis. It is possible, however, that I did not fully understand the plan of Avanesov's commission. He promised to send the proposals in writing tomorrow.

The most important question, however, has been and remains the regulation of our foreign trade out of Russia in connection with our overall economic work. It is necessary for someone to know and decide what may be imported and what may not, what may be exported and what we must keep for ourselves. The decisions needed here are not on the plane of legislative regulation, set lists, but practical flexible ones, always adjusted to economic requirements taken as a whole. This obviously should be the task of Gosplan, which comes, in turn, under the heading of development of state industry. But this is a different matter, which I have written about more than once. Avanesov's commission has only confirmed that *this kind* of calculation of our imports and exports has not been made up to now.

Trotsky

[*The Trotsky Papers,* vol. 2, pp. 778-80. Translated from the Russian by the editor.]

To Comrades Frumkin and Stomonyakov Copy to Trotsky

In view of my increasing sickness, I cannot be present at the plenum. I am conscious how awkwardly, and even worse than awkwardly, I am behaving in relation to you, but all the same, I cannot possibly speak.

Today I have received the enclosed letter from Comrade Trotsky with which I agree in all essentials, with the exception perhaps of the last lines about the State Planning Commission. I will write Trotsky of my agreement with him and ask him to take upon himself, in view of my sickness, the defense of my position at the plenum.

I think that this defense ought to be divided into three parts. *First,* the defense of the fundamental principle of the monopoly of foreign trade, its full and final confirmation; *second,* delegate to a special commission the detailed consideration of those practical plans for realizing this monopoly which are advanced by Avanesov—at least half of this commission ought to consist of representatives from the Commissariat of Foreign Trade; *third,* the question of the work of the State Planning Commission ought to be considered separately. And by the way, I think that there will be no disagreement between me and Trotsky if he confines himself to the demand that the work of the State Planning Commission, carried on under the aegis of the development of state industry, should give its opinion about all parts of the activity of the People's Commissariat of Foreign Trade.

I hope to write again today or tomorrow and send you my declaration on the essence of the given problem at the plenum of the Central Committee. At any rate, I think that this question is of such fundamental importance that in case I do not get the agreement of the plenum, I ought to carry it into the party congress and before that announce the existing disagreement in the fraction of our party at the coming congress of the soviets.

Lenin

Dictated to L.F.
December 12, 1922.

[Trotsky, *The Stalin School of Falsification,* pp. 59-60. Spelling, capitalization, and punctuation slightly revised. This letter is not included in the *Collected Works*.]

To L.D. Trotsky

Comrade Trotsky
Copy to Frumkin and Stomonyakov

Comrade Trotsky:

I have received your comments on Krestinsky's letter and Avanesov's plans. I think that you and I are in maximum agreement, and I believe that the State Planning Commission question, as presented in this case, rules out (or postpones) any discussion on whether the State Planning Commission needs to have any administrative rights.

At any rate, it is my request[4] that at the forthcoming plenum you should undertake the defense of our common standpoint on the unquestionable need to maintain and consolidate the foreign-trade monopoly. Since the preceding plenum passed a decision in this respect which runs entirely counter to the foreign-trade monopoly, and since there can be no concessions on this matter, I believe, as I say in my letter to Frumkin and Stomonyakov, that in the event of our defeat on this question we must refer the question to a party congress. This will require a brief exposition of our differences before the party group of the forthcoming congress of soviets. If I have time, I shall write this, and I would be very glad if you did the same. Hesitation on this question is doing us unprecedented harm, and the negative arguments boil down entirely to accusations of shortcomings in the apparatus. But our apparatus is everywhere imperfect, and to abandon the monopoly because of an imperfect apparatus would be throwing out the baby with the bath water.

Lenin

December 13, 1922

[Lenin, *Collected Works,* vol. 45, pp. 601-02.]

Letter to J.V. Stalin for members of the RCP(B) CC

I am now through with putting my business in order, and am in a position to leave without worry.[5] I have also come to an arrangement with Trotsky to stand up for my views on the foreign-trade monopoly. There is only one thing that is worrying me extremely—it is that I am unable to speak at the congress of soviets. On Tuesday, I shall have the doctors in to see me and we shall discuss whether there is any chance at all of my doing so. I would regard my missing it as a great inconvenience, to put it no stronger. I have had the outline of my speech written several days ago.[6] I propose, therefore, without suspending preparations by some other speaker in my place, to keep open until Wednesday the possibility that I will perhaps personally make a speech, much shorter than the usual one, say, lasting forty-five minutes. Such a speech would in no way prevent a substitute (whomsoever you would authorize for that purpose) from making a speech, but I think it would be useful both in the political and in the personal sense because it would remove any cause for great agitation. Please have this in mind, and if the opening of the congress should be further delayed, inform me in good time through my secretary.

Lenin

December 15, 1922

I am resolutely opposed to any delay on the question of the foreign-trade monopoly. If the idea should arise, for whatever reason (including the proposition that my participation in the question is desirable), to postpone it until the next plenum, I should most resolutely object to this, because I am sure that Trotsky will be able to stand up for my views just as well as I myself. That is the first thing. The second is that your statement and Zinoviev's and, according to rumor, Kamenev's as well confirm that some members of the CC have already altered their earlier opinion; third, and most important: any further hesitation on this highly important question is absolutely intolerable and will tend to frustrate any work.

Lenin

December 15, 1922

[Lenin, *Collected Works*, vol. 45, pp. 602-03.]

To L.D. Trotsky

Comrade Trotsky:

I consider that we have quite reached agreement. I ask you to declare our solidarity at the plenum. I hope that our decision will be passed, because some of those who had voted against it in October have now partially or altogether switched to our side.

If for some reason our decision should not be passed, we shall apply to the group of the congress of soviets, and declare that we are referring the question to the party congress.

In that case, inform me and I shall send in my statement.

Yours,
Lenin

PS: If this question should be removed from the present plenum (which I do not expect, and against which you should of course protest as strongly as you can on our common behalf), I think that we should apply to the group of the congress of soviets anyway and demand that the question be referred to the party congress because any further hesitation is absolutely intolerable.

You can keep all the material I have sent you until after the plenum.

[December 15, 1922]

[Lenin, *Collected Works*, vol. 45, p. 604.]

To L.D. Trotsky

Comrade Trotsky:

I am sending on to you Frumkin's letter[7] which I have received today. I also think that it is absolutely necessary to have done with this question once and for all. If there are any fears that I am being worried by this question and that it could even have an effect on my health, I think that this is absolutely wrong because I am infinitely more worried by the delay which makes our policy on one of the most basic questions quite unstable. That is why I call your attention to the enclosed letter and ask you to support an immediate discussion of this question. I am sure that if we are threatened with the danger of failure, it would be much better to fail before the party congress and at once to apply to the group of the congress, than to fail after the congress. Perhaps an acceptable compromise is that we pass a decision just now confirming the monopoly, and still bring up the question at the party congress, making an arrangement about this right away. I do not believe that we could accept any other compromise either in our own interests or the interests of the cause.

Lenin

December 15, 1922

[Lenin, *Collected Works,* vol. 45, pp. 604-05]

To L.D. Trotsky

It looks as though it has been possible to take the position without a single shot, by a simple maneuver. I suggest that we should not stop and should continue the offensive and for that purpose put through a motion to raise at the party congress the question of consolidating our foreign trade and the measures to improve its implementation. This is to be announced in the group of the congress of soviets. I hope that you will not object to this and will not refuse to give a report in the group.

N. Lenin

December 21, 1922

[Lenin, *Collected Works*, vol. 45, p. 606.]

Letter to L.B. Kamenev for the Members of the Political Bureau of the Central Committee of the Russian Communist Party (Bolsheviks)

September 29 [1922]
Comrade Kamenev! No doubt you have already received from Stalin the resolution of his commission on incorporating the independent republics in the RSFSR.

If you have not received it, get it from the secretary and read it immediately, please. I discussed it yesterday with Sokolnikov and today with Stalin. Tommorow I will be seeing Mdivani (a Georgian Communist suspected of "separatist" sentiments).

In my opinion, the question is of prime importance. Stalin is rather in too much of a hurry. You must—since at one time you intended to take up the question and have also studied it to some extent—think the matter through and Zinoviev likewise.

Stalin has already agreed to make one concession—to say in paragraph 1 in place of "entry" into the RSFSR:

"Formal union with the RSFSR in a Union of Soviet Republics of Europe and Asia."

The spirit of this concession is, I hope, clear: we see ourselves as equals in law with the Ukrainian SSR and the others and enter with them into a new union, a new federation, "The Union of Soviet Republics of Europe and Asia."

Paragraph 2 will then also have to be amended. Something like creating an "All-Federation Central Executive Committee of the Union of Soviet Republics of Europe and Asia" to meet side by side with CEC of the RSFSR.

If the latter meets once a week and the former meets once a week (or even once every two weeks), it should not be difficult to arrange this.

It is important not to give the supporters of "independence" grist for their mill, not to destroy their *independence*, but rather to establish a *new stage*, a federation of republics *with equal rights*.

The second part of paragraph 2 could stand as is: dissatisfaction (with decisions of STO [Council of Labor and Defense] and SNK [Council of People's Commissars]) will be appealed to the All-Federation CEC *without suspending execution* (the same goes for the RSFSR).

Paragraph 3 could stand with an editorial amendment: "[The services of foreign affairs, foreign trade, defense, communications, and posts and telegraphs of the republics. . .] will be merged into *all-federation* people's commissariats with headquarters in Moscow, and the corresponding people's commissariats of the RSFSR will have their authorized representatives with a small staff in all the republics *belonging to the Union of Republics of Europe and Asia.*"

The second part of paragraph 3 stands; perhaps it might be more equitable to say: "[these representatives will be appointed] after agreement with the CECs of the member republics of the Union of Soviet Republics of Europe and Asia."

The third part ["The participation of the representatives of the republics concerned in the commissariats of Foreign Affairs and Foreign Trade must be regarded as useful"] needs more consideration. Shouldn't "useful" be replaced by *"obligatory"*? Or shouldn't we insert a *conditional* obligation, if only in the form of *interpellation*, accepting decisions without interpellation applying only in matters of "special emergency importance"?

Paragraph 4, ["The commissariats of Finance, Food, Labor, and Economics of the republics will be strictly subject to the directives of the corresponding commissariats of the RSFSR"] perhaps add "merged by agreement of the CECs"?

Paragraph 5, ["The other commissariats of the republics . . . will be regarded as independent"] perhaps add "with the establishment of combined or general conferences and meetings having a *purely consultative* character (or *merely* consultative character)"?

Corresponding changes in first and second addenda.

Stalin has agreed to delay presenting the resolution to the Politburo of the CC until my arrival. I shall arrive on Monday, October 2. I would like to see you along with Rykov for a couple of hours in the morning, say, between noon and two o'clock, or if necessary in the evening, say, between five and seven or six and eight.

This is my initial proposal. On the basis of discussions with

Mdivani and other comrades, I will make additions or alterations. I strongly urge your doing likewise and sending me your reply.

Yours, Lenin

PS: Send copies to *all* members of the Politburo.

[Lenin, *Sochineniya* (Collected Works), 5th ed., vol. 45 (Moscow: Izdatelstvo Politicheskoi Literatury, 1970), pp. 211-13. Translated from Russian by the editor. This document does not appear in the English *Collected Works*. The text of Stalin's "autonomization plan" is in Lewin, *Lenin's Last Struggle*, pp. 146-47. Relevant passages have been interpolated in brackets to make Lenin's comments clear.]

Memo to L.B. Kamenev on Combating Great Russian Chauvinism

Comrade Kamenev:

I declare war to the death on Great Russian chauvinism. I shall eat it with all my healthy teeth as soon as I get rid of this accursed bad tooth.

It must be *absolutely* insisted that the Union Central Executive Committee should be *presided over* in turn by a

Russian,
Ukrainian,
Georgian, etc.
Absolutely!

Yours,
Lenin

[October 6, 1922]

[Lenin, *Collected Works,* vol. 33, p. 372 and *Sochineniya,* vol. 45, p. 214. The version in the English edition is corrupt, substituting "the Political Bureau" for L.B. Kamenev in the title, and omitting the salutation. In addition, *Velikorusskii shovinizm* (Great Russian chauvinism) is rendered by "dominant nation chauvinism."]

THE NATIONALITIES QUESTION

I suppose I have been very remiss[2] with respect to the workers of Russia for not having intervened energetically and decisively enough in the notorious question of autonomization, which, it appears, is officially called the question of the Union of Soviet Socialist Republics.

When this question arose last summer, I was ill; and then in autumn I relied too much on my recovery and on the October and December plenary meetings giving me an opportunity of intervening in this question. However, I did not manage to attend the October plenary meeting (when this question came up) or the one in December, and so the question passed me by almost completely.

I have only had time for a talk with Comrade Dzerzhinsky, who came from the Caucasus and told me how this matter stood in Georgia. I have also managed to exchange a few words with Comrade Zinoviev and express my apprehensions on this matter. From what I was told by Comrade Dzerzhinsky, who was at the head of the commission sent by the CC to "investigate" the Georgian incident, I could only draw the greatest apprehensions. If matters had come to such a pass that Ordzhonikidze could go to the extreme of applying physical violence, as Comrade Dzerzhinsky informed me, we can imagine what a mess we have got ourselves into. Obviously the whole business of "autonomization" was radically wrong and badly timed.

It is said that a united apparatus was needed. Where did that assurance come from? Did it not come from that same Russian apparatus which, as I pointed out in one of the preceding sections of my diary,[3] we took over from tsarism and slightly anointed with Soviet oil?

There is no doubt that that measure should have been delayed somewhat until we could say that we vouched for our apparatus as our own. But now, we must, in all conscience, admit the contrary; the apparatus we call ours is, in fact, still quite alien to us; it is a bourgeois and tsarist hotchpotch and there has been no possibility of getting rid of it in the course of the past five years without the help of other countries and because we have been "busy" most of the time with military engagements and the fight against famine.

It is quite natural that in such circumstances the "freedom to secede from the union" by which we justify ourselves will be a mere scrap of paper, unable to defend the non-Russians from the onslaught of that really Russian man, the Great Russian chauvinist, in substance a rascal and a tyrant, such as the typical Russian bureaucrat is. There is no doubt that the infinitesimal percentage of Soviet and sovietized workers will drown in that tide of chauvinistic Great Russian riffraff like a fly in milk.

It is said in defense of this measure that the people's commissariats directly concerned with national psychology and national education were set up as separate bodies. But there the question arises: can these people's commissariats be made quite independent? And secondly: were we careful enough to take measures to provide the non-Russians with a real safeguard against the truly Russian bully? I do not think we took such measures although we could and should have done so.

I think that Stalin's haste and his infatuation with pure administration, together with his spite against the notorious "nationalist-socialism," played a fatal role here. In politics spite generally plays the basest of roles.

I also fear that Comrade Dzerzhinsky, who went to the Caucasus to investigate the "crime" of those "nationalist-socialists," distinguished himself there by his truly Russian frame of mind (it is common knowledge that people of other nationalities who have become Russified overdo this Russian frame of mind)[4] and that the impartiality of his whole commission was typified well enough by Ordzhonikidze's "manhandling." I think that no provocation or even insult can justify such Russian manhandling and that Comrade Dzerzhinsky was inexcusably guilty in adopting a light-hearted attitude towards it.

For all the citizens in the Caucasus, Ordzhonikidze was the authority. Ordzhonikidze had no right to display that irritability to which he and Dzerzhinsky referred. On the contrary, Ordzhonikidze should have behaved with a restraint which cannot be demanded of any ordinary citizen, still less of a man accused of a "political" crime. And, to tell the truth, those nationalist-socialists were citizens who were accused of a political crime, and the terms of the accusation were such that it could not be described otherwise.

Here we have an important question of principle: how is internationalism to be understood?[5]

Lenin

December 30, 1922
Taken down by M.V.

Continuation of the notes.
December 31, 1922

In my writings on the national question, I have already said that an abstract presentation of the question of nationalism in general is of no use at all. A distinction must necessarily be made between the nationalism of an oppressor nation and that of an oppressed nation, the nationalism of a big nation and that of a small nation.

In respect of the second kind of nationalism we, nationals of a big nation, have nearly always been guilty, in historic practice, of an infinite number of cases of violence; furthermore, we commit violence and insult an infinite number of times without noticing it. It is sufficient to recall my Volga reminiscences of how non-Russians are treated; how the Poles are not called by any other name than "Polyachiska," how the Tatar is nicknamed "Prince," how the Ukrainians are always "Khokhols" and the Georgians and other Caucasian nationals always "Kapkasians."

That is why internationalism on the part of oppressors or "great" nations, as they are called (though they are great only in their violence, only great as bullies), must consist not only in the observance of the formal equality of nations but even in an inequality of the oppressor nation, the great nation, that must make up for the inequality which obtains in actual practice. Anybody who does not understand this has not grasped the real proletarian attitude to the national question, he is still essentially petty bourgeois in his point of view and is, therefore, sure to descend to the bourgeois point of view.

What is important for the proletarian? For the proletarian it is not only important, it is absolutely essential that he should be assured that the non-Russians place the greatest possible trust in the proletarian class struggle. What is needed to ensure this? Not merely formal equality. In one way or another, by one's attitude or by concessions, it is necessary to compensate the non-Russians for the lack of trust, for the suspicion and the insults to which the government of the "dominant" nation subjected them in the past.

I think it is unnecessary to explain this to Bolsheviks, to Communists, in greater detail. And I think that in the present instance, as far as the Georgian nation is concerned, we have a typical case in which a genuinely proletarian attitude makes profound caution, thoughtfulness, and a readiness to compromise a matter of necessity for us. The Georgian who is neglectful of this aspect of the question, or who carelessly flings about accusations of "nationalist-socialism" (whereas he himself is a real and true "nationalist-socialist," and even a vulgar Great Russian bully), violates, in substance, the interests of proletarian class solidarity, for nothing holds up the development and strengthening of proletarian class solidarity so much as national injustice; "offended" nationals are not sensitive to anything so much as to the feeling of equality and the violation of this equality, if only through negligence or jest—to the violation of that equality by their proletarian comrades. That is why in this case it is better to overdo rather than underdo the concessions and leniency towards the national minorities. That is why, in this case, the fundamental interest of proletarian solidarity, and consequently of the proletarian class struggle, requires that we never adopt a formal attitude to the national question, but always take into account the specific attitude of the proletarian of the oppressed (or small) nation towards the oppressor (or great) nation.

Lenin

Taken down by M.V.
December 31, 1922

Continuation of the notes
December 31, 1922

What practical measures must be taken in the present situation?

Firstly, we must maintain and strengthen the union of socialist republics. Of this there can be no doubt. This measure is necessary for us and it is necessary for the world communist proletariat in its struggle against the world bourgeoisie and its defense against bourgeois intrigues.

Secondly, the union of socialist republics must be retained for its diplomatic apparatus. By the way, this apparatus is an exceptional component of our state apparatus. We have not allowed a single influential person from the old tsarist apparatus into it. All sections with any authority are composed of Communists. That is why it has already won for itself (this may be said boldly) the name of a reliable communist apparatus purged to an incomparably greater extent of the old tsarist, bourgeois, and petty-bourgeois elements than that which we have had to make do with in other people's commissariats.

Thirdly, exemplary punishment must be inflicted on Comrade Ordzhonikidze (I say this all the more regretfully as I am one of his personal friends and have worked with him abroad) and the investigation of all the material which Dzerzhinsky's commission has collected must be completed or started over again to correct the enormous mass of wrongs and biased judgments which it doubtlessly contains. The political responsibility for all this truly Great Russian nationalist campaign must, of course, be laid on Stalin and Dzerzhinsky.

Fourthly, the strictest rules must be introduced on the use of the national language in the non-Russian republics of our union, and these rules must be checked with special care. There is no doubt that our apparatus being what it is, there is bound to be, on the pretext of unity in the railway service, unity in the fiscal service and so on, a mass of truly Russian abuses. Special ingenuity is necessary for the struggle against these abuses, not to mention special sincerity on the part of those who undertake this struggle. A detailed code will be required, and only the nationals living in the republic in question can draw it up at all successfully. And then we cannot be sure in advance that as a result of this work we shall not take a step backward at our next congress of soviets, i.e., retain the Union of Soviet Socialist Republics only for military and diplomatic affairs, and in all other respects restore full independence to the individual people's commissariats.

It must be borne in mind that the decentralization of the people's commissariats and the lack of coordination in their work as far as Moscow and other centers are concerned can be compensated sufficiently by party authority if it is exercised with sufficient prudence and impartiality; the harm that can result to our state from a lack of unification between the national apparatuses and the Russian apparatus is infinitely less than that which will be done not only to us, but to the whole International, and to the hundreds of millions of the peoples of Asia, which is destined to follow us on to the stage of history in the near future. It would be unpardonable opportunism if, on the eve of the debut of the East, just as it is awakening, we undermined our prestige with its peoples, even if only by the slightest crudity or injustice towards our own non-Russian nationalities. The need to rally against the imperialists of the West, who are defending the capitalist world, is one thing. There can be no doubt about that and it would be superfluous for me to speak about my unconditional approval of it. It is another thing when we ourselves lapse, even if only in trifles, into imperialist attitudes towards oppressed nationalities, thus undermining all our principled sincerity, all our principled defense of the struggle against imperialism. But the morrow of world history will be a day when the awakening peoples oppressed by imperialism are finally aroused and the decisive long and hard struggle for their liberation begins.

Lenin

December 31, 1922
Taken down by M. V.

[Lenin, *Collected Works,* vol. 36, pp. 605-11.]

To L.D. Trotsky

Top secret
Personal

Dear Comrade Trotsky:

It is my earnest request that you should undertake the defense of the Georgian case in the Party CC. This case is now under "persecution" by Stalin and Dzerzhinsky, and I cannot rely on their impartiality. Quite to the contrary. I would feel at ease if you agreed to undertake its defense. If you should refuse to do so for any reason, return the whole case to me. I shall consider it a sign that you do not accept.

With best comradely greetings,[6]
Lenin

[March 5, 1923]

[Lenin, *Collected Works,* vol. 45, p. 607.]

To P.G. Mdivani, F.Y. Makharadze and Others

Top secret

Copy to Comrades Trotsky and Kamenev

Dear Comrades:

I am following your case with all my heart. I am indignant over Ordzhonikidze's rudeness and the connivance of Stalin and Dzerzhinsky. I am preparing for you notes and a speech.

Respectfully yours,
Lenin

March 6, 1923

[Lenin, *Collected Works,* vol. 45, p. 608.]

Thoughts on the Party: The National Question and the Education of the Party Youth

Goethe said long ago that old truths have to be won afresh again and again. This applies to individuals, to parties, and to entire classes. Our party must win for itself afresh, that is, must think out anew, its national program, and consciously check it in actual experience.

Both the domestic policy and the international policy of our party are determined by two fundamental lines—the revolutionary class movement of the Western proletariat and the national revolutionary movement of the East. We have said before how important it is for us to forge strong living ties between the education of our youth—indeed, of the whole party—and the actual course of the proletarian movement throughout the world. (The education of the party, like that of the individual, is never finished; as long as you live, you learn.) Here we must say that not the least useful political exercise for the orientation and self-education of the party is a clear understanding of the national question. In saying *not the least* we may risk being misunderstood. After all, what we have in the West is the proletariat, the struggle for power, while in the East, "all in all," it is only a matter of liberating predominantly peasant nations from an alien yoke. Of course, considered abstractly, these two movements belong to different epochs of social development; but historically they are linked together, directed from two sides against one and the same mighty foe: imperialism. And if we should fail to understand the colossal importance of the national revolutionary factor, its immeasurable explosive power, we would risk hopelessly compromising the revolutionary movement of the West, and ourselves along with it, for many years if not forever.[7]

From the experience of our revolution we have firmly mastered the importance of correct relations between the proletariat and the peasantry, that is, relations corresponding to their class forces and the course of development of the revolutionary movement throughout the world. We have learned to decline the word *smychka* (bond)[8] in all its cases, and that is not accidental—it must be admitted that sometimes we even bring this word in where it is quite irrelevant! But we have thoroughly mastered the basic question. Our government is not called a workers' and peasants' government for nothing. If the success of our revolution depends on correct collaboration between the proletariat and the peasantry, the success of the world revolution depends, above all, on correct collaboration between the West European proletariat and the peasant, national-revolutionary East. Russia is a gigantic junction of the proletarian West and the peasant East; a junction and at the same time a proving ground.

In Russia itself, however, the question of relations between the proletariat and the peasantry is not at all homogeneous. One part of the question is the relations between the Great Russian proletariat and the Great Russian peasantry. Here the question stands in its purely class content. This strips and simplifies the task, thereby rendering it easier to solve. The relations between the Great Russian proletariat, which plays first fiddle in our Union state, and the Azerbaidzhani,Turkestani, Georgian, or Ukrainian peasantry, however, are something else again. There, in the formerly oppressed "borderlands," all social, class, economic, administrative, and cultural questions are sharply refracted through a national prism. There, misunderstandings between proletariat and peasantry (and we have seen not a few in these last few years) inevitably assume a national coloring. This also applies to a considerable extent to the proletariat of the formerly oppressed nations. What in Moscow or Petrograd will be understood as a simple practical conflict between the center and the localities, town and country, textile workers and metal workers, can easily assume in Georgia, Azerbaidzhan, and even in the Ukraine, the form of a conflict between "great-power" Moscow and the demands of small and weaker nations. In certain cases this is the truth of the matter; in others it can appear to be true. Our task consists, first, in preventing it from being true, and, second, in preventing it from seeming true. And this is a very big task, which we must accomplish at all costs, by both constitutional and administrative methods, and above all by party methods.

In what does the danger consist as regards an incorrect policy toward the peasantry? In the fact that the peasantry may cease to be led by the proletariat and fall under the leadership of the bourgeoisie. But this danger is ten times greater when it is a question of the peasant masses—and to a considerable extent also, the young and numerically weak proletariat—of *the small and backward nations that were oppressed by tsarism.* The national link between classes is also a *smychka,* one that has often shown itself in history to be a very strong and tenacious bond. The Georgian Mensheviks, the Ukrainian Petlyurists, the Armenian Dashnaks, the Azerbaidzhani Mussavatists, [9] and the rest were condemned to insignificance by our correct, that is, attentive and courteous, attitude toward the national demands of those people whose ancient historical resentments were being exploited by those parties. Conversely, a lack of understanding or an insufficient understanding on our part of the enormous historical importance of winning the complete and unconditional trust of the formerly oppressed nations would inevitably lend each and every demand, every resentment, every discontent of the indigenous working masses a *national*-oppositional coloring. On that basis a nationalist ideology would create, or more exactly, would re-create, a stong "bond" between the bourgeoisie and the toilers, wholly directed against the revolution.

The dictatorship of the working class has opened up for the first time in history the possibility of a correct solution to the national question. The Soviet system establishes a completely favorable state framework for this: elastic, resilient, and at the same time always capable of giving expression both to the centripetal tendencies of the revolution, surrounded as it is by innumerable and irreconcilable enemies, and to the planning requirements of a socialist economy. But we should fall into crude self-delusion if we conceitedly supposed that we have already solved the national question. Actually, great-power chauvinism is often hidden under this complacency (and it can be found even in the ranks of our party). It is not of the aggressive kind, but slumbering and not liking to be disturbed. A "solution" to the national question can be secured only by ensuring to every nation completely unconstrained access to world culture in the language the given nation considers to be its mother tongue. This presumes a great material and cultural advance by our entire union, and we are still far away from that. It is beyond our power to arbitrarily shorten the time that such an advance must take. But one thing *is* in our power: to show and prove to all the small, weak, and backward nations and nationalities formerly oppressed by tsarism that if very important and considerable demands of theirs are not satisfied, this is due to objective conditions common to the whole union, and not at all to inattention, and not at all to great-power partiality. This must be done not in programmatic declarations, but in our day-to-day state work. And this task, the winning of the complete and unconditional trust of the small and weak nations, confirmed by all their experience, is a paramount party task.

The civil war cut the deepest and clearest channel in the consciousness of the millions of people living in the Soviet Union. In the motives and aims of this war, so far as our party was concerned, there was not an atom of nationalism or "imperialism." The war was essentially a class revolutionary war and in this form it embraced the entire territory of the old tsarist empire, even at moments overflowing the old frontiers. The civil war intersected national groupings in different directions and at different angles, and often bore heavily on certain parts of the present union. During this very severe struggle to save the revolution, the laws of war took precedence over all other laws. Bridges were blown up regardless of what damage would result to economic life. Buildings were taken over for headquarters and barracks from which schoolchildren and their teachers had to be evicted. A harsh military regime cannot but bear heavily on cultural life in general and national culture in particular. Contributing to this was the fact that in particular cases the backwardness of a Red Army unit, the ill will of certain elements in the Communist organization in such a unit, and the inadequate efforts of the political commissars concerned gave rise to ignoring and even roughly trampling upon national feelings and moods. But these were all isolated and passing phenomena. The civil war welded together with blood the working people of all nationalities in struggle against their class oppressors. But in general, by its very essence, it could not be a school of everyday coexistence and cooperation. It could not go beyond formal and "constitutional" principles to practical, material, and moral equality of the citizens of small and backward nationalities with citizens of the former ruling nationality in *enjoying all those benefits, tangible and intangible, which can and must be ensured by belonging to the Soviet Union.* A feeling of national resentment has been accumulated in the formerly oppressed nations over decades and centuries. And this heritage, as with the oppressed position of women it should be said, cannot be disposed of merely by declarations, however sincere they may be and even if they are given legislative character. It is necessary that a woman should feel, in ordinary life, in everyday experience, that there are no external restrictions and constraints upon her and no contemptuous or condescending attitude is being taken toward her. On the contrary, she must feel that she not only has her "rights" but is being given fraternal collaboration directed toward helping her to rise to a higher level. It is necessary that a small nation should feel that a radical and irreversible change has taken place in the consciousness of the former "ruling" nation. It should feel that all departures by members of this nation from practical and moral equality, from actual, living national fraternity will be punished as strikebreaking and treason by the "ruling" nation itself, that is, by its ruling class. Precisely now, with the onset of more organic work, both economic and cultural, the small nations will observe with watchful attention how they are affected by the general economic, political, juridical, and cultural measures of the government of the Soviet Union, that is, primarily what line our party is carrying out in these questions.

Our enemies seek and will continue to seek opportunities for themselves in this sphere. What a rabid international campaign the Social Democrats waged and are still waging around the Georgian question, depicting the eviction of the Mensheviks from Georgia as the suppression of the Georgian nation! We have shown, and with complete justification, that the purging of the Menshevik agents of imperialism from Georgia was a question of life and death for our entire revolution. For us it is beyond question that the proletarian revolution wholly coincides in its aims and consequences with the interests of the small and oppressed peoples. But the living, struggling, as yet uncompleted revolution may in its advance clash with and, without wishing to, inflict blows upon national interests and sentiments. It is not to be doubted that the invasion of Georgia by the Red Army, going to the aid of the Georgian insurgents, not only was interpreted by the charlatans of international Menshevism as a "predatory" policy on the part of the Soviet power, but could also be understood in that sense, and was in fact so understood, by a certain section of the Georgian peasantry and even of the Georgian workers. In struggling against this mood and these views it is absolutely insufficient to show, even with documentation, that the Georgian Mensheviks had deliberately provided an opening for world imperialism that was of the greatest danger to the revolution. The backward section of the Georgian working people that was gripped by national mistrust of the Red Army is distinguished by this fact: it cannot grasp the significance of revolutionary events in their European and worldwide setting. The only convincing policy for us can be a policy that in deeds shows the Georgian peasantry that its national-cultural interests, its national feelings, its national self-respect, which in the past has too often been insulted, find today all the satisfaction that is possible under the objective circumstances.

It is very possible that we can expect a certain exacerbation of national sensitivity and even national mistrust among those nationalities which formerly were oppressed and which, of course, demand of the revolution, and quite rightly, that it guarantee them against any sort of relapse into national inequality in the future. On this basis, it is quite possible that a penetration or intensification of nationalistic tendencies (predominantly *defensive*-nationalistic) may take place even among the Communists of the small nations. Such phenomen, however, as a general rule are not of an independent nature but are reflexive, symptomatic. Just as anarchist-adventurist tendencies in working-class circles are usually a sign and result of the opportunist character of the leaders of the labor organizations, so nationalist tendencies among the Communists of the small nations are a sign that the aims of great-powerism are not yet everywhere eradicated in the general state machine or even in some corners of the ruling party itself.

The danger in this direction is all the greater because the young generation of party members have not, on the whole, come up against the national question in politics. In tsarist Russia this question inescapably confronted the revolutionary party in the form of national oppression and played an outstanding role in our day-to-day agitation. Party theory accorded a big place to the national question. The "old men" passed through all this—although even here cases of recidivism have not been rare. The youth were born to politics in a country without national oppression. They know about the question of military defense of the republic; they went on to questions of the economy. The national question hardly faced them in any real way. For this reason it sometimes seems to them that it is something already settled, like religion, for instance. Is there really, they ask, anything to be said or thought about such a matter?

Among the small or backward nations themselves there is often to be observed insufficient attention to the national question on the part of the more revolutionary elements, including the proletarians. Having adhered to the Russian Communist Party and at once enlarged their own horizons, these young, sincere, ardent revolutionists are sometimes inclined to look upon the national question on their own doorstep not as a problem to be solved but as a mere obstacle to be jumped over. It is certainly the case that a struggle against their own domestic nationalism, even if it has grown out of former oppression, is an important task for revolutionary elements everywhere. But on soil that has been plowed by the old oppression, this struggle must assume a patient, propagandist character and must rely on thoughtfully meeting national demands, not on ignoring them.

A brushing aside of the national question is sometimes found in the case of quite old comrades on the grounds that it is, they say, a temporary "concession," something like our "Narodnik" agrarian program,[10] or NEP. Well, this comparison can be accepted, conditionally. It would of course be easier to build socialism if there were no need to make national "concessions"; that is, if there had not been oppression in the past, and if in the present there were not differences in language and national culture. It would also be easier to build socialism if we did not have millions of peasants. One can go even further and say: It would be better for the proletarian revolution if Asia constituted a capitalist arena of class struggle like Europe. But putting the question like that is utterly remote from life. Essentially, inattention or a contemptuous attitude to the national question often conceals a lifeless, confused, rationalistic attitude toward history. The mighty revolutionary realism of our party, on the contrary, consists in taking facts as they are and combining them practically in the interests of the revolution.

If, on the eve of October, we had closed our eyes to the peasantry we would, of course, not have been any nearer to socialism today, and indeed we should not have got so far as Soviet power. Only in these years since October has our party fully understood the significance of the peasantry: The "old men" understood in practice what previously they had only known in theory, and the youth, having come up against the question in practice, is now comprehending its experience theoretically. *In the field of the national question the party as a whole undoubtedly needs a refresher course, and the youth a beginners' course.* And this course must be undertaken in good time and according to a very stiff program, for whoever ignores the national question risks getting bogged down in it.

An attentive attitude toward national demands does not mean at all, of course, the cultivation of economic separation. That could only be of advantage to the local ("national") bureaucracy but certainly not to the masses. It is quite obvious that a centralized administration of the railways throughout the Union does not at all exclude the use of national languages on the railways. And when evaluating demands and programs for autonomy it is proper to strictly and attentively distinguish between the purely bureaucratic, "prestige and precedence" pretensions of the administrative upper circles and the genuine, everyday, vital interests and demands of the masses. The former are sometimes extremely Russified in relation to the local population, and at the same time separatist in relation to the center.

The widest independence in the national-cultural sphere is in principle fully compatible with economic centralization, insofar as centralization is required by national and production-technique conditions. But state coordination of economic centralization with national-cultural decentralization—in life, in practice—is a big and complex task. Its implementation requires prudence, thoughtfulness, and self-control. Undoubtedly, the nationalities that formerly suffered oppression and that still bear the marks of it may show themselves inclined to uphold their autonomy also in those fields that could be essentially centralized without any loss to national independence and with great administrative or economic benefit to all. But even in such doubtful matters it is necessary first of all to do everything that can be done so that at least the leading circles of the small or backward nation may appreciate the advantages and benefits of centralization. They can then help the masses to appreciate the measure in question, not as some sort of pressure from the center but as a measure that meets the interests of all and is being put into effect by consent. In politics it is impossible to think rationalistically, and in the national question less than anywhere else.

Two more words in conclusion. Not long ago I had occasion to hear from a certain not-so-young Communist that to bring forward the importance of the national factor in the revolution is—it is embarrassing but it must be confessed—Menshevism and liberalism. Here already we see what it really means to turn things and concepts upside down! The position of Menshevism on the national question is this: While Menshevism is in opposition, it is nationally sentimental and given to democratic appeals, never daring to put the question sharply, that is, on the plane of calling on the oppressed to revolt. When the national bourgeoisie is in danger, or when Menshevism itself is in power, it is filled to the brim with awareness of the importance and responsibility of the great-power mission entrusted to it by the bourgeoisie and continues the centralizing oppressive policy, dressing it up with charges of nationalism against . . . the oppressed nations. Bolshevism showed its revolutionary farsightedness in the fact that it knew how to appreciate from the class point of view the enormous revolutionary importance of the national factor. And in this spirit and direction Bolshevism will continue in the future to educate the youth.

March 19, 1923

[Trotsky, *Pokolenie Oktyabrya* (Generation of October) (Moscow, 1924), pp. 28-37. Translated from the Russian by Brian Pearce.]

BIOGRAPHICAL NOTES

Avanesov, Varlaam Aleksandrovich (1884-1930)—Member of Russian Social Democratic Labor Party from 1903. In 1917-19, secretary of Presidium of All-Russia Central Executive Committee. In 1920-24, deputy people's commissar of Rabkrin.

Bukharin, Nikolai Ivanovich (1888-1938)—Joined Bolsheviks in 1906. In 1918, was a spokesman of the "Left Communists" but emerged after Lenin's death as chief theoretician for right-wing prokulak tendency. From 1926 to 1929 chairman of the Comintern, succeeding Zinoviev. In 1928, organized Right Opposition against Stalin's forced collectivization of peasantry and forced industrialization. In 1929, Right Opposition was crushed and he was forced to capitulate. Defendant in the March 1938 Moscow show trial. "Confessed" and was shot.

Dzerzhinsky, Feliks Edmundovich (1877-1926)—A founder of Social Democratic Party of Poland and Lithuania. In 1906, was elected to the Central Committee of the Russian party. After the revolution, he organized and became chairman of All-Russia Extraordinary Commission for Combating Counterrevolution and Sabotage (Cheka).

Eastman, Max (1883-1969)—Editor of **The Masses** before World War I, then editor of **The Liberator**. An early supporter of Russian Left Opposition although not a member of any party. Translated several of Trotsky's books and was the first to acquaint American public with issues of Trotsky-Stalin stuggle. In mid-1930s, began a retreat from Marxism, repudiating socialism in 1940. Became an anticommunist and an editor of the **Reader's Digest**.

Eltsin, Boris Mikhailovich (1879-1937?)—Joined Russian Social Democratic Labor Party in 1899. In 1917, head of Ekaterinoslav Soviet. Member of Left Opposition. Directed small group of Oppositionists still at liberty in 1928-29. Arrested along with his two sons, also Oppositionists. Disappeared in labor camps.

Eltsin, Viktor Borisovich—Son of Boris Eltsin. One of Trotsky's secretaries in 1927-28. Arrested along with father and brother. Spent five years in prison and then deported to Archangel. Subsequent fate unknown.

Fotieva, Lydia Alexandrovna (1881-)—Member of Russian Social Democratic Labor Party from 1904. From 1918, Lenin's secretary and secretary of the Council of People's Commissars, and Council of Labor and Defense. Survived the purge. In 1956, as part of "de-Stalinization," was awarded the Order of Lenin.

Frumkin, Moisei Ilyich (1878-1939)—Joined Russian Social Democratic Labor Party in 1898. From April 1922, deputy people's commissar for foreign trade of the RSFSR. Held prominent posts in Soviet trade and finance. In 1928-29 and again later, supported Right Opposition. Expelled from party in 1937.

Glyasser, Maria Ignatyevna (1890-1951)—Joined Bolsheviks in 1917. From 1918 to 1924, worked in the Secretariat of the Council of People's Commissars. One of Lenin's private secretaries. Subsequently worked in the Lenin Institute.

Kabanidze—L.A. Fotieva, in her memoirs **Iz Vospominaniy o Lenine** (Moscow: Gosizdat, Polit. Lit., 1964), p. 75, identifies Kabanidze as the Georgian oppositionist struck by Ordzhonikidze.

Kalinin, Mikhail Ivanovich (1875-1946)—Active since 1898. Member of first illegal Marxist study circles. In 1919, became chairman of All-Russia Central Executive Committee and a member of Bolshevik Central Committee. Survived the purges. From 1938 to 1946, headed Presidium of Supreme Soviet of USSR.

Kamenev, Lev Borisovich (1883-1936)—Joined Russian Social Democratic Labor Party in 1901. Head of Bolshevik Duma fraction before World War I. Arrested and exiled to Siberia in November 1914. After February Revolution in 1917, returned to Petrograd and, with Stalin, led Bolsheviks until Lenin's arrival in April. With Zinoviev (q.v.) opposed October insurrection. After Lenin's death, emerged as a member of ruling triumvirate (Zinoviev, Kamenev, Stalin). Followed Zinoviev into Joint Opposition with Trotsky in 1926-27. Expelled from party as Oppositionist in December 1927 but recanted and was readmitted. Expelled again in 1932 and again readmitted after recanting. In 1935, after Kirov assassination, sentenced to five years' imprisonment for "moral complicity" with the murder. In 1936, was rearraigned in first Moscow show trial. "Confessed" and was executed.

Kavtaradze, Sergei Ivanovich (1885-)—Joined Russian Social Democratic Labor Party in 1903. In 1917, was a leader of Bolsheviks in Georgia and editor of the Bolshevik paper. After establishment of Soviet power in Georgia, was people's commissar of justice. In 1922-23, chairman of the Council of People's Commissars in Georgia. Supported Left Opposition and was expelled from party in 1927. Exiled to Siberia. After assassination of Sergei Kirov (1934), recanted in a personal letter to Stalin. Was pardoned but did not rejoin the party. Arrested again in 1936 and accused, with Budu Mdivani, of plotting to kill Stalin. Reported in Maryinsk and Kolyma labor camps in 1936. Rehabilitated in 1940. Became assistant people's commissar for foreign affairs. After World War II, Soviet ambassador to Rumania.

Kerzhentsev, Platon Mikhailovich (1881-1940)—Joined Russian Social Democratic Labor Party in 1904. In 1918-20, deputy editor of **Izvestia.** Held posts in foreign service. President of Rabkrin Council for the Scientific Organization of Labor in 1923-24. In 1923, founded "League of Time," with a journal **Vremya** (Time) to promote rationalization of work.

Kirov, Sergei Mironovich (1886-1934)—A member of Political Bureau and head of party organization in Leningrad. Was the leader of a tendency favoring liberalization of regime. His assassination in December 1934 was followed by a wave of terror against Trotskyists, Zinovievists, and disgruntled Stalinists.

Krestinsky, Nikolai Nikolayevich (1883-1938)—Joined Russian Social Democratic Labor Party in 1903. From December 1919 to March 1921, secretary of Bolshevik Central Committee. From October 1921, ambassador of RSFSR to Germany. Was a leading figure in third Moscow show trial (March 1938). Created a stir by at first repudiating his "confession." Executed in 1938, posthumously rehabilitated during "de-Stalinization."

Krupskaya, Nadezhda Konstantinova (1869-1939)—Joined Russian Social Democratic Labor Party in 1898. Wife and political associate of Lenin. Worked on editorial boards of Bolshevik papers before the revolution. Afterward, worked in public education.

Krzhizhanovsky, Gleb Maksimilianovich (1872-1959)—Joined Russian Social Democracy in 1893. Together with Lenin organized League of Struggle for the Emancipation of the Working Class in St. Petersburg. Graduated from Petersburg Technological Institute as electrical engineer in 1894. Become politically inactive after 1907. A member of the Bolshevik fraction in the Moscow Soviet after the February 1917 revolution. In 1920, headed the State Commission for the Electrification of Russia. Director of State Planning Commission 1921-30. From 1929 to 1939, vice-president of the Soviet Academy of Sciences.

Kuibyshev, Valerian Vladimirovich (1888-1935)—Joined Russian Social Democratic Labor Party in 1904. During civil war held military and diplomatic posts. Elected to Bolshevik Central Committee in 1922. Became head of the Central Control Commission in 1923, later of Rabkrin as well. Became member of the Politburo in 1927. In 1934, was reportedly part of a group favoring liberalization of regime. Died, apparently of natural causes, but defendants in the third Moscow show trial (March 1938) were accused of having murdered him.

Ludwig, Emil (1881-1948)—German biographer and dramatist. Emigrated to Switzerland in 1907. Served as war correspondent in World War I. The Nazis burned his works.

Makharadze, Filipp Yeseyevich (1868-1941)—Joined Russian Social Democratic Labor Party in 1903. From March 1921 to February 1922, chairman of the Revolutionary Committee in Georgia. From 1922, chairman of the Georgian Central Executive Committee. Escaped the purges.

Mdivani, Polikarp Gurgenovich (Budu) (1877-1937)—Joined Russian Social Democratic Labor Party in 1903. During civil war, was head of Political Department of Tenth Army. In 1920-21, a member of the Caucasus Bureau of Bolshevik Central Committee. In 1924, made Soviet trade representative in France. Expelled for "Trotskyist oppositional activity" in 1928. Rehabilitated in 1931. From 1931 to 1936, people's commissar for light industry and first deputy chairman of the Georgian Council of People's Commissars. Expelled from the party again for "anti-party activities" in 1936. Arrested in 1937, given secret trial and executed.

Molotov, Vyacheslav Mikhailovich (1890-)—Joined Russian Social Democratic Labor Party in 1906. Became candidate member of Politburo in 1921, full member in 1926. Consistent supporter of Stalin in political struggles. In 1930, became chairman of Council of People's Commissars and in 1939 also took over portfolio of foreign affairs. In 1957, dropped from Central Committee for opposing "de-Stalinization" and made ambassador to Outer Mongolia. In 1960, named Soviet representative to the International Atomic Energy Agency in Vienna. The Twenty-second Party Congress (1961) recommended his expulsion from the party. Retired from public life in 1962.

Oldenburg, S.S. (d. 1940)—Political correspondent for **Russkaya Mysl** (Russian Thought), a white-guard journal published in Prague in 1922.

Ordzhonikidze, Grigory Konstantinovich (Sergo) (1886-1937)—Joined Russian Social Democratic Labor Party in 1903. Held military posts during civil war. A close personal friend and political supporter of Stalin. From 1926, chairman of Central Control Commission and Rabkrin. From 1930, chairman of Supreme Economic Council. Reportedly opposed continuation of the purge. Died under mysterious circumstances.

Pokrovsky, Mikhail Nikolayevich (1868-1932)—Joined the Russian Social Democratic Labor Party in 1905. In 1918, appointed deputy people's commissar for education of the RSFSR. A prominent Stalinist historian.

Pyatakov, Georgi Leonidovich (1890-1937)—Joined Russian Social Democratic Labor Party in 1910. A prominent theoretician and economist. Supporter of Left Opposition, 1923-28. Expelled from party in 1927. Capitulated. Played an important role in the development of Soviet industry in the earlier five-year plans. Purged in the second Moscow show trial (January 1937). Executed.

Radek, Karl Berngardovich (1885-1939?)—Active in Polish and German Social Democratic parties prior to World War I. Returned to Russia with Lenin in April 1917 and joined Bolsheviks. Held diplomatic posts during civil war and was Comintern representative in Germany during 1923 revolution. A member of Left Opposition, he was expelled from party in December 1927, but quickly capitulated and was reinstated. During early thirties, was the principal journalistic interpreter of Stalinist foreign policy. Sentenced to ten years' imprisonment at the second Moscow show trial (January 1937) and probably died in prison.

Rakovsky, Khristian Georgievich (1873-1941)—A leading figure in Balkan revolutionary movement before World War I. In 1918, became chairman of Ukrainian Soviet and later Soviet ambassador in London and Paris. An early leader of Left Opposition, was expelled from the party in 1927 and exiled to Siberia. Capitulated in 1934. In 1938, he was one of principal defendants in third Moscow show trial, where he was sentenced to twenty years' imprisonment. Died in prison.

Rykov, Aleksei Ivanovich (1881-1938)—Joined Russian Social Democratic Labor Party in 1899. Succeeded Lenin as head of state. With Bukharin, led right-wing tendency in party during NEP period. Removed from post as premier in 1930. Was a defendant in the third Moscow show trial (March 1938). "Confessed" and was executed.

Smirnov, Aleksandr Petrovich (1877-1938)—Joined Russian Social Democratic movement in 1896. After October Revolution, was deputy people's commissar for internal affairs and deputy people's commissar for food. In 1933, was accused of forming an "antiparty group" designed to remove Stalin. Dropped from the Central Committee and later (December 1934) expelled from the party. His name figures prominently in "confessions" extracted from the defendants in the Moscow trials, but he himself was not brought to the dock.

Sokolnikov, Grigory Yakovlevich (1888-1939)—Joined Russian Social Democratic Labor Party in 1905. Member of Soviet delegation at Brest-Litovsk peace negotiations. People's commissar of finance from 1922 to 1926. Founded an opposition grouping but did not join Joint Opposition. Ambassador to London 1927-33. Expelled from party and arrested in 1936. Sentenced to ten years in prison at second Moscow show trial (January 1937). Died or was executed in prison.

Stomonyakov, Boris Spiridonovich (1882-1941)—Joined Russian Social Democratic Labor Party in 1902. From 1920 to 1925, Soviet trade representative in Berlin.

Sverdlov, Yakov Mikhailovich (1885-1919)—Joined Russian Social Democratic Labor Party in 1901. One of ablest organizers in Bolshevik Party. From 1917 to 1919, head of Secretariat of the Central Committee. From November 1917, chairman of All-Russia Central Executive Committee.

Tsintsadze, Kote Maksimovich (1887-1937?)—Joined Russian Social Democratic Labor Party in 1904. Was active in the Caucasus. After establishment of Soviet power in Georgia, chairman of Cheka in Georgia and a member of Central Committee of Georgian CP and Central Executive Committee of Georgian Republic. Expelled from the party in 1927 as a Left Oppositionist and deported to Siberia. Official Soviet sources list his date of death as 1930, but was reported alive in Verkhne-Uralsk Prison in 1933. According to same report, was shot on Stalin's orders in 1937.

Tsyurupa, Aleksandr Dmitrievich (1870-1928)—Joined Russian Social Democracy in 1898. In 1922-23, people's commissar of Rabkrin. In 1923-25, chairman of Gosplan. In 1925-26, people's commissar for domestic and foreign trade. A member of Bolshevik Central Committee from 1923.

Ulyanova, Maria Ilyinichna (1878-1937)—Lenin's younger sister. Joined Russian Social Democracy in 1898. From March 1917 to spring 1929, a member of editorial board and executive secretary of **Pravda.** Backed Bukharin against Stalin in 1928-29 and was dismissed from **Pravda.**

Volodicheva, Maria Akinovna (1881-)—Joined Bolsheviks in 1917. After October Revolution to July 1918, secretary of press bureau of Council of People's Commissars. Served as one of Lenin's private secretaries during his last illness.

Yermansky, O.A. (1866-1941)—In 1918, a member of Central Committee of Menshevik Party. In 1921, left Mensheviks and became involved in scientific work in Moscow.

Zinoviev, Grigory Yevseyevich (1883-1936)—Joined Russian Social Democratic Labor Party in 1901. Lenin's closest associate during World War I. He and Kamenev opposed Central Committee decision to go ahead with October insurrection and published a statement to that effect in a semi-Menshevik newspaper. After Lenin's death, emerged as apparent leader of ruling triumvirate (Zinoviev, Kamenev, Stalin). Broke with Stalin in 1925 and joined Trotsky's Left Opposition forming Joint Opposition in 1926. Expelled at Fifteenth Party Congress (December 1927) and banished to Siberia. Capitulated in 1928 and was readmitted to party. In 1932, again expelled and again capitulated. In 1935, after Kirov assassination, was sentenced to ten years' imprisonment on trumped-up charges of complicity in the murder. A principal defendant in first Moscow show trial (August 1936). "Confessed" and was executed.

IMPERIALISM: THE HIGHEST STAGE OF CAPITALISM

CONTENTS

Preface to the Russian Edition

The pamphlet here presented to the reader was written in Zürich in the spring of 1916. In the conditions in which I was obliged to work there I naturally suffered somewhat from a shortage of French and English literature and from a serious dearth of Russian literature. However, I made use of the principal English work, *Imperialism,* J. A. Hobson's book, with all the care that, in my opinion, that work deserves.

This pamphlet was written with an eye to the tsarist censorship. Hence, I was not only forced to confine myself strictly to an exclusively theoretical, mainly economic analysis of facts, but to formulate the few necessary observations on politics with extreme caution, by hints, in that Æsopian language—in that cursed Æsopian language—to which tsarism compelled all revolutionaries to have recourse whenever they took up their pens to write a "legal" work.[1]

It is very painful, in these days of liberty, to read these cramped passages of the pamphlet, crushed, as they seem, in an iron vise, distorted on account of the censor. Of how imperialism is the eve of the socialist revolution; of how social-chauvinism (socialism in words, chauvinism in deeds) is the utter betrayal of socialism, complete desertion to the side of the bourgeoisie; of how the split in the labour movement is bound up with the objective conditions of imperialism, etc., I had to speak in a "slavish" tongue, and I must refer the reader who is interested in the question to the volume, which is soon to appear, in which are reproduced the articles I wrote abroad in the years 1914-17. Special attention must be drawn, however, to a passage on pages 119-20.[2] In order to show, in a guise acceptable to the censors, how shamefully the

[1] "Æsopian," after the Greek fable writer Æsop, was the term applied to the allusive and roundabout style adopted in "legal" publications by revolutionaries in order to evade the censorship.—*Ed.*

[2] *Cf.* pp. 121-22 in this volume.—*Ed.*

capitalists and the social-chauvinist deserters (whom Kautsky opposes with so much inconsistency) lie on the question of annexations; in order to show with what cynicism they *screen* the annexations of *their* capitalists, I was forced to quote as an example —Japan! The careful reader will easily substitute Russia for Japan, and Finland, Poland, Courland, the Ukraine, Khiva, Bokhara, Estonia or other regions peopled by non-Great Russians, for Korea.

I trust that this pamphlet will help the reader to understand the fundamental economic question, *viz.*, the question of the economic essence of imperialism, for unless this is studied, it will be impossible to understand and appraise modern war and modern politics

Petrograd, April 26, 1917

Preface to the French and German Editions

I

As was indicated in the preface to the Russian edition, this pamphlet was written in 1916, with an eye to the tsarist censorship. I am unable to revise the whole text at the present time, nor, perhaps, is this advisable, since the main purpose of the book was and remains: to present, on the basis of the summarised returns of irrefutable bourgeois statistics, and the admissions of bourgeois scholars of all countries, a *general picture* of the world capitalist system in its international relationships at the beginning of the twentieth century—on the eve of the first world imperialist war.

To a certain extent it will be useful for many Communists in advanced capitalist countries to convince themselves by the example of this pamphlet, *legal, from the standpoint of the tsarist censor,* of the possibility—and necessity—of making use of even the slight remnants of legality which still remain at the disposal of the Communists, say, in contemporary America or France, after the recent wholesale arrests of Communists, in order to explain the utter falsity of social-pacifist views and hopes for "world democracy." The most essential of what should be added to this censored pamphlet I shall try to present in this preface.

II

In the pamphlet I proved that the war of 1914-18 was imperialistic (that is, an annexationist, predatory, plunderous war) on the part of both sides; it was a war for the division of the world, for the partition and repartition of colonies, "spheres of influence" of finance capital, etc.

Proof of what was the true social, or rather, the true class character of the war is naturally to be found, not in the diplomatic history of the war, but in an analysis of the *objective* position of the ruling *classes in all* belligerent countries. In order to depict this objective position one must not take examples or isolated data (in view of the extreme complexity of social life it is always quite easy to select any number of examples or separate data to prove any point one desires), but the *whole* of the data concerning the *basis* of economic life in *all* the belligerent countries and the *whole* world.

It is precisely irrefutable summarised data of this kind that I quoted in describing the *partition of the world* in the period of 1876 to 1914 (in chapter VI) and the distribution of the *railways* all over the world in the period of 1890 to 1913 (in chapter VII). Railways combine within themselves the basic capitalist industries: coal, iron and steel; and they are the most striking index of the development of international trade and bourgeois-democratic civilisation. In the preceding chapters of the book I showed how the railways are linked up with large-scale industry, with monopolies, syndicates, cartels, trusts, banks and the financial oligarchy. The uneven distribution of the railways, their uneven development—sums up, as it were, modern world monopolist capitalism. And this summing up proves that imperialist wars are absolutely inevitable under *such* an economic system, *as long as* private property in the means of production exists.

The building of railways seems to be a simple, natural, democratic, cultural and civilising enterprise; that is what it is in the opinion of bourgeois professors, who are paid to depict capitalist slavery in bright colours, and in the opinion of petty-bourgeois philistines. But as a matter of fact the capitalist threads, which in thousands of different intercrossings bind these enterprises with private property in the means of production in general, have converted this work of construction into an instrument for oppressing *a thousand million* people (in the colonies and semi-colonies), that is, more than half the population of the globe, which inhabits the subject countries, as well as the wage slaves of capitalism in the lands of "civilisation."

Private property based on the labour of the small proprietor, free competition, democracy, *i.e.*, all the catchwords with which the capitalists and their press deceive the workers and the peasants—are things of the past. Capitalism has grown into a world system of colonial oppression and of the financial strangulation of the overwhelming majority of the people of the world by a handful of "advanced" countries. And this "booty" is shared between two or three powerful world marauders armed to the teeth (America, Great Britain, Japan), who involve the whole world in *their* war over the sharing of *their* booty.

III

The Brest-Litovsk Peace Treaty dictated by monarchist Germany, and later on, the much more brutal and despicable Versailles Treaty dictated by the "democratic" republics of America and France and also by "free" England, have rendered very good service to humanity by exposing both the hired coolies of the pen of imperialism and the petty-bourgeois reactionaries, although they call themselves pacifists and socialists, who sang praises to "Wilsonism," and who insisted that peace and reform were possible under imperialism.

The tens of millions of dead and maimed left by the war—a war for the purpose of deciding whether the British or German group of financial marauders is to receive the lion's share—and the two "peace treaties," mentioned above, open the eyes of the millions and tens of millions of people who are downtrodden, oppressed, deceived and duped by the bourgeoisie with unprecedented rapidity. Thus, out of the universal ruin caused by the war a world-wide revolutionary crisis is arising which, in spite of the protracted and difficult stages it may have to pass, cannot end in any other way than in a proletarian revolution and in its victory.

The Basle Manifesto of the Second International which in 1912 gave an appraisal of the war that ultimately broke out in 1914, and not of war in general (there are all kinds of wars, including revolutionary wars), this Manifesto is now a monument exposing the shameful bankruptcy and treachery of the heroes of the Second International.

That is why I reproduce this Manifesto as a supplement to the present edition [1] and again I call upon the reader to note that the

[1] *Cf.* V. I. Lenin, *The Imperialist War,* Collected Works, Vol. XVIII, N. Y., pp. 468-72.—*Ed.*

heroes of the Second International are just as assiduously avoiding the passages of this Manifesto which speak precisely, clearly and definitely of the connection between that impending war and the proletarian revolution, as a thief avoids the place where he has committed a theft.

IV

Special attention has been devoted in this pamphlet to a criticism of "Kautskyism," the international ideological trend represented in all countries of the world by the "prominent theoreticians" and leaders of the Second International (Otto Bauer and Co. in Austria, Ramsay MacDonald and others in England, Albert Thomas in France, etc., etc.) and multitudes of socialists, reformists, pacifists, bourgeois-democrats and parsons.

This ideological trend is, on the one hand, a product of the disintegration and decay of the Second International, and, on the other hand, it is the inevitable fruit of the ideology of the petty bourgeoisie, who, by the whole of their conditions of life, are held captive to bourgeois and democratic prejudices.

The views held by Kautsky and his like are a complete renunciation of the very revolutionary principles of Marxism which he championed for decades, especially in his struggle against socialist opportunism (Bernstein, Millerand, Hyndman, Gompers, etc.). It is not a mere accident, therefore, that the "Kautskyans" all over the world have now united in practical politics with the extreme opportunists (through the Second, or the Yellow, International) and with the bourgeois governments (through bourgeois coalition governments in which socialists take part).

The growing world proletarian revolutionary movement in general, and the Communist movement in particular, demands that the theoretical errors of "Kautskyism" be analysed and exposed. The more so since pacifism and "democracy" in general, which have no claim to Marxism whatever, but which, like Kautsky and Co., are obscuring the profundity of the contradictions of imperialism and the inevitable revolutionary crisis to which it gives rise, are still very widespread all over the world. It is the bounden duty of the party of the proletariat to combat these tendencies and to win away from the bourgeoisie the small proprietors who are duped by them, and the millions of toilers who live in more or less petty-bourgeois conditions of life.

V

A few words must be said about chapter VIII entitled: "The Parasitism and Decay of Capitalism." As already pointed out in the text, Hilferding, ex-Marxist, and now a comrade-in-arms of Kautsky, one of the chief exponents of bourgeois reformist policy in the Independent Social-Democratic Party of Germany, has taken a step backward compared with the *frankly* pacifist and reformist Englishman, Hobson, on this question. The international split of the whole labour movement is now quite evident (Second and Third Internationals). Armed struggle and civil war between the two trends is now a recognised fact: the support given to Kolchak and Denikin in Russia by the Mensheviks and Socialist-Revolutionaries against the Bolsheviks; the fight the Scheidemanns, Noskes and Co. have conducted in conjunction with the bourgeoisie against the Spartacists in Germany; the same thing in Finland, Poland, Hungary, etc. What is the economic basis of this historically important world phenomenon?

Precisely the parasitism and decay of capitalism which are the characteristic features of its highest historical stage of development, *i.e.,* imperialism. As has been shown in this pamphlet, capitalism has now brought to the front a *handful* (less than one-tenth of the inhabitants of the globe; less than one-fifth, if the most "generous" and liberal calculations were made) of very rich and very powerful states which plunder the whole world simply by "clipping coupons." Capital exports produce an income of eight to ten billion francs per annum, according to pre-war prices and pre-war bourgeois statistics. Now, of course, they produce much more than that.

Obviously, out of such enormous *super-profits* (since they are obtained over and above the profits which capitalists squeeze out of the workers of their "home" country) it is quite *possible to bribe* the labour leaders and the upper stratum of the labour aristocracy.

And the capitalists of the "advanced" countries are bribing them; they bribe them in a thousand different ways, direct and indirect, overt and covert.

This stratum of bourgeoisified workers, or the "labour aristocracy," who are quite philistine in their mode of life, in the size of their earnings and in their outlook, serves as the principal prop of the Second International, and, in our days, the principal *social* (not military) *prop of the bourgeoisie.* They are the real *agents of the bourgeoisie in the labour movement,* the labour lieutenants of the capitalist class, real channels of reformism and chauvinism. In the civil war between the proletariat and the bourgeoisie they inevitably, and in no small numbers, stand side by side with the bourgeoisie, with the "Versaillese" against the "Communards."

Not the slightest progress can be made toward the solution of the practical problems of the Communist movement and of the impending social revolution unless the economic roots of this phenomenon are understood and unless its political and sociological significance is appreciated.

Imperialism is the eve of the proletarian social revolution. This has been confirmed since 1917 on a world-wide scale.

N. Lenin

July 6, 1920

Imperialism, the Highest Stage of Capitalism

During the last fifteen or twenty years, especially since the Spanish-American War (1898), and the Anglo-Boer War (1899-1902), the economic and also the political literature of the two hemispheres has more and more often adopted the term "imperialism" in order to define the present era. In 1902, a book by the English economist, J. A. Hobson, *Imperialism,* was published in London and New York. This author, who adopts the point of view of bourgeois social reformism and pacifism which, in essence, is identical with the present point of view of the ex-Marxist, K. Kautsky, gives an excellent and comprehensive description of the principal economic and political characteristics of imperialism. In 1910, there appeared in Vienna the work of the Austrian Marxist, Rudolf Hilferding, *Finance Capital.* In spite of the mistake the author commits on the theory of money, and in spite of a certain inclination on his part to reconcile Marxism with opportunism, this work gives a very valuable theoretical analysis, as its sub-title tells us, of "the latest phase of capitalist development." Indeed, what has been said of imperialism during the last few years, especially in a great many magazine and newspaper articles, and also in the resolutions, for example, of the Chemnitz and Basle Congresses which took place in the autumn of 1912, has scarcely gone beyond the ideas put forward, or, more exactly, summed up by the two writers mentioned above.

Later on we shall try to show briefly, and as simply as possible, the connection and relationships between the *principal* economic features of imperialism. We shall not be able to deal with non-economic aspects of the question, however much they deserve to be dealt with.[1] We have put references to literature and other notes which, perhaps, would not interest all readers, at the end of this pamphlet.[2]

[1] By "non-economic" Lenin meant political; the pamphlet was intended for legal publication and so these aspects were left out in order to enable it to pass the tsarist censorship.—*Ed.*

[2] These references are not given in this edition.—*Ed.*

CHAPTER I

Concentration of Production and Monopolies

THE enormous growth of industry and the remarkably rapid process of concentration of production in ever-larger enterprises represent one of the most characteristic features of capitalism. Modern censuses of production give very complete and exact data on this process.

In Germany, for example, for every 1,000 industrial enterprises, large enterprises, *i.e.*, those employing more than 50 workers, numbered three in 1882, six in 1895 and nine in 1907; and out of every 100 workers employed, this group of enterprises employed 22, 30 and 37 respectively. Concentration of production, however, is much more intense than the concentration of workers, since labour in the large enterprises is much more productive. This is shown by the figures available on steam engines and electric motors. If we take what in Germany is called industry in the broad sense of the term, that is, including commerce, transport, etc., we get the following picture: Large-scale enterprises: 30,588 out of a total of 3,265,623, that is to say, 0.9 per cent. These large-scale enterprises employ 5,700,000 workers out of a total of 14,400,000, that is, 39.4 per cent; they use 6,660,000 steam horse power out of a total of 8,800,000, that is, 75.3 per cent and 1,200,000 kilowatts of electricity out of a total of 1,500,000, that is, 77.2 per cent.

Less than one-hundredth of the total enterprises utilise *more than three-fourths* of the steam and electric power! Two million nine hundred and seventy thousand small enterprises (employing up to five workers), representing 91 per cent of the total, utilise only 7 per cent of the steam and electric power. Tens of thousands of large-scale enterprises are everything; millions of small ones are nothing.

In 1907, there were in Germany 586 establishments employing

one thousand and more workers. They employed nearly *one-tenth* (1,380,000) of the total number of workers employed in industry and utilised *almost one-third* (32 per cent) of the total steam and electric power employed.[1] As we shall see, money capital and the banks make this superiority of a handful of the largest enterprises still more overwhelming, in the most literal sense of the word, since millions of small, medium, and even some big "masters" are in fact in complete subjection to some hundreds of millionaire financiers.

In another advanced country of modern capitalism, the United States, the growth of the concentration of production is still greater. Here statistics single out industry in the narrow sense of the word and group enterprises according to the value of their annual output. In 1904 large-scale enterprises with an annual output of one million dollars and over numbered 1,900 (out of 216,180, *i.e.*, 0.9 per cent). These employed 1,400,000 workers (out of 5,500,000, *i.e.*, 25.6 per cent) and their combined annual output was valued at $5,600,000,000 (out of $14,800,000,000, *i.e.*, 38 per cent). Five years later, in 1909, the corresponding figures were: large-scale enterprises: 3,060 out of 268,491, *i.e.*, 1.1 per cent; employing: 2,000,000 workers out of 6,600,000, *i.e.*, 30.5 per cent; output: $9,000,000,000 out of $20,700,000,000, *i.e.*, 43.8 per cent.[2]

Almost half the total production of all the enterprises of the country was carried on by a *hundredth part* of those enterprises! These 3,000 giant enterprises embrace 268 branches of industry. From this it can be seen that, at a certain stage of its development, concentration itself, as it were, leads right to monopoly; for a score or so of giant enterprises can easily arrive at an agreement, while on the other hand, the difficulty of competition and the tendency towards monopoly arise from the very dimensions of the enterprises. This transformation of competition into monopoly is one of the most important—if not the most important—phenomena of modern capitalist economy, and we must deal with it in greater detail. But first we must clear up one possible misunderstanding.

[1] *Annalen des Deutschen Reichs* (*Annals of the German Empire*), 1911, pp. 165-169.

[2] *Statistical Abstract of the United States*, 1912, p. 202.

American statistics say: 3,000 giant enterprises in 250 branches of industry, as if there were only a dozen large-scale enterprises for each branch of industry.

But this is not the case. Not in every branch of industry are there large-scale enterprises; and, moreover, a very important feature of capitalism in its highest stage of development is so-called "combined production," that is to say, the grouping in a single enterprise of different branches of industry, which either represent the consecutive stages in the working up of raw materials (for example, the smelting of iron ore into pig iron, the conversion of pig iron into steel, and then, perhaps, the manufacture of steel goods)—or are auxiliary to one another (for example, the utilisation of waste or of by-products, the manufacture of packing materials, etc.).

"Combination," writes Hilferding, "levels out the fluctuations of trade and therefore assures to the combined enterprises a more stable rate of profit. Secondly, combination has the effect of eliminating trading. Thirdly, it has the effect of rendering possible technical improvements, and, consequently, the acquisition of superprofits over and above those obtained by the 'pure' (*i.e., non-combined*) enterprises. Fourthly, it strengthens the position of the combined enterprises compared with that of 'pure' enterprises in the competitive struggle in periods of serious depression, when the fall in prices of raw materials does not keep pace with the fall in prices of manufactured articles."[3]

The German bourgeois economist, Heymann, who has written a book especially on "mixed," that is, combined, enterprises in the German iron industry, says: "Pure enterprises perish, crushed between the high price of raw material and the low price of the finished product." Thus we get the following picture:

"There remain, on the one hand, the great coal companies, producing millions of tons yearly, strongly organized in their coal syndicate, and on the other, the great steel works, closely allied to the coal mines, having their own steel syndicate. These giant enterprises, producing 400,000 tons of steel per annum, with correspondingly extensive coal, ore and blast furnace plants, as well as the manufacturing of finished goods, employing 10,000 workers quartered in company houses, some-

[3] Rudolf Hilferding, *Das Finanzkapital* (*Finance Capital*), Vienna, 1910, p. 239.

times owning their own ports and railroads, are today the standard type of German iron and steel plant. And concentration still continues. Individual enterprises are becoming larger and larger. An ever increasing number of enterprises in one given industry, or in several different industries, join together in giant combines, backed up and controlled by half a dozen Berlin banks. In the German mining industry, the truth of the teachings of Karl Marx on concentration is definitely proved, at any rate in a country like ours where it is protected by tariffs and freight rates. The German mining industry is ripe for expropriation."[4]

Such is the conclusion which a conscientious bourgeois economist, and such are exceptional, had to arrive at. It must be noted that he seems to place Germany in a special category because her industries are protected by high tariffs. But the concentration of industry and the formation of monopolist manufacturers' combines, cartels, syndicates, etc., could only be accelerated by these circumstances. It is extremely important to note that in free-trade England, concentration *also* leads to monopoly, although somewhat later and perhaps in another form. Professor Hermann Levy, in his special work of research entitled *Monopolies, Cartels and Trusts,* based on data on British economic development, writes as follows:

"In Great Britain it is the size of the enterprise and its capacity which harbour a monopolist tendency. This, for one thing, is due to the fact that the great investment of capital per enterprise, once the concentration movement has commenced, gives rise to increasing demands for new capital for the new enterprises and thereby renders their launching more difficult. Moreover (and this seems to us to be the more important point) every new enterprise that wants to keep pace with the gigantic enterprises that have arisen on the basis of the process of concentration would produce such an enormous quantity of surplus goods that it could only dispose of them either by being able to sell them profitably as a result of an enormous increase in demand or by immediately forcing down prices to a level that would be unprofitable both for itself and for the monopoly combines."

[4] Hans Gideon Heymann, *Die gemischten Werke im deutschen Grosseisengewerbe* (*Combined Plants in the German Big Iron Industry*), Stuttgart, 1904, pp. 256 and 278.

In England, unlike other countries where protective tariffs facilitate the formation of cartels, monopolist alliances of *entrepreneurs,* cartels and trusts arise in the majority of cases only when the number of competing enterprises is reduced to "a couple of dozen or so." "Here the influence of the concentration movement on the formation of large industrial monopolies in a whole sphere of industry stands out with crystal clarity."[5]

Fifty years ago, when Marx was writing *Capital,* free competition appeared to most economists to be a "natural law." Official science tried, by a conspiracy of silence, to kill the works of Marx, which by a theoretical and historical analysis of capitalism showed that free competition gives rise to the concentration of production, which, in turn, at a certain stage of development, leads to monopoly. Today, monopoly has become a fact. The economists are writing mountains of books in which they describe the diverse manifestations of monopoly, and continue to declare in chorus that "Marxism is refuted." But facts are stubborn things, as the English proverb says, and they have to be reckoned with, whether we like it or not. The facts show that differences between capitalist countries, *e.g.,* in the matter of protection or free trade, only give rise to insignificant variations in the form of monopolies or in the moment of their appearance; and that the rise of monopolies, as the result of the concentration of production, is a general and fundamental law of the present stage of development of capitalism.

For Europe, the time when the new capitalism *definitely* superseded the old can be established with fair precision: it was the beginning of the twentieth century. In one of the latest compilations on the history of the "formation of monopolies," we read:

"A few isolated examples of capitalist monopoly could be cited from the period preceding 1860; in these could be discerned the embryo of the forms that are common today; but all this undoubtedly represents pre-history. The real beginning of modern monopoly goes back, at the earliest, to the 'sixties. The first important period of development of monopoly commenced with the international industrial depression of

[5] Hermann Levy, *Monopole, Kartelle und Trusts* (*Monopolies, Cartels and Trusts*), Jena, 1909, pp. 286, 290, 298.

the 'seventies and lasted until the beginning of the 'nineties.... If we examine the question on a European scale, we will find that the development of free competition reached its apex in the 'sixties and 'seventies. Then it was that England completed the construction of its old style capitalist organisation. In Germany, this organisation had entered into a fierce struggle with handicraft and domestic industry, and had begun to create for itself its own forms of existence....

"The great revolutionisation commenced with the crash of 1873, or rather, the depression which followed it and which, with hardly discernible interruptions in the early 'eighties, and the unusually violent, but short-lived boom about 1889, marks twenty-two years of European economic history.... During the short boom of 1889-90, the system of cartels was widely resorted to in order to take advantage of the favourable business conditions. An ill-considered policy drove prices still higher than would have been the case otherwise and nearly all these cartels perished ingloriously in the smash. Another five-year period of bad trade and low prices followed, but a new spirit reigned in industry; the depression was no longer regarded as something to be taken for granted: it was regarded as nothing more than a pause before another boom.

"The cartel movement entered its second epoch: instead of being a transitory phenomenon, the cartels became one of the foundations of economic life. They are winning one field after another, primarily, the raw materials industry. At the beginning of the 'nineties the cartel system had already acquired—in the organisation of the coke syndicate on the model of which the coal syndicate was later formed—a cartel technique which could hardly be improved. For the first time the great boom at the close of the nineteenth century and the crisis of 1900-03 occurred entirely—in the mining and iron industries at least—under the *ægis* of the cartels. And while at that time it appeared to be something novel, now the general public takes it for granted that large spheres of economic life have been, as a general rule, systematically removed from the realm of free competition."[6]

Thus, the principal stages in the history of monopolies are the

[6] Th. Vogelstein: *Die finanzielle Organisation der kapitalistischen Industrie und die Monopolbildungen* (*Financial Organisation of Capitalist Industry and the Formation of Monopolies*) in *Grundriss der Sozialökonomik* (*Outline of Social Economics*), 1914, *Tüb.*, Sec. VI, pp. 222 *et seq.* See also by the same author: *Organisationsformen des Eisenindustrie und der Textilindustrie in England und Amerika*, Bd. I., Lpz. 1910 (*The Organisational Forms of the Iron and Textile Industries of England and America*, Vol. I, Leipzig, 1910).

following: 1) 1860-70, the highest stage, the apex of development of free competition; monopoly is in the barely discernible, embryonic stage. 2) After the crisis of 1873, a wide zone of development of cartels; but they are still the exception. They are not yet durable. They are still a transitory phenomenon. 3) The boom at the end of the nineteenth century and the crisis of 1900-03. Cartels become one of the foundations of the whole of economic life. Capitalism has been transformed into imperialism.

Cartels come to an agreement on the conditions of sale, terms of payment, etc. They divide the markets among themselves. They fix the quantity of goods to be produced. They fix prices. They divide the profits among the various enterprises, etc.

The number of cartels in Germany was estimated at about 250 in 1896 and at 385 in 1905, with about 12,000 firms participating.[7] But it is generally recognised that these figures are underestimations. From the statistics of German industry for 1907 we quoted above, it is evident that even 12,000 large enterprises control certainly more than half the steam and electric power used in the country. In the United States, the number of trusts in 1900 was 185, and in 1907, 250.

American statistics divide all industrial enterprises into three categories, according to whether they belong to individuals, to private firms or to corporations. These latter in 1904 comprised 23.6 per cent, and in 1909, 25.9 per cent (*i.e.,* more than one-fourth of the total industrial enterprises in the country). These employed in 1904, 70.6 per cent, and in 1909, 75.6 per cent (*i.e.,* more than three-fourths) of the total wage earners. Their output amounted at these two dates to $10,900,000,000 and to $16,300,000,000, *i.e,* to 73.7 per cent and 79 per cent of the total respectively.

Not infrequently cartels and trusts concentrate in their hands seven or eight tenths of the total output of a given branch of

[7] Dr. Riesser, *Die deutschen Grossbanken und ihre Konzentration im Zusammenhang mit der Entwicklung der Gesamtwirtschaft in Deutschland* (*The German Big Banks and their Concentration in Connection with the Development of the General Economy in Germany*), fourth ed., 1912, p. 149; *cf.* also Robert Liefmann, *Kartelle und Trusts und die Weiterbildung der volkswirtschaftlichen Organisation* (*Cartels and Trusts and the Further Development of Economic Organisation*), second ed., 1910, p. 25.

industry. The Rhine-Westphalian Coal Syndicate, at its foundation in 1893, controlled 86.7 per cent of the total coal output of the area. In 1910, it controlled 95.4 per cent.[8] The monopoly so created assures enormous profits, and leads to the formation of technical productive units of formidable magnitude. The famous Standard Oil Company in the United States was founded in 1900:[9]

"It has an authorised capital of $150,000,000. It issued $100,000,000 common and $106,000,000 preferred stock. From 1900 to 1907 the following dividends were paid on this stock: 48, 48, 45, 44, 36, 40, 40, 40 per cent, in the respective years, *i.e.*, in all, $367,000,000. From 1882 to 1907, out of a total net profits to the amount of $889,000,000, $606,000,000 were distributed in dividends, and the rest went to reserve capital.... In 1907 the various works of the United States Steel Corporation employed no less than 210,180 workers and other employees. The largest enterprise in the German mining industry, the Gelsenkirchen Mining Company (*Gelsenkirchner Bergwerksgesellschaft*) employed in 1908 46,048 persons."[10]

In 1902, the United States Steel Corporation had already produced 9,000,000 tons of steel.[11] Its output constituted in 1901, 66.3 per cent, and in 1908, 56.1 per cent of the total output of steel in the United States.[12] The output of mineral ore was 43.9 per cent and 46.3 per cent respectively.

The report of the American Government Commission on Trusts states:

"The superiority of the trust over competitors is due to the magnitude of its enterprises and their excellent technical equipment. Since its

[8] Dr. Fritz Kestner, *Der Organisationszwang. Eine Untersuchung über die Kämpfe zwischen Kartellen und Aussenseitern* (*The Compulsion to Organise. An Investigation of the Struggles between Cartels and Outsiders*), Berlin, 1912, p. 11.

[9] Holding company was formed in 1899 to replace trust agreement of 1882.—*Ed.*

[10] Robert Liefmann, *Beteiligungs- und Finanzierungsgesellschaften. Eine Studie über den modernen Kapitalismus und das Effektenwesen* (*Holding and Finance Companies—A Study in Modern Capitalism and Securities*), first ed., Jena, 1909, pp. 212 and 218.

[11] Dr. S. Tschierschky, *Kartelle und Trusts, Göttingen*, 1903, p. 13.

[12] Vogelstein, *Organisationsformen* (*Forms of Organisation*), p. 275.

inception, the Tobacco Trust has devoted all its efforts to the substitution of mechanical for manual labour on an extensive scale. With this end in view, it bought up all patents that had anything to do with the manufacture of tobacco and spent enormous sums for this purpose. Many of these patents at first proved to be of no use, and had to be modified by the engineers employed by the trust. At the end of 1906, two subsidiary companies were formed solely to acquire patents. With the same object in view, the trust built its own foundries, machine shops and repair shops. One of these establishments, that in Brooklyn, employs on the average 300 workers; here experiments are carried out on inventions concerning the manufacture of cigarettes, cheroots, snuff, tinfoil for packing, boxes, etc. Here, also, inventions are perfected.[13]

"Other trusts also employ so-called developing engineers whose business it is to devise new methods of production and to test technical improvements. The United States Steel Corporation grants big bonuses to its workers and engineers for all inventions suitable for raising technical efficiency, or for reducing cost of production."[14]

In German large-scale industry, *e.g.*, in the chemical industry, which has developed so enormously during these last few decades, the promotion of technical improvement is organised in the same way. By 1908, the process of concentration production had already given rise to two main groups which, in their way, were in the nature of monopolies. First these groups represented "dual alliances" of two pairs of big factories, each having a capital of from twenty to twenty-one million marks: on the one hand, the former Meister Factory at Höchst and the Cassella Factory at Frankfort-on-Main; and on the other hand, the aniline and soda factory at Ludwigshafen and the former Bayer Factory at Elberfeld. In 1905, one of these groups, and in 1908 the other group, each concluded a separate agreement with yet another big factory. The result was the formation of two "triple alliances," each with a capital of from forty to fifty million marks. And

[13] *Report of the Commission of Corporations on the Tobacco Industry*, Washington, 1909, p. 266, cited according to Dr. Paul Tafel, *Die nordamerikanischen Trusts und ihre Wirkungen auf den Fortschritt der Technik* (*North American Trusts and their Effect on Technical Progress*), Stuttgart, 1913, p. 48.

[14] Dr. P. Tafel, *ibid.*, pp. 48-49.

these "alliances" began to come "close" to one another, to reach "an understanding" about prices, etc.[15]

Competition becomes transformed into monopoly. The result is immense progress in the socialisation of production. In particular, the process of technical invention and improvement becomes socialised.

This is no longer the old type of free competition between manufacturers, scattered and out of touch with one another, and producing for an unknown market. Concentration has reached the point at which it is possible to make an approximate estimate of all sources of raw materials (for example, the iron ore deposits) of a country and even, as we shall see, of several countries, or of the whole world. Not only are such estimates made, but these sources are captured by gigantic monopolist combines. An approximate estimate of the capacity of markets is also made, and the combines divide them up amongst themselves by agreement. Skilled labour is monopolised, the best engineers are engaged; the means of transport are captured: railways in America, shipping companies in Europe and America. Capitalism in its imperialist stage arrives at the threshold of the most complete socialisation of production. In spite of themselves, the capitalists are dragged, as it were, into a new social order, a transitional social order from complete free competition to complete socialisation.

Production becomes social, but appropriation remains private. The social means of production remain the private property of a few. The general framework of formally recognised free competition remains, but the yoke of a few monopolists on the rest of the population becomes a hundred times heavier, more burdensome and intolerable.

The German economist, Kestner, has written a book especially on the subject of "the struggle between the cartels and outsiders," *i.e.*, enterprises outside the cartels. He entitled his work *Compulsory Organisation,* although, in order to present capitalism in its true light, he should have given it the title: "Compulsory Sub-

[15] Riesser, *op. cit.*, third ed., pp. 547-48. The newspapers (June 1916) report the formation of a new gigantic trust which is to combine the chemical industry of Germany.

mission to Monopolist Combines." This book is edifying if only for the list it gives of the modern and civilised methods that monopolist combines resort to in their striving towards "organisation."

They are as follows: 1) Stopping supplies of raw materials ("one of the most important methods of compelling adherence to the cartel"); 2) Stopping the supply of labour by means of "alliances" (*i.e.*, of agreements between employers and the trade unions by which the latter permit their members to work only in cartelised enterprises); 3) Cutting off deliveries; 4) Closing of trade outlets; 5) Agreements with the buyers, by which the latter undertake to trade only with the cartels; 6) Systematic price cutting (to ruin "outside" firms, *i.e.*, those which refuse to submit to the monopolists. Millions are spent in order to sell goods for a certain time below their cost price; there were instances when the price of benzine was thus lowered from 40 to 22 marks, *i.e.*, reduced almost by half!); 7) Stopping credits; 8) Boycott.

This is no longer competition between small and large-scale industry, or between technically developed and backward enterprises. We see here the monopolies throttling those which do not submit to them, to their yoke, to their dictation. This is how this process is reflected in the mind of a bourgeois economist:

> "Even in the purely economic sphere," writes Kestner, "a certain change is taking place from commercial activity in the old sense of the word towards organisational-speculative activity. The greatest success no longer goes to the merchant whose technical and commercial experience enables him best of all to understand the needs of the buyer, and who is able to discover and effectively awake a latent demand; it goes to the speculative genius [?!] who knows how to estimate, or even only to sense in advance the organisational development and the possibilities of connections between individual enterprises and the banks." [16]

Translated into ordinary human language this means that the development of capitalism has arrived at a stage when, although commodity production still "reigns" and continues to be regarded

[16] Kestner, *op. cit.*, p. 241.—*Ed.*

as the basis of economic life, it has in reality been undermined and the big profits go to the "geniuses" of financial manipulation. At the basis of these swindles and manipulations lies socialised production; but the immense progress of humanity, which achieved this socialisation, goes to benefit the speculators. We shall see later how "on these grounds" reactionary, petty-bourgeois critics of capitalist imperialism dream of going *back* to "free," "peaceful" and "honest" competition.

"The prolonged raising of prices which results from the formation of cartels," says Kestner, "has hitherto been observed only in relation to the most important means of production, particularly coal, iron and potassium, but has never been observed for any length of time in relation to manufactured goods. Similarly, the increase in profits resulting from that has been limited only to the industries which produce means of production. To this observation we must add that the raw materials industry not only has secured advantages from the cartel formation in regard to the growth of income and profitableness, to the detriment of the finished goods industry, but that it has secured also a *dominating position* over the latter, which did not exist under free competition."[17]

The words which we have italicised reveal the essence of the case which the bourgeois economists admit so rarely and so unwillingly, and which the modern defenders of opportunism, led by K. Kautsky, so zealously try to evade and brush aside. Domination, and violence that is associated with it, such are the relationships that are most typical of the "latest phase of capitalist development"; this is what must inevitably result, and has resulted, from the formation of all-powerful economic monopolies.

We will give one more example of the methods employed by the cartels. It is particularly easy for cartels and monopolies to arise when it is possible to capture all the sources of raw materials, or at least, the most important of them. It would be wrong, however, to assume that monopolies do not arise in other industries in which it is impossible to corner the sources of raw materials. The cement industry, for instance, can find its raw materials everywhere. Yet in Germany it is strongly cartelised. The cement

[17] Kestner, *op. cit.*, p. 254.

manufacturers have formed regional syndicates: South German, Rhine-Westphalian, etc. The prices fixed are monopoly prices: 230 to 280 marks a carload (at a cost price of 180 marks!). The enterprises pay a dividend of from 12 per cent to 16 per cent—and let us not forget that the "geniuses" of modern speculation know how to pocket big profits besides those they draw by way of dividends. Now, in order to prevent competition in such a profitable industry, the monopolists resort to sundry stratagems. For example, they spread disquieting rumours about the situation in their industry. Anonymous warnings are published in the newspapers, like the following: "Investors, don't place your capital in the cement industry!" They buy up "outsiders" (those outside the syndicates) and pay them "indemnities" of 60,000, 80,000 and even 150,000 marks.[18] Monopoly everywhere hews a path for itself without scruple as to the means, from "modestly" buying off competitors to the American device of "employing" dynamite against them.

The statement that cartels can abolish crises is a fable spread by bourgeois economists who at all costs desire to place capitalism in a favourable light. On the contrary, when monopoly appears in *certain* branches of industry, it increases and intensifies the anarchy inherent in capitalist production *as a whole*. The disparity between the development of agriculture and that of industry, which is characteristic of capitalism, is increased. The privileged position of the most highly cartelised industry, so-called *heavy* industry, especially coal and iron, causes "a still greater lack of concerted organisation" in other branches of production—as Jeidels, the author of one of the best works on the relationship of the German big banks to industry, puts it.[19]

"The more developed an economic system is," writes Liefmann, one of the most unblushing apologists of capitalism, "the more it resorts to risky enterprises, or enterprises abroad, to those which need a great

[18] Ludwig Eschwege, *Zement*, in *Die Bank*, 1909, Vol. I, p. 115 *et seq.*

[19] Otto Jeidels, *Das Verhältnis der deutschen Grossbanken zur Industrie, mit besonderer Berücksichtigung der Eisenindustrie* (*The Relationship of the German Big Banks to Industry, with Special Reference to the Iron Industry*), Leipzig, 1905, p. 271.

deal of time to develop, or finally, to those which are only of local importance."[20]

The increased risk is connected in the long run with the prodigious increase of capital, which overflows the brim, as it were, flows abroad, etc. At the same time the extremely rapid rate of technical progress gives rise more and more to disturbances in the co-ordination between the various spheres of national economy, to anarchy and crisis. Liefmann is obliged to admit that:

"In all probability mankind will see further important technical revolutions in the near future which will also affect the organisation of the economic system...." (For example, electricity and aviation.) "As a general rule, in such periods of radical economic change, speculation develops on a large scale."[21]

Crises of every kind—economic crises more frequently, but not only these—in their turn increase very considerably the tendency towards concentration and monopoly. In this connection, the following reflections of Jeidels on the significance of the crisis of 1900, which, as we have already seen, marked the turning point in the history of modern monopoly, are exceedingly instructive.

"Side by side with the giant plants in the basic industries, the crisis of 1900 found many plants organised on lines that today would be considered obsolete, the 'pure' [non-combined] plants, which had arisen on the crest of the industrial boom. The fall in prices and the falling off in demand put these 'pure' enterprises into a precarious position, which did not affect the big combined enterprises at all, or only affected them for a very short time. As a consequence of this the crisis of 1900 resulted in a far greater concentration of industry than former crises, like that of 1873. The latter crisis also produced a sort of selection of the best equipped enterprises, but owing to the level of technical development at that time, this selection could not place the firms which successfully emerged from the crisis in a position of monopoly. Such a durable monopoly exists to a high degree in the gigantic enterprises in the modern iron and steel and electrical industries, and to a lesser degree, in the engineering industry and certain metal, transport and

[20] Robert Liefmann, *Beteiligungs- und Finanzierungsgesellschaften (Holding and Finance Companies)*, p. 434.

[21] *Ibid.*, pp. 465-6.

other branches in consequence of their complicated technique, their extensive organisation and the magnitude of their capital."[22]

Monopoly! This is the last word in the "latest phase of capitalist development." But we shall only have a very insufficient, incomplete, and poor notion of the real power and the significance of modern monopolies if we do not take into consideration the part played by the banks.

[22] Jeidels, *op. cit.*, p. 108.

CHAPTER II

The Banks and Their New Role

THE principal and primary function of banks is to serve as an intermediary in the making of payments. In doing so they transform inactive money capital into active capital, that is, into capital producing a profit; they collect all kinds of money revenues and place them at the disposal of the capitalist class.

As banking develops and becomes concentrated in a small number of establishments the banks become transformed, and instead of being modest intermediaries they become powerful monopolies having at their command almost the whole of the money capital of all the capitalists and small business men and also a large part of the means of production and of the sources of raw materials of the given country and in a number of countries. The transformation of numerous modest intermediaries into a handful of monopolists represents one of the fundamental processes in the transformation of capitalism into capitalist imperialism. For this reason we must first of all deal with the concentration of banking.

In 1907-08, the combined deposits of the German joint stock banks, each having a capital of more than a million marks, amounted to 7,000,000,000 marks, while in 1912-13, they amounted to 9,800,000,000 marks. Thus, in five years their deposits increased by 40 per cent. Of the 2,800,000,000 increase, 2,750,000,000 was divided amongst 57 banks, each having a capital of more than 10,000,000 marks. The distribution of the deposits between big and small banks was as follows:[1]

PERCENTAGE OF TOTAL DEPOSITS

Year	IN 9 BIG BERLIN BANKS	IN THE OTHER 48 BANKS WITH A CAPITAL OF MORE THAN 10 MILLION MARKS	IN 115 BANKS WITH A CAPITAL OF 1 TO 10 MILLION MARKS	IN THE SMALL BANKS WITH A CAPITAL OF LESS THAN 1 MILLION MARKS
1907-08	47	32.5	16.5	4
1912-13	49	36	12.	3

[1] Alfred Lansburgh, *Fünf Jahre deutsches Bankwesen* (*Five Years of German Banking*), in *Die Bank*, No. 8, 1913, S. 728.

The small banks are being pushed aside by the big banks, of which nine concentrate in their hands almost half the total deposits. But we have left out of account many important details, for instance, the transformation of numerous small banks practically into branches of big banks, etc. Of this we shall speak later on.

At the end of 1913, Schulze-Gaevernitz estimated the deposits in the nine big Berlin banks at 5,100,000,000 marks, out of a total of about 10,000,000,000 marks. Taking into account not only the deposits, but the total resources of these banks, this author wrote:

"At the end of 1909, the nine big Berlin banks, *together* with their *affiliated banks* controlled 11,276,000,000 marks... that is, about 83 per cent of the total German bank capital. The Deutsche Bank, *which together with its affiliated banks* controls nearly 3,000,000,000 marks, represents, parallel with the Prussian State Railway Administration, the biggest and also the most decentralised accumulation of capital in the old world."[2]

We have emphasised the reference to the "affiliated" banks because this is one of the most important features of modern capitalist concentration. Large-scale enterprises, especially the banks, not only completely absorb small ones, but also "join" them to themselves, subordinate them, bring them into their "own" group or *concern* (to use the technical term) by having "holdings" in their capital, by purchasing or exchanging shares, by controlling them through a system of credits, etc., etc. Professor Liefmann has written a voluminous "work" of about 500 pages describing modern "holding and finance companies,"[3] unfortunately adding "theoretical" reflections of a very poor quality to what is frequently partly digested raw material. To what results this "holding" system leads in regard to concentration is best illustrated in the book written

[2] Schulze-Gaevernitz. *Die deutsche Kreditbank, Grundriss der Sozialokonomik* (*The German Credit Bank* in *Outline of Social Economics*), Sec. V, Part II, *Tübingen*, 1915, pp. 12 and 137.

[3] Robert Liefmann, *Beteiligungs- und Finanzierungsgesellschaften. Eine Studie über den modernen Kapitalismus und das Effektenwesen* (*Holding and Finance Companies—A Study in Modern Capitalism and Securities*), first ed., Jena, 1909, p. 212.

on the big German banks by the banker Riesser. But before examining his data, we will quote an example of the "holding" system.

The Deutsche Bank group is one of the biggest, if not the biggest banking group. In order to trace the main threads which connect all the banks in this group, it is necessary to distinguish between holdings of the first, second and third degree, or what amounts to the same thing, between dependence (of the lesser establishments on the Deutsche Bank) in the first, second and third degree. We then obtain the following picture:[4]

THE DEUTSCHE BANK PARTICIPATES:

	PERMANENTLY	FOR AN INDEFINITE PERIOD	OCCASIONALLY	TOTAL
1st degree	in 17 banks	in 5 banks	in 8 banks	in 30 banks
2nd degree	of which 9 participate in 34 others		of which 5 participate in 14 others	of which 14 participate in 48 others
3rd degree	of which 4 participate in 7 others		of which 2 participate in 2 others	of which 6 participate in 9 others

Included in the eight banks dependent on the Deutsche Bank in the "first degree," "occasionally," there are three foreign banks: one Austrian, the Wiener Bankverein, and two Russian, the Siberian Commercial Bank and the Russian Bank for Foreign Trade. Altogether, the Deutsche Bank group comprises, directly and indirectly, partially and totally, no less than 87 banks; and the capital—its own and others which it controls—is estimated at between two and three billion marks.

It is obvious that a bank which stands at the head of such a group, and which enters into agreement with a half dozen other banks only slightly smaller than itself for the purpose of conducting big and profitable operations like floating state loans, is

[4] A. Lansburgh, *Das Beteiligungssystem im deutschen Bankwesen* (*The Holding System in German Banking*), in *Die Bank*, 1910, I, p. 500 *et seq.*

no longer a mere "intermediary" but a combine of a handful of monopolists.

The rapidity with which the concentration of banking proceeded in Germany at the end of the nineteenth and the beginning of the twentieth centuries is shown by the following data which we quote in an abbreviated form from Riesser:

SIX BIG BERLIN BANKS

Year	BRANCHES IN GERMANY	DEPOSIT BANKS AND EXCHANGE OFFICES	CONSTANT HOLDINGS IN GERMAN JOINT STOCK BANKS	TOTAL ESTABLISHMENTS
1895	16	14	1	42
1900	21	40	8	80
1911	104	276	63	450

We see the rapid extension of a close network of canals which cover the whole country, centralising all capital and all revenues, transforming thousands and thousands of scattered economic enterprises into a single national, capitalist, and then into an international, capitalist, economic unit. The "decentralisation" that Schulze-Gaevernitz, as an exponent of modern bourgeois political economy, speaks of in the passage previously quoted, really means the subordination of an increasing number of formerly relatively "independent," or rather, strictly local economic units, to a single centre. In reality it is *centralisation,* the increase in the role, the importance and the power of monopolist giants.

In the older capitalist countries this "banking network" is still more close. In Great Britain (including Ireland) in 1910, there were in all 7,151 branches of banks. Four big banks had more than 400 branches each (from 447 to 689); four had more than 200 branches each, and eleven more than 100 each.

In France, *three* big banks (Crédit Lyonnais, the Comptoir National d'Escompte and the Société Générale) extended their operations and their network of branches in the following manner:[5]

[5] Eugen Kaufmann, *Das französische Bankwesen* (*French Banking*), Tübingen, 1911, pp. 356 and 362.

Year	Number of branches and offices: IN THE PROVINCES	IN PARIS	TOTAL	Capital in million francs: OWN CAPITAL	BORROWED CAPITAL
1870	47	17	64	200	427
1890	192	66	258	265	1,245
1909	1,033	196	1,229	887	4,363

In order to show the "connections" of a big modern bank, Riesser gives the following figures of the number of letters dispatched and received by the Disconto-Gesellschaft, one of the biggest banks in Germany and in the world, the capital of which amounted to 300,000,000 marks in 1914:

Year	LETTERS RECEIVED	LETTERS DISPATCHED
1852	6,135	6,292
1870	85,800	87,513
1900	533,102	626,043

In 1875, the big Paris bank, the Crédit Lyonnais, had 28,535 accounts. In 1912 it had 633,539.[6]

These simple figures show perhaps better than long explanations how the concentration of capital and the growth of their turnover is radically changing the significance of the banks. Scattered capitalists are transformed into a single collective capitalist. When carrying the current accounts of a few capitalists, the banks, as it were, transact a purely technical and exclusively auxiliary operation. When, however, these operations grow to enormous dimensions we find that a handful of monopolists control all the operations, both commercial and industrial, of the whole of capitalist society. They can, by means of their banking connections, by running current accounts and transacting other financial operations, first *ascertain exactly* the position of the various capitalists, then *control* them, influence them by restricting or enlarging, facilitating or hindering their credits, and finally they can *entirely determine* their fate, determine their income, deprive them of capi-

[6] Jean Lescure, *L'épargne en France (Savings in France)*, Paris, 1914, p. 52.

tal, or, on the other hand, permit them to increase their capital rapidly and to enormous dimensions, etc.

We have just mentioned the 300,000,000 marks' capital of the Disconto-Gesellschaft of Berlin. The increase of the capital of this bank was one of the incidents in the struggle for hegemony between two of the biggest Berlin banks—the Deutsche Bank and the Disconto.

In 1870, the Deutsche Bank, a new enterprise, had a capital of only 15,000,000 marks, while that of the Disconto was 30,000,000 marks. In 1908, the first had a capital of 200,000,000, while the second had 170,000,000. In 1914, the Deutsche Bank increased its capital to 250,000,000 and the Disconto, by merging with a very important bank, the Schaffhausenscher Bankverein, increased its capital to 300,000,000. And, of course, while this struggle for hegemony goes on the two banks more and more frequently conclude "agreements" of an increasingly durable character with each other. This development of banking compels specialists in the study of banking questions—who regard economic questions from a standpoint which does not in the least exceed the bounds of the most moderate and cautious bourgeois reformism—to arrive at the following conclusions:

The German review, *Die Bank*, commenting on the increase of the capital of the Disconto-Gesellschaft to 300,000,000 marks, writes:

> "Other banks will follow this same path and in time the three hundred men, who today govern Germany economically, will gradually be reduced to fifty, twenty-five or still fewer. It cannot be expected that this new move towards concentration will be confined to banking. The close relations that exist between certain banks naturally involve the bringing together of the manufacturing concerns which they favour.... One fine morning we shall wake up in surprise to see nothing but trusts before our eyes, and to find ourselves faced with the necessity of substituting state monopolies for private monopolies. However, we have nothing to reproach ourselves with, except with us having allowed things to follow their own course, slightly accelerated by the manipulation of stocks." [7]

[7] A. Lansburgh, *Die Bank mit den 300 Millionen* (*The 300 Million Mark Bank*), in *Die Bank*, 1914, I, p. 426.

This is an example of the impotence of bourgeois journalism which differs from bourgeois science only in that the latter is less sincere and strives to obscure essential things, to conceal the wood by trees. To be "surprised" at the results of concentration, to "reproach" the government of capitalist Germany, or capitalist "society" ("us"), to fear that the introduction of stocks and shares might "accelerate" concentration in the same way as the German "cartel specialist" Tschierschky fears the American trusts and "prefers" the German cartels on the grounds that they may not, like the trusts, "accelerate technical and economic progress to an excessive degree"[8]—is not this impotence?

But facts remain facts There are no trusts in Germany; there are "only" cartels—but Germany is *governed* by not more than three hundred magnates of capital, and the number of these is constantly diminishing. At all events, banks in all capitalist countries, no matter what the law in regard to them may be, greatly intensify and accelerate the process of concentration of capital and the formation of monopolies.

The banking system, Marx wrote half a century ago in *Capital*, "presents indeed the form of common bookkeeping and distribution of means of production on a social scale, but only the form."[9] The figures we have quoted on the growth of bank capital, on the increase in the number of the branches and offices of the biggest banks, the increase in the number of their accounts, etc., present a concrete picture of this "common bookkeeping" of the *whole* capitalist class; and not only of the capitalists, for the banks collect, even though temporarily, all kinds of financial revenues of small business men, office clerks, and of a small upper stratum of the working class. It is "common distribution of means of production" that, from the formal point of view, grows out of the development of modern banks, the most important of which, numbering from three to six in France, and from six to eight in Germany, control billions and billions. In point of fact, however, the distribution of means

[8] Tschierschky, *op. cit.*, p. 128.

[9] Karl Marx, *Capital* (Three Volumes), new and revised edition, International Publishers, New York, 1967, Volume III, p. 606.—*Ed.*

of production is by no means "common," but private, *i.e.*, it conforms to the interests of big capital, and primarily, of very big monopoly capital, which operates in conditions in which the masses of the population live in want, in which the whole development of agriculture hopelessly lags behind the development of industry, and within industry itself the "heavy industries" exact tribute from all other branches of industry.

The savings banks and post offices are beginning to compete with the banks in the matter of socialising capitalist economy; they are more "decentralised," *i.e.*, their influence extends to a greater number of localities, to more remote places, to wider sections of the population. An American commission has collected the following data on the comparative growth of deposits in banks and savings banks:[10]

DEPOSITS (*in billions of marks*)

	ENGLAND		FRANCE		GERMANY		
Year	BANKS	SAVINGS BANKS	BANKS	SAVINGS BANKS	BANKS	CREDIT SOCIETIES	SAVINGS BANKS
1880	8.4	1.6	?	0.9	0.5	0.4	2.6
1888	12.4	2.0	1.5	2.1	1.1	0.4	4.5
1908	23.2	4.2	3.7	4.2	7.1	2.2	13.9

As they pay interest at the rate of 4 per cent and 4¼ per cent on deposits, the savings banks must seek "profitable" investments for their capital, they must deal in bills, mortgages, etc. The boundaries between the banks and the savings banks "become more and more obliterated." The Chambers of Commerce at Bochum and Erfurt, for example, demand that savings banks be prohibited from engaging in "purely" banking business, such as discounting bills. They demand the limitation of the "banking" operations of the post office.[11] The banking magnates seem to be afraid that state monopoly will steal upon them from an unexpected quarter. It goes without saying, however, that this fear is no more than the expression, as it were, of the rivalry between two department man-

[10] *Cf. Statistics of the National Monetary Commission*, quoted in *Die Bank*, 1910, I, p. 1200.

[11] *Die Bank*, 1913, I, 811, 1022; 1914, p. 743.

agers in the same office; for, on the one hand, the billions entrusted to the savings banks are in the final analysis actually controlled by *these very same* bank magnates, while, on the other hand, state monopoly in capitalist society is nothing more than a means of increasing and guaranteeing the income of millionaires on the verge of bankruptcy in one branch of industry or another.

The change from the old type of capitalism, in which free competition predominated, to the new capitalism, in which monopoly reigns, is expressed, among other things, by a decrease in the importance of the Stock Exchange. The German review, *Die Bank*, wrote:

"For a long time now, the Stock Exchange has ceased to be the indispensable intermediary of circulation that it was formerly when the banks were not yet able to place the bulk of new issues with their clients." [12]

"Every bank is a Stock Exchange, and the bigger the bank, and the more successful the concentration of banking, the truer does this proverb become." [13]

"While formerly, in the 'seventies, the Stock Exchange, flushed with the exuberance of youth" (a "subtle" allusion to the crash of 1873, and to the company promotion scandals), "opened the era of the industrialisation of Germany, nowadays the banks and industry are able to 'do it alone.' The domination of our big banks over the Stock Exchange ... is nothing else than the expression of the completely organised German industrial state. If the domain of the automatically functioning economic laws is thus restricted, and if the domain consciously regulated by the banks is considerably increased, the national economic responsibility of a very small number of guiding heads is infinitely increased," [14] so wrote Professor Schulze-Gaevernitz, an apologist of German imperialism, who is regarded as an authority by the imperialists of all countries, and who tries to gloss over a "detail," *viz.*, that

[12] *Die Bank*, 1914, I, p. 316.

[13] Oskar Stillich, *Geld und Bankwesen* (*Money and Banking*), Berlin, 1907, p. 169.

[14] Schulze-Gaevernitz, *Die deutsche Kreditbank*, *Grundriss der Sozialökonomik* (*German Credit Bank* in *Outline of Social Economics*), Tübingen, 1915. Schulze-Gaevernitz, *ibid.*, p. 151.

the "conscious regulation" of economic life by the banks consists in the fleecing of the public by a handful of "completely organised" monopolists. For the task of a bourgeois professor is not to lay bare the mechanism of the financial system, or to divulge all the machinations of the finance monopolists, but, rather, to present them in a favourable light.

In the same way, Riesser, a still more authoritative economist and himself a bank man, makes shift with meaningless phrases in order to explain away undeniable facts. He writes:

"...The Stock Exchange is steadily losing the feature which is absolutely essential for national economy as a whole and for the circulation of securities in particular—that of being an exact measuring-rod and an almost automatic regulator of the economic movements which converge on it." [15]

In other words, the old capitalism, the capitalism of free competition, and its indispensable regulator, the Stock Exchange, are passing away. A new capitalism has come to take its place, which bears obvious features of something transitory, which is a mixture of free competition and monoply. The question naturally arises: to *what* is this new, "transitory" capitalism leading? But the bourgeois scholars are afraid to raise this question.

"Thirty years ago, employers, freely competing against one another, performed nine-tenths of the work connected with their businesses other than manual labour. At the present time, nine-tenths of this business 'brain work' is performed by *officials*. Banking is in the forefront of this evolution." [16]

This admission by Schulze-Gaevernitz brings us once again to the question as to what this new capitalism, capitalism in its imperialist stage, is leading to.

Among the few banks which remain at the head of all capitalist economy as a result of the process of concentration, there is naturally to be observed an increasingly marked tendency towards monopolist agreements, towards a *bank trust*. In America, there are not nine, but *two* big banks, those of the billionaires Rocke-

[15] Riesser, *op. cit.*, fourth ed., p. 629.

[16] *Die Bank*, 1912, p. 435.

feller and Morgan, which control a capital of eleven billion marks.[17] In Germany, the absorption of the Schaffhausenscher Bankverein by the Disconto-Gesellschaft, to which we referred above, was commented on in the following terms by the *Frankfurter Zeitung*, one of the organs of the Stock Exchange interests:

"The concentration movement of the banks is narrowing the circle of establishments from which it is possible to obtain large credits, and is consequently increasing the dependence of big industry upon a small number of banking groups. In view of the internal links between industry and finance, the freedom of movement of manufacturing companies in need of bank capital is restricted. For this reason, big industry is watching the growing trustification of the banks with mixed feelings. Indeed we have repeatedly seen the beginnings of certain agreements between the individual big banking concerns, which aim at limiting competition." [18]

Again, the final word in the development of the banks is monopoly.

The close ties that exist between the banks and industry are the very things that bring out most strikingly the new role of the banks. When a bank discounts a bill for an industrial firm, opens a current account for it, etc., these operations, taken separately, do not in the least diminish the independence of the industrial firm, and the bank plays no other part than that of a modest intermediary. But when such operations are multiplied and become an established practice, when the bank "collects" in its own hands enormous amounts of capital, when the running of a current account for the firm in question enables the bank—and this is what happens—to become better informed of the economic position of the client, then the result is that the industrial capitalist becomes more completely dependent on the bank.

At the same time a very close personal union is established between the banks and the biggest industrial and commercial enterprises the merging of one with another through the acquisition of shares, through the appointment of bank directors to the Supervisory Boards (or Boards of Directors) of industrial and com-

[17] *Die Bank*, 1912, p. 435.
[18] Quoted by Schulze-Gaevernitz, *ibid.*, p. 155.

mercial enterprises, and *vice versa.* The German economist, Jeidels, has compiled very complete data on this form of concentration of capital and of enterprises. Six of the biggest Berlin banks were represented by their directors in 344 industrial companies; and by their board members in 407 other companies. Altogether, they supervised a total of 751 companies. In 289 of these companies they either had two of their representatives on each of the respective Supervisory Boards, or held the posts of chairmen. These industrial and commercial companies are engaged in the most varied branches of industry: in insurance, transport, restaurants, theatres, art industry, etc. On the other hand, there were on the Supervisory Boards of these six banks (in 1910) fifty-one of the biggest manufacturers, among whom were directors of Krupp, of the powerful "Hapag" (Hamburg-American Line), etc. From 1895 to 1910, each of these six banks participated in the share and bond issues of several hundreds of industrial companies (the number ranging from 281 to 419).[19]

The "personal union" between the banks and industry is completed by the "personal union" between both and the state.

> "Seats on the Supervisory Board," writes Jeidels, "are freely offered to persons of title, also to ex-civil servants, who are able to do a great deal to facilitate [!!] relations with the authorities.... Usually on the Supervisory Board of a big bank there is a member of parliament or a Berlin city councillor."[20]

The building, so to speak, of the great capitalist monopolies is therefore going on full steam ahead in all "natural" and "supernatural" ways. A sort of division of labour amongst some hundreds of kings of finance who reign over modern capitalist society is being systematically developed.

> "Simultaneously with this widening of the sphere of activity of certain big industrialists" (sharing in the management of banks, etc.) "and together with the allocation of provincial bank managers to definite industrial regions, there is a growth of specialisation among the managers of the big banks.... Generally speaking, this specialisation is only

[19] Jeidels, *op. cit.;* Riesser, *op. cit.—Ed.*

[20] Jeidels, *op. cit.,* pp. 149, 152.—*Ed.*

conceivable when banking is conducted on a large scale, and particularly when it has widespread connections with industry. This division of labour proceeds along two lines: on the one hand, the relations with industry as a whole are entrusted to one manager, as his special function; on the other, each manager assumes the supervision of several isolated enterprises, or enterprises with allied interests, or in the same branch of industry, sitting on their Boards of Directors" (capitalism has reached the stage of organised *control* of individual enterprises). "One specialises in German industry, sometimes even in West German industry alone" (the West is the most industrialised part of Germany). "Others specialise in relations with foreign states and foreign industry, in information about manufacturers, in Stock Exchange questions, etc. Besides, each bank manager is often assigned a special industry or locality, where he has a say as a member of the Board of Directors; one works mainly on the Board of Directors of electric companies, another in the chemical, brewing or sugar beet industry; a third in a few isolated industrial enterprises but at the same time in non-industrial, *i.e.,* insurance companies.... It is certain that, as the extent and diversification of the big banks' operations increase, the division of labour among their directors also spreads, with the object and result of lifting them somewhat out of pure banking and making them better experts, better judges of the general problems of industry and the special problems of each branch of industry, thus making them more capable of action within the respective bank's industrial sphere of influence. This system is supplemented by the banks' endeavours to have elected to their own Board of Directors, or to those of their subsidiary banks, men who are experts in industrial affairs, such as manufacturers, former officials, especially those formerly in the railway service or in mining," etc.[21]

We find the same system, with only slight difference, in French banking. For instance, one of the three biggest French banks, the Crédit Lyonnais, has organised a financial research service (*Service des études financières*), which permanently employs over fifty engineers, statisticians, economists, lawyers, etc., at a cost of six or seven hundred thousand francs annually. The service is in turn divided into eight sections, of which one deals with industrial establishments, another with general statistics, a third with railway and

[21] Jeidels, *op. cit.,* pp. 156-57.

steamship companies, a fourth with securities, a fifth with financial reports, etc.[22]

The result is twofold: on the one hand the merging, to an ever greater extent, or, as N. Bukharin aptly calls it, the coalescence of bank and industrial capital; and on the other hand, a transformation of the banks into institutions of a truly "universal character." On this question we think it necessary to quote the exact terms used by Jeidels, who has best studied the subject:

> "An examination of the sum total of industrial relationships reveals the *universal character* of the financial establishments working on behalf of industry. Unlike other kinds of banks and contrary to the requirements often laid down in literature—according to which banks ought to specialise in one kind of business or in one branch of industry in order to maintain a firm footing—the big banks are striving to make their industrial connections as varied and far-reaching as possible, according to locality and branch of business, and are striving to do away with the inequalities in the distribution among localities and branches of business resulting from the historical development of individual banking houses.... One tendency is to make the ties with industry general; another tendency is to make these ties durable and close. In the six big banks both these tendencies are realised, not in full, but to a considerable extent and to an equal degree." [23]

Quite often industrial and commercial circles complain of the "terrorism" of the banks. And it is not surprising that such complaints are heard, for the big banks "command," as will be seen from the following example: on November 19, 1901, one of the big Berlin "D" bank (such is the name given to the four biggest banks whose names begin with the letter D [24]) wrote to the Board of Directors of the German Central Northwest Cement Syndicate in the following terms:

[22] Eugen Kaufmann, *Die Organisation der französischen Depositen-Grossbanken* (*Organisation of the Big French Deposit Banks*), in *Die Bank*, 1909, II, pp. 851 *et seq.*

[23] Jeidels, *op. cit.*, p. 180.

[24] *I.e.*, Deutsche Bank, Disconto-Gesellschaft, Dresdner Bank and Darmstädter Bank.—*Ed.*

"As we learn from the notice you published in the *Reichsanzeiger* of the 18th instant, we must reckon with the possibility that the next general meeting of your company, fixed for the 30th of this month, may decide on measures which are likely to effect changes in your undertakings which are unacceptable to us. We deeply regret that, for these reasons, we are obliged henceforth to withdraw the credit which has been hitherto allowed you.... But if the said next general meeting does not decide upon measures which are unacceptable to us and if we receive suitable guarantees on this matter for the future, we shall be quite willing to open negotiations with you on the grant of a new credit." [25]

As a matter of fact, this is small capital's old complaint about being oppressed by big capital, but in this case it was a whole syndicate that fell into the category of "small" capital! The old struggle between big and small capital is being resumed on a new and higher stage of development. It stands to reason that undertakings, financed by big banks handling billions, can accelerate technical progress in a way that cannot possibly be compared with the past. The banks, for example, set up special technical research societies, and only "friendly" industrial enterprises benefit from their work. To this category belong the Electric Railway Research Association and the Central Bureau of Scientific and Technical Research.

The directors of the big banks themselves cannot fail to see that new conditions of national economy are being created. But they are powerless in the face of these phenomena.

"Anyone who has watched, in recent years, the changes of incumbents of directorships and seats on the Supervisory Boards of the big banks, cannot fail to have noticed that power is gradually passing into the hands of men who consider the active intervention of the big banks in the general development of industry to be indispensable and of increasing importance. Between these new men and the old bank directors, disagreements of a business and often of a personal nature are growing on this subject. The question that is in dispute is whether or not the banks, as credit institutions, will suffer from this intervention in industry, whether they are sacrificing tried principles and an assured profit to engage in a field of activity which has nothing in common

[25] Oskar Stillich, *Geld und Bankwesen*, Berlin, 1907, p. 147.

with their role as intermediaries in providing credit, and which is leading the banks into a field where they are more than ever before exposed to the blind forces of trade fluctuations. This is the opinion of many of the older bank directors, while most of the young men consider active intervention in industry to be a necessity as great as that which gave rise, simultaneously with big modern industry, to the big banks and modern industrial banking. The two parties to this discussion are agreed only on one point: and that is, that as yet there are neither firm principles nor a concrete aim in the new activities of the big banks." [26]

The old capitalism has had its day. The new capitalism represents a transition towards something. It is hopeless, of course, to seek for "firm principles and a concrete aim" for the purpose of "reconciling" monopoly with free competition. The admission of the practical men has quite a different ring from the official praises of the charms of "organised" capitalism sung by its apologists, Schulze-Gaevernitz, Liefmann and similar "theoreticians."

At precisely what period were the "new activities" of the big banks finally established? Jeidels gives us a fairly exact answer to this important question:

"The ties between the banks and industrial enterprises, with their new content, their new forms and their new organs, namely, the big banks which are organised on both a centralised and a decentralised basis, were scarcely a characteristic economic phenomenon before the 'nineties; in one sense, indeed, this initial date may be advanced to the year 1897, when the important 'mergers' took place and when, for the first time, the new form of decentralised organisation was introduced to suit the industrial policy of the banks. This starting point could perhaps be placed at an even later date, for it was the crisis [of 1900] that enormously accelerated and intensified the process of concentration of industry and banking, consolidated that process, for the first time transformed the connection with industry into the monopoly of the big banks, and made this connection much closer and more active." [27]

Thus, the beginning of the twentieth century marks the turning point from the old capitalism to the new, from the domination of capital in general to the domination of finance capital.

[26] Jeidels, *op. cit.*, pp. 183-84.
[27] *Ibid.*, p. 181.

CHAPTER III

Finance Capital and Financial Oligarchy

"A steadily increasing proportion of capital in industry," Hilferding writes, "does not belong to the industrialists who employ it. They obtain the use of it only through the medium of the banks, which, in relation to them, represent the owners of the capital. On the other hand, the bank is forced to keep an increasing share of its funds engaged in industry. Thus, to an increasing degree the bank is being transformed into an industrial capitalist. This bank capital, *i.e.*, capital in money form which is thus really transformed into industrial capital, I call 'finance capital.'...Finance capital is capital controlled by banks and employed by industrialists."[1]

This definition is incomplete in so far as it is silent on one extremely important fact: the increase of concentration of production and of capital to such an extent that it leads, and has led, to monopoly. But throughout the whole of his work, and particularly in the two chapters which precede the one from which this definition is taken, Hilferding stresses the part played by ***capitalist monopolies.***

The concentration of production; the monopoly arising therefrom; the merging or coalescence of banking with industry—this is the history of the rise of finance capital and what gives the term "finance capital" its content.

We now have to describe how, under the general conditions of commodity production and private property, the "domination" of capitalist monopolies inevitably becomes the domination of a financial oligarchy. It should be noted that the representatives of German bourgeois science—and not only of German science—like Riesser, Schulze-Gaevernitz, Liefmann and others are all apologists of imperialism and of finance capital. Instead of revealing the "mechanics" of the formation of an oligarchy, its methods, its revenues "innocent and sinful," its connections with parliaments, etc., they

[1] R. Hilferding, *Das Finanzkapital*, 1912, p. 283.

conceal, obscure and embellish them. They evade these "vexed questions" by a few vague and pompous phrases: appeals to the "sense of responsibility" of bank directors, praising "the sense of duty" of Prussian officials; by giving serious study to petty details, to ridiculous bills of parliament—for the "supervision" and "regulation" of monopolies; by playing with theories, like, for example, the following "scientific" definition, arrived at by Professor Liefmann: ***"Commerce is an occupation having for its object: collecting goods, storing them and making them available."*** (The Professor's boldface italics.) From this it would follow that commerce existed in the time of primitive man, who knew nothing about exchange, and that it will exist under socialism!

But the monstrous facts concerning the monstrous rule of the financial oligarchy are so striking that in all capitalist countries, in America, France and Germany, a whole literature has sprung up, written from the *bourgeois* point of view, but which, nevertheless, gives a fairly accurate picture and criticism—petty-bourgeois, naturally—of this oligarchy.

The "holding system," to which we have already briefly referred above, should be placed at the corner-stone. The German economist, Heymann, probably the first to call attention to this matter, describes it in this way:

> "The head of the concern controls the parent company; the latter reigns over the subsidiary companies which in their turn control still other subsidiaries. Thus, it is possible with a comparatively small capital to dominate immense spheres of production. As a matter of fact, if holding 50 per cent of the capital is always sufficient to control a company, the head of the concern needs only one million to control eight millions in the second subsidiaries. And if this "interlocking" is extended, it is possible with one million to control sixteen, thirty-two or more millions." [2]

Experience shows that it is sufficient to own 40 per cent of the shares of a company in order to direct its affairs,[3] since a certain number of small, scattered shareholders find it impossible, in prac-

[2] Heymann, *Die gemischten Werke im deutschen Grosseisengewerbe,* Stuttgart 1904, pp. 268-69.

[3] R. Liefmann, *Beteiligungsgesellschaften,* p. 258.

tice, to attend general meetings, etc. The "democratisation" of the ownership of shares, from which the bourgeois sophists and opportunist "would-be" Social-Democrats expect (or declare that they expect) the "democratisation of capital," the strengthening of the role and significance of small-scale production, etc., is, in fact, one of the ways of increasing the power of financial oligarchy. Incidentally, this is why, in the more advanced, or in the older and more "experienced" capitalist countries, the law allows the issue of shares of very small denomination. In Germany, it is not permitted by the law to issue shares of less value than one thousand marks, and the magnates of German finance look with an envious eye at England, where the issue of one-pound shares is permitted. Siemens, one of the biggest industrialists and "financial kings" in Germany, told the Reichstag on June 7, 1900, that "the one-pound share is the basis of British imperialism."[4] This merchant has a much deeper and more "Marxian" understanding of imperialism than a certain disreputable writer, generally held to be one of the founders of Russian Marxism, who believes that imperialism is a bad habit of a certain nation....

But the "holding system" not only serves to increase enormously the power of the monopolists; it also enables them to resort with impunity to all sorts of shady tricks to cheat the public, for the directors of the parent company are not legally responsible for the subsidiary companies, which are supposed to be "independent," and *through the medium* of which they can "pull off" *anything*. Here is an example taken from the German review, *Die Bank*, for May 1914:

"The Spring Steel Company of Kassel was regarded some years ago as being one of the most profitable enterprises in Germany. Through bad management its dividends fell within the space of a few years from 15 per cent to nil. It appears that the Board, without consulting the shareholders, had loaned *six million marks* to one of the subsidiary companies, the Hassia, Ltd., which had a nominal capital of only some hundreds of thousands of marks. This commitment, amounting to nearly treble the capital of the parent company, was never mentioned

[4] Schulze-Gaevernitz in "*Grdr. d. S.-Oek.*," V, 2, p. 110.

in its balance sheets. This omission was quite legal, and could be kept up for two whole years because it did not violate any provision of company law. The chairman of the Supervisory Board, who as the responsible head had signed the false balance sheets, was, and still is, the president of the Kassel Chamber of Commerce. The shareholders only heard of the loan to the Hassia, Ltd., long afterwards, when it had long been proved to have been a mistake" (this word the writer should have put in quotation marks), "and when Spring Steel shares had dropped nearly 100 points, because those in the know had got rid of them....

"*This typical example of balance-sheet jugglery, quite common in joint stock companies,* explains why their Boards of Directors are more willing to undertake risky transactions than individual dealers. Modern methods of drawing up balance sheets not only make it possible to conceal doubtful undertakings from the average shareholder, but also allow the people most concerned to escape the consequence of unsuccessful speculation by selling their shares in time while the individual dealer risks his own skin in everything he does.

"The balance sheets of many joint stock companies put us in mind of the palimpsests of the Middle Ages from which the visible inscription had first to be erased in order to discover beneath it another inscription giving the real meaning of the document." (Palimpsests are parchment documents from which the original inscription has been obliterated and another inscription imposed.)

"The simplest and, therefore, most common procedure for making balance sheets indecipherable is to divide a single business into several parts by setting up subsidiary companies—or by annexing such. The advantages of this system for various objects—legal and illegal—are so evident that it is now quite unusual to find an important company in which it is not actually in use." [5]

As an example of an important monopolist company widely employing this system, the author quotes the famous General Electric Company (Allgemeine Elektrizitäts Gesellschaft—A.E.G.) to which we shall refer below. In 1912, it was calculated that this company held shares in from *175 to 200* other companies, controlling them,

[5] Ludwig Eschwege, *Tochtergesellschaften* (*Subsidiary Companies*), in *Die Bank*, 1914, I, pp. 544-46.

of course, and thus having control of a total capital of *1,500,000,000 marks!*[6]

All rules of control, the publication of balance sheets, the drawing up of balance sheets according to a definite form, the public auditing of accounts, etc., the things about which well-intentioned professors and officials—that is, those imbued with the good intention of defending and embellishing capitalism—discourse to the public, are of no avail. For private property is sacred, and no one can be prohibited from buying, selling, exchanging or mortgaging shares, etc.

The extent to which this "holding system" has developed in the big Russian banks may be judged by the figures given by E. Agahd, who was for fifteen years an official of the Russo-Chinese Bank and who, in May 1914, published a book, not altogether correctly entitled *Big Banks and the World Market.*[7] The author divides the big Russian banks into two main categories: a) banks that come under a "holding system," and b) "independent" banks—"independence," however, being arbitrarily taken to mean independence of *foreign* banks. The author divides the first group into three sub-groups: 1) German participation, 2) British participation, and 3) French participation, having in view the "participation" and domination of the big foreign banks of the particular country mentioned. The author divides the capital of the banks into "productively" invested capital (in industrial and commercial undertakings), and "speculatively" invested capital (in Stock Exchange and financial operations), assuming, from his petty-bourgeois reformist point of view, that it is possible, under capitalism, to separate the first form of investment from the second and to abolish the second form.

Here are the figures he supplies:

[6] Kurt Heinig, *Der Weg des Elektrotrusts* (*The Path of the Electric Trust*), in *Die Neue Zeit*, 1911-1912, Vol. II, p. 484.

[7] E. Agahd, *Grossbanken und Weltmarkt. Die wirtschaftliche und politische Bedeutung der Grossbanken im Weltmark unter Berücksichtung ihres Einflusses auf Russlands Volkswirtschaft und die deutsch-russischen Beziehungen. Berl.* ("Big Banks and the World Market. The economic and political significance of the big banks on the world market, with reference to their influence on Russia's national economy and German-Russian relations." Berlin, 1914, pp. 11-17.)

BANK ASSETS

(*According to reports for October-November, 1913, in millions of rubles*)

GROUPS OF RUSSIAN BANKS	CAPITAL INVESTED		
	PRODUCTIVE	SPECULATIVE	TOTAL
A. 1) Four banks: Siberian Commercial Bank, Russian Bank, International Bank, and Discount Bank	413.7	859.1	1,272.8
2) Two banks: Commercial and Industrial and Russo-British	239.3	169.1	408.4
3) Five banks: Russian-Asiatic, St. Petersburg Private, Azov-Don, Union Moscow, Russo-French Commercial	711.8	661.2	1,373.0
Total: (11 banks)	1,364.8	1,689.4	3,054.2
B. Eight banks: Moscow Merchants, Volga-Kama, Junker and Co., St. Petersburg Commercial (formerly Wawelberg), Bank of Moscow (formerly Riabushinsky), Moscow Discount, Moscow Commercial, Private Bank of Moscow	504.2	391.1	895.3
Total: (19 banks)	1,869.0	2,080.5	3,949.5

According to these figures, of the approximately four billion rubles making up the "working" capital of the big banks, *more than three-fourths,* more than three billion, belonged to banks which in reality were only "subsidiary companies" of foreign banks, and chiefly of the Paris banks (the famous trio: Union Parisien, Paris et Pays-Bas and Société Générale), and of the Berlin banks (particularly the Deutsche Bank and Disconto-Gesellschaft). Two of the most important Russian banks, the Russian Bank for Foreign Trade and the St. Petersburg International Commercial, between 1906 and 1912 increased their capital from 44,000,000 to 98,000,000 rubles, and their reserve from 15,000,000 to 39,000,000 "employing three-fourths German capital." The first belongs to the Deutsche Bank group and the second to the Disconto-Gesellschaft. The worthy Agahd is indignant at the fact that the majority of the shares are held by the Berlin banks, and that, therefore, the Russian shareholders are powerless. Naturally, the country which exports capital skims the cream: for example, the Deutsche Bank, while introducing the shares of the Siberian Commercial Bank on the Berlin market, kept them in its portfolio for a whole year, and then sold them at the rate of 193 for 100, that is, at nearly twice their nominal value, "earning" a profit of nearly 6,000,000 rubles, which Hilferding calls "promoters' profits."

Our author puts the total "resources" of the principal St. Petersburg banks at 8,235,000,000 rubles, about 8¼ billions and the "holdings," or rather, the extent to which foreign banks dominated them, he estimates as follows: French banks, 55 per cent; English, 10 per cent; German, 35 per cent. The author calculates that of the total of 8,235,000,000 rubles of functioning capital, 3,687,000,000 rubles, or over 40 per cent, fall to the share of the syndicates, Produgol and Prodamet [8]—and the syndicates in the oil, metallurgical and cement industries. Thus, the merging of bank and industrial capital has also made great strides in Russia owing to the formation of capitalist monpolies.

Finance capital, concentrated in a few hands and exercising a virtual monopoly, exacts enormous and ever-increasing profits from the floating of companies, issue of stock, state loans, etc., tightens the grip of financial oligarchies and levies tribute upon the whole of society for the benefit of monopolists. Here is an example, taken from a multitude of others, of the methods of "business" of the American trusts, quoted by Hilferding: in 1887, Havemeyer founded the Sugar Trust by amalgamating fifteen small firms, whose total capital amounted to $6,500,000. Suitably "watered," as the Americans say, the capital of the trust was increased to $50,000,000. This "over-capitalisation" anticipated the monopoly profits, in the same way as the United States Steel Corporation anticipated its profits by buying up as many iron fields as possible. In fact, the Sugar Trust set up monopoly prices on the market, which secured it such profits that it could pay 10 per

[8] Abbreviated names of the syndicates, "Russian Society for Trade in the Mineral Fuels of the Donetz Basin," and "Society for the Sale of the Products of Russian Metallurgical Works," organized in 1906 and 1901 respectively.—*Ed.*

cent dividend on capital "watered" *sevenfold, or about 70 per cent on the capital actually invested at the time of the creation of the trust!* In 1909, the capital of the Sugar Trust was increased to $90,000,000. In twenty-two years, it had increased its capital more than tenfold.

In France the role of the "financial oligarchy" (*Against the Financial Oligarchy in France,* the title of the well-known book by Lysis, the fifth edition of which was published in 1908) assumed a form that was only slightly different. Four of the most powerful banks enjoy, not a relative, but an "absolute monopoly" in the issue of bonds. In reality, this is a "trust of the big banks." And their monopoly ensures the monopolist profits from bond issues. Usually a country borrowing from France does not get more than 90 per cent of the total of the loan, the remaining 10 per cent goes to the banks and other middlemen. The profit made by the banks out of the Russo-Chinese loans of 400,000,000 francs amounted to 8 per cent; out of the Russian (1904) loan of 800,000,000 francs the profit amounted to 10 per cent; and out of the Moroccan (1904) loan of 62,500,000 francs, to 18.75 per cent. Capitalism, which began its development with petty usury capital, ends its development with gigantic usury capital. "The French," says Lysis, "are the usurers of Europe." All the conditions of economic life are being profoundly modified by this transformation of capitalism. With a stationary population, and stagnant industry, commerce and shipping, the "country" can grow rich by usury. "Fifty persons, representing a capital of 8,000,000 francs, can control *2,000,000,000* francs deposited in four banks." The "holding system," with which we are already familiar, leads to the same result. One of the biggest banks, the Société Générale, for instance, issues 64,000 bonds for one of its subsidiary companies, the Egyptian Sugar Refineries. The bonds are issued at 150 per cent, *i.e.,* the bank gaining 50 centimes on the franc. The dividends of the new company are then found to be fictitious. The "public" lost from 90 to 100 million francs. One of the directors of the Société Générale was a member of the board of directors of the Egyptian Sugar Refineries. Hence it is not surprising that the author is driven to the conclusion that "the French Republic is a financial monarchy"; "it is the complete domination of the financial oligarchy; the latter controls the press and the government." [9]

The extraordinarily high rate of profit obtained from the issue of securities, which is one of the principal functions of finance capital, plays a large part in the development and consolidation of the financial oligarchy.

"There is not within the country a single business of this type that brings in profits even approximately equal to those obtained from the flotation of foreign loans," [10] says the German magazine, *Die Bank*.

"No banking operation brings in profits comparable with those obtained from the issue of securities!" [11]

According to the *German Economist,* the average annual profits made on the issue of industrial securities were as follows:

	PER CENT		PER CENT
1895	38.6	1898	67.7
1896	36.1	1899	66.9
1897	66.7	1900	55.2

"In the ten years from 1891 to 1900, *more than a billion* marks of profits were 'earned' by issuing German industrial securities." [12]

While, during periods of industrial boom, the profits of finance capital are disproportionately large, during periods of depression, small and unsound businesses go out of existence, while the big banks take "holdings" in their shares, which are bought up cheaply or in profitable schemes for their "reconstruction" and "reorganisation." In the "reconstruction" of undertakings which have been running at a loss,

"the share capital is written down, that is, profits are distributed on a smaller capital and subsequently are calculated on this smaller basis. If the income has fallen to zero, new capital is called in, which, com-

[9] Lysis, *Contre l'oligarchie financière en France* (*Against the Financial Oligarchy in France*) fifth ed., Paris, 1908, pp. 11, 12, 26, 39, 40, 47-48.

[10] *Die Bank*, 1913, II, p. 630.

[11] Stillich, *op. cit.*, p. 143.—*Ed.*

[12] Stillich, *ibid.;* also Werner Sombart, *Die deutsche Volkswirtschaft im 19. Jahrhundert* (*German National Economy in the Nineteenth Century*), second ed., Berlin, 1909, p. 526, Appendix.

bined with the old and less remunerative capital, will bring in an adequate return."

"Incidentally," adds Hilferding, "these reorganisations and reconstructions have a twofold significance for the banks: first, as profitable transactions; and secondly, as opportunities for securing control of the companies in difficulties."[13]

Here is an instance. The Union Mining Company of Dortmund, founded in 1872, with a share capital of nearly 40,000,000 marks, saw the market price of shares rise to 170 after it had paid a 12 per cent dividend in its first year. Finance capital skimmed the cream and earned a "trifle" of something like 28,000,000 marks. The principal sponsor of this company was that very big German Disconto-Gesellschaft which so successfully attained a capital of 300,000,000 marks. Later, the dividends of the Union declined to nil: the shareholders had to consent to a "writing down" of capital, that is, to losing some of it in order not to lose it all. By a series of "reconstructions," more than 73,000,000 marks were written off the books of the Union in the course of thirty years.

"At the present time, the original shareholders of this company possess only 5 per cent of the nominal value of their shares."[14]

But the bank "made a profit" out of every "reconstruction."

Speculation in land situated in the suburbs of rapidly growing towns is a particularly profitable operation for finance capital. The monopoly of the banks merges here with the monopoly of ground rent and with monopoly in the means of communication, since the increase in the value of the land and the possibility of selling it profitably in allotments, etc., is mainly dependent on good means of communication with the centre of the town; and these means of communication are in the hands of large companies which are connected by means of the holding system and by the distribution of positions on the directorates, with the interested banks. As a result we get what the German writer, L. Eschwege, a contributor to *Die Bank,* who has made a special study of real estate business and mortgages, etc., calls the formation of a "bog." Frantic specu-

[13] Hilferding, *op. cit.,* pp. 142-143.

[14] Stillich, *op. cit.,* p. 138, and Liefmann, p. 51.

lation in suburban building lots: collapse of building enterprises (like that of the Berlin firm of Boswau and Knauer, which grabbed 100,000,000 marks with the help of the "sound and solid" Deutsche Bank—the latter acting, of course, discreetly behind the scenes through the holding system and getting out of it by losing "only" 12,000,000 marks), then the ruin of small proprietors and of workers who get nothing from the fraudulent building firms, underhand agreements with the "honest" Berlin police and the Berlin administration for the purpose of getting control of the issue of building sites, tenders, building licenses, etc.[15]

"American ethics," which the European professors and well-meaning bourgeois so hypocritically deplore, have, in the age of finance capital, become the ethics of literally every large city, no matter what country it is in.

At the beginning of 1914, there was talk in Berlin of the proposed formation of a "transport trust," *i. e.,* of establishing "community of interests" between the three Berlin passenger transport undertakings: the Metropolitan electric railway, the tramway company and the omnibus company.

"We know," wrote *Die Bank,* "that this plan has been contemplated since it became known that the majority of the shares in the bus company has been acquired by the other two transport companies.... We may believe those who are pursuing this aim when they say that by uniting the transport services, they will secure economies part of which will in time benefit the public. But the question is complicated by the fact that behind the transport trust that is being formed are the banks, which, if they desire, can subordinate the means of transportation, which they have monopolised, to the interests of their real estate business. To be convinced of the reasonableness of such a conjecture, we need only recall that at the very formation of the Elevated Railway Company the traffic interests became interlocked with the real estate interests of the big bank which financed it, and this interlocking even created the prerequisites for the formation of the transport enterprise. Its eastern line, in fact, was to run through land which, when it became certain the line was to be laid down, this bank sold to a real estate

[15] Ludwig Eschwege, *Der Sumpf (The Bog)*, in *Die Bank,* 1913, II, p. 952, *et seq.; ibid.,* 1912, I, p. 223 *et seq.*

firm at an enormous profit for itself and for several partners in the transactions."[16]

A monopoly, once it is formed and controls thousands of millions, inevitably penetrates into *every* sphere of public life, regardless of the form of government and all other "details." In the economic literature of Germany one usually comes across the servile praise of the integrity of the Prussian bureaucracy, and allusions to the French Panama scandal and to political corruption in America. But the fact is that *even* the bourgeois literature devoted to German banking matters constantly has to go far beyond the field of purely banking operations and to speak, for instance, of "the attraction of the banks" in reference to the increasing frequency with which public officials take employment with the banks.

"How about the integrity of a state official who in his inmost heart is aspiring to a soft job in the Behrenstrasse?"[17] (the street in Berlin in which the head office of the Deutsche Bank is situated).

In 1909, the publisher of *Die Bank,* Alfred Lansburgh, wrote an article entitled "The Economic Significance of Byzantinism," in which he incidentally referred to Wilhelm II's tour of Palestine, and to "the immediate result of this journey," the construction of the Bagdad railway, that fatal "standard product of German enterprise, which is more responsible for the 'encirclement' than all our political blunders put together."[18] (By encirclement is meant the policy of Edward VII to isolate Germany by surrounding her with an imperialist anti-German alliance.) In 1912, another contributor to this magazine, Eschwege, to whom we have already referred, wrote an article entitled "Plutocracy and Bureaucracy," in which he exposes the case of a German official named Volker, who was a zealous member of the Cartel Committee and who, some time later, obtained a lucrative post in the biggest cartel, *i.e.,* the Steel Syndicate.[19] Similar cases, by no means casual, forced

[16] *Verkehrstrust (Transport Trust),* in *Die Bank,* 1914, I, pp. 89-90.
[17] *Der Zug zur Bank (The Attraction of the Banks),* in *Die Bank,* 1909, I, p. 79.
[18] *Ibid.,* p. 307.
[19] *Die Bank,* 1912, II, p. 825.—*Ed.*

this bourgeois author to admit that "the economic liberty guaranteed by the German Constitution has become in many departments of economic life, a meaningless phrase" and that under the existing rule of the plutocracy, "even the widest political liberty cannot save us from being converted into a nation of unfree people." [20]

As for Russia, we will content ourselves by quoting one example. Some years ago, all the newspapers announced that Davidov, the director of the Credit Department of the Treasury, had resigned his post to take employment with a certain big bank at a salary which, according to the contract, was to amount to over one million rubles in the course of several years. The function of the Credit Department is to "co-ordinate the activities of all the credit institutions of the country"; it also grants subsidies to banks in St. Petersburg and Moscow amounting to between 800 and 1,000 million rubles.[21]

It is characteristic of capitalism in general that the ownership of capital is separated from the application of capital to production, that money capital is separated from industrial or productive capital, and that the rentier, who lives entirely on income obtained from money capital, is separated from the entrepreneur and from all who are directly concerned in the management of capital. Imperialism, or the domination of finance capital, is that highest stage of capitalism in which this separation reaches vast proportions. The supremacy of finance capital over all other forms of capital means the predominance of the rentier and of the financial oligarchy; it means the crystallisation of a small number of financially "powerful" states from among all the rest. The extent to which this process is going on may be judged from the statistics on emissions, *i.e.*, the issue of all kinds of securities.

In the Bulletin of the International Statistical Institute, A. Neymarck [22] has published very comprehensive and complete compara-

[20] *Ibid.*, 1913, II, p. 962.

[21] E. Agahd, *op. cit.*, p. 202.

[22] A. Neymarck, *Bulletin de l'institut international de statistique* (*Bulletin of the International Statistical Institute*), Vol. XIX, Book II, The Hague, 1912. Data concerning small states, second column, are approximately calculated by adding 20 per cent to the 1902 figures.

tive figures covering the issue of securities all over the world, which have been repeatedly quoted in economic literature. The following are the totals he gives for four decades:

TOTAL ISSUES IN BILLIONS OF FRANCS (*Decades*)

1871-1880	76.1
1881-1890	64.5
1891-1900	100.4
1901-1910	197.8

In the 1870's, the total amount of issues for the whole world was high, owing particularly to the loans floated in connection with the Franco-Prussian War, and the company-promoting boom which set in in Germany after the war. In general, the increase is not very rapid during the three last decades of the nineteenth century, and only in the first ten years of the twentieth century is an enormous increase observed of almost 100 per cent. Thus the beginning of the twentieth century marks the turning point, not only in regard to the growth of monopolies (cartels, syndicates, trusts), of which we have already spoken, but also in regard to the development of finance capital.

Neymarck estimates the total amount of issued securities current in the world in 1910 at about 815,000,000,000 francs. Deducting from this amounts which might have been duplicated, he reduces the total to 575-600,000,000,000, which is distributed among the various countries as follows (we will take 600,000,000,000):

FINANCIAL SECURITIES CURRENT IN 1910

(*In billions of francs*)

Great Britain	142	479 (Great Britain, United States, France, Germany)	Japan	12
United States	132		Holland	12.5
France	110		Belgium	7.5
Germany	95		Spain	7.5
Russia	31		Switzerland	6.25
Austria-Hungary	24		Denmark	3.75
Italy	14		Sweden, Norway, Rumania, etc.	2.5
			Total	600.00

From these figures we at once see standing out in sharp relief four of the richest capitalist countries, each of which controls securities to amounts ranging from 100 to 150 billion francs. Two of these countries, England and France, are the oldest capitalist countries, and, as we shall see, possess the most colonies; the other two, the United States and Germany, are in the front rank as regards rapidity of development and the degree of extension of capitalist monopolies in industry. Together, these four countries own 479,000,000,000 francs, that is, nearly 80 per cent of the world's finance capital. Thus, in one way or another, nearly the whole world is more or less the debtor to and tributary of these four international banker countries, the four "pillars" of world finance capital.

It is particularly important to examine the part which export of capital plays in creating the international network of dependence and ties of finance capital.

CHAPTER IV

The Export of Capital

UNDER the old capitalism, when free competition prevailed, the export of *goods* was the most typical feature. Under modern capitalism, when monopolies prevail, the export of *capital* has become the typical feature.

Capitalism is commodity production at the highest stage of development, when labour power itself becomes a commodity. The growth of internal exchange, and particularly of international exchange, is the characteristic distinguishing feature of capitalism. The uneven and spasmodic character of the development of individual enterprises, of individual branches of industry and individual countries, is inevitable under the capitalist system. England became a capitalist country before any other, and in the middle of the nineteenth century, having adopted free trade, claimed to be the "workshop of the world," the great purveyor of manufactured goods to all countries, which in exchange were to keep her supplied with raw materials. But in the last quarter of the nineteenth century, *this* monopoly was already undermined. Other countries, protecting themselves by tariff walls, had developed into independent capitalist states. On the threshold of the twentieth century, we see a new type of monopoly coming into existence. Firstly, there are monopolist capitalist combines in all advanced capitalist countries; secondly, a few rich countries, in which the accumulation of capital reaches gigantic proportions, occupy a monopolist position. An enormous "superabundance of capital" has accumulated in the advanced countries.

It goes without saying that if capitalism could develop agriculture, which today lags far behind industry everywhere, if it could raise the standard of living of the masses, who are everywhere still poverty-stricken and underfed, in spite of the amazing advance in technical knowledge, there could be no talk of a superabundance of capital. This "argument" the petty-bourgeois critics of capitalism advance on every occasion. But if capitalism did these things it would not be capitalism; for uneven development and wretched conditions of the masses are fundamental and inevitable conditions and premises of this mode of production. As long as capitalism remains what it is, surplus capital will never be utilised for the purpose of raising the standard of living of the masses in a given country, for this would mean a decline in profits for the capitalists; it will be used for the purpose of increasing those profits by exporting capital abroad to the backward countries. In these backward countries profits are usually high, for capital is scarce, the price of land is relatively low, wages are low, raw materials are cheap. The possibility of exporting capital is created by the fact that numerous backward countries have been drawn into international capitalist intercourse; main railways have either been built or are being built there; the elementary conditions for industrial development have been created, etc. The necessity for exporting capital arises from the fact that in a few countries capitalism has become "over-ripe" and (owing to the backward state of agriculture and the impoverished state of the masses) capital cannot find "profitable" investment.

Here are approximate figures showing the amount of capital invested abroad by the three principal countries:[1]

CAPITAL INVESTED ABROAD

(In billions of francs)

Year	GREAT BRITAIN	FRANCE	GERMANY
1862	3.6	—	—
1872	15.0	10 (1869)	—
1882	22.0	15 (1880)	?
1893	42.0	20 (1890)	?
1902	62.0	27-37	12.5
1914	75-100	60	44.0

[1] Hobson, *Imperialism*, London, 1902, p. 58; Riesser, *op. cit.*, pp. 395 and 404; P. Arndt in *Weltwirtschaftliches Archiv* (*World Economic Archive*), Vol. VII, 1916, p. 35; Neymarck in *Bulletin de l'institut international de statistique;* Hilferding, *Finanzkapital*, p. 437; Lloyd George, Speech in the House of Commons, May 4, 1915, reported in *Daily Telegraph*, May 5, 1915; B. Harms, *Probleme der Welt-*

This table shows that the export of capital reached formidable dimensions only in the beginning of the twentieth century. Before the war the capital invested abroad by the three principal countries amounted to between 175,000,000,000 and 200,000,000,000 francs. At the modest rate of 5 per cent, this sum should have brought in from 8 to 10 billions a year. This provided a solid basis for imperialist oppression and the exploitation of most of the countries and nations of the world; a solid basis for the capitalist parasitism of a handful of wealthy states!

How is this capital invested abroad distributed among the various countries? *Where* does it go? Only an approximate answer can be given to this question, but sufficient to throw light on certain general relations and ties of modern imperialism.

APPROXIMATE DISTRIBUTION OF FOREIGN CAPITAL (ABOUT 1910)

(In billions of marks)

CONTINENT	GT. BRITAIN	FRANCE	GERMANY	TOTAL
Europe	4	23	18	45
America	37	4	10	51
Asia, Africa and Australia	29	8	7	44
Total	70	35	35	140

The principal spheres of investment of British capital are the British colonies, which are very large also in America (for example, Canada) not to mention Asia, etc. In this case, enormous exports of capital are bound up with the possession of enormous colonies, of the importance of which for imperialism we shall speak later. In regard to France, the situation is quite different. French capital exports are invested mainly in Europe, particularly in Russia (at

wirtschaft (*Problems of World Economy*), Jena, 1912, p. 235 *et seq.;* Dr. Sigmund Schilder, *Entwicklungstendenzen der Weltwirtschaft* (*Trends of Development of World Economy*), Berlin, 1912, Vol. I, p. 150; George Paish, Great Britain's Capital Investments, etc., in *Journal of the Royal Statistical Society,* Vol. LXXIV, 1910-11, p. 167; Georges Diouritch, *L'expansion des banques allemandes à l'étranger, ses rapports avec le développement économique de l'Allemagne* (*Expansion of German Banks Abroad, in Connection with the Economic Development of Germany*), Paris, 1909, p. 84.

least ten billion francs). This is mainly *loan* capital, in the form of government loans and not investments in industrial undertakings. Unlike British colonial imperialism, French imperialism might be termed usury imperialism. In regard to Germany, we have a third type; the German colonies are inconsiderable, and German capital invested abroad is divided fairly evenly between Europe and America.

The export of capital greatly affects and accelerates the development of capitalism in those countries to which it is exported. While, therefore, the export of capital may tend to a certain extent to arrest development in the countries exporting capital, it can only do so by expanding and deepening the further development of capitalism throughout the world.

The countries which export capital are nearly always able to obtain "advantages," the character of which throws light on the peculiarities of the epoch of finance capital and monopoly. The following passage, for instance, occurred in the Berlin review, *Die Bank,* for October 1913:

> "A comedy worthy of the pen of Aristophanes is being played just now on the international capital market. Numerous foreign countries, from Spain to the Balkan states, from Russia to the Argentine, Brazil and China, are openly or secretly approaching the big money markets demanding loans, some of which are very urgent. The money market is not at the moment very bright and the political outlook is not yet promising. But not a single money market dares to refuse a foreign loan for fear that its neighbour might first anticipate it and so secure some small reciprocal service. In these international transactions the creditor nearly always manages to get some special advantages: an advantage of a commercial-political nature, a coaling station, a contract to construct a harbour, a fat concession, or an order for guns."[2]

Finance capital has created the epoch of monopolies, and monopolies introduce everywhere monopolist methods: the utilisation of "connections" for profitable transactions takes the place of competition on the open market. The most usual thing is to stipulate that part of the loan that is granted shall be spent on purchases in the country of issue, particularly on orders for war materials,

[2] *Die Bank,* 1913, pp. 1024-25.

or for ships, etc. In the course of the last two decades (1890-1910), France often resorted to this method. The export of capital abroad thus becomes a means for encouraging the export of commodities. In these circumstances transactions between particularly big firms assume a form "bordering on corruption," as Schilder [8] "delicately" puts it. Krupp in Germany, Schneider in France, Armstrong in England are instances of firms which have close connections with powerful banks and governments and cannot be "ignored" when arranging a loan.

France granted loans to Russia in 1905 and by the commercial treaty of September 16, 1905, she "squeezed" concessions out of her to run till 1917. She did the same thing when the Franco-Japanese commercial treaty was concluded on August 19, 1911. The tariff war between Austria and Serbia, which lasted with a seven months' interval, from 1906 to 1911, was partly caused by competition between Austria and France for supplying Serbia with war materials. In January 1912, Paul Deschanel stated in the Chamber of Deputies that from 1908 to 1911 French firms had supplied war materials to Serbia to the value of 45,000,000 francs.

A report from the Austro-Hungarian Consul at Sao-Paulo (Brazil) states:

> "The construction of the Brazilian railways is being carried out chiefly by French, Belgian, British and German capital. In the financial operations connected with the construction of these railways the countries involved also stipulate for orders for the necessary railway materials."

Thus, finance capital, almost literally, one might say, spreads its net over all countries of the world. Banks founded in the colonies, or their branches, play an important part in these operations. German imperialists look with envy on the "old" colonising nations which are "well established" in this respect. In 1904, Great Britain had 50 colonial banks with 2,279 branches (in 1910 there were 72 banks with 5,449 branches); France had 20 with 136 branches; Holland 16 with 68 branches; and Germany had a "mere" 13 with

[8] Schilder, *op. cit.*, Vol. I, pp. 346, 350 and 371.

70 branches.[4] The American capitalists, in their turn, are jealous of the English and German: "In South America," they complained in 1915, "five German banks have forty branches and five English banks have seventy branches.... England and Germany have invested in Argentina, Brazil, and Uruguay in the last twenty-five years approximately four thousand million dollars, and as a result enjoy together 46 per cent of the total trade of these three countries."[5]

The capital exporting countries have divided the world among themselves in the figurative sense of the term. But finance capital has also led to the *actual* division of the world.

[4] Riesser, *op. cit.*, fourth edition, pp. 374-75; Diouritch, p. 283.

[5] *The Annals of the American Academy of Political and Social Science*, Vol. LIX, May 1915, p. 301. In the same volume on p. 331, we read that the well-known statistician Paish, in the last annual issue of the financial magazine *Statist*, estimated the amount of capital exported by England, Germany, France, Belgium and Holland at 40,000,000,000 dollars, *i.e.*, 200,000,000,000 francs.

CHAPTER V

The Division of the World Among Capitalist Combines

MONOPOLIST capitalist combines—cartels, syndicates, trusts—divide among themselves, first of all, the whole internal market of a country, and impose their control, more or less completely, upon the industry of that country. But under capitalism the home market is inevitably bound up with the foreign market. Capitalism long ago created a world market. As the export of capital increased, and as the foreign and colonial relations and the "spheres of influence" of the big monopolist combines expanded, things "naturally" gravitated towards an international agreement among these combines, and towards the formation of international cartels.

This is a new stage of world concentration of capital and production, incomparably higher than the preceding stages. Let us see how this super-monopoly develops.

The electrical industry is the most typical of the modern technical achievements of capitalism of the *end* of the nineteenth and beginning of the twentieth centuries. This industry has developed most in the two most advanced of the new capitalist countries, the United States and Germany. In Germany, the crisis of 1900 gave a particularly strong impetus to its concentration. During the crisis, the banks, which by this time had become fairly well merged with industry, greatly accelerated and deepened the collapse of relatively small firms and their absorption by the large ones.

"The banks," writes Jeidels, "in refusing a helping hand to the very companies which are in greatest need of capital bring on first a frenzied boom and then the hopeless failure of the companies which have not been attached to them closely long enough."[1]

As a result, after 1900, concentration in Germany proceeded by leaps and bounds. Up to 1900 there had been seven or eight

[1] Jeidels, *op. cit.*, p. 232.

"groups" in the electrical industry. Each was formed of several companies (altogether there were twenty-eight) and each was supported by from two to eleven banks. Between 1908 and 1912 all the groups were merged into two, or possibly one. The diagram below shows the process:

GROUPS IN THE GERMAN ELECTRICAL INDUSTRY

Prior to 1900:	FELTEN & GUILLAUME	LAHMEYER	UNION A.E.G.	SIEMENS & HALSKE	SCHUCKERT & CO.	BERGMANN	KUMMER
	FELTEN & LAHMEYER		A.E.G.	SIEMENS & HALSKE-SCHUCKERT		BERGMANN	*Failed in 1900*
By 1912:	A.E.G. (GENERAL ELECTRIC CO.)			SIEMENS & HALSKE-SCHUCKERT			

(In close "co-operation" since 1908)

The famous A.E.G. (General Electric Company), which grew up in this way, controls 175 to 200 companies (through shareholdings), and a total capital of approximately 1,500,000,000 marks. Abroad, it has thirty-four direct agencies, of which twelve are joint stock companies, in more than ten countries. As early as 1904 the amount of capital invested abroad by the German electrical industry was estimated at 233,000,000 marks. Of this sum, 62,000,000 were invested in Russia. Needless to say, the A.E.G. is a huge combine. Its manufacturing companies alone number no less than sixteen, and their factories make the most varied articles, from cables and insulators to motor cars and aeroplanes.

But concentration in Europe was a part of the process of concentration in America, which developed in the following way:

GENERAL ELECTRIC COMPANY

United States:	Thomson-Houston Co. establishes a firm in Europe	Edison Co. establishes in Europe the French Edison Co. which transfers its patents to the German firm
Germany:	Union Electric Co.	Gen'l Electric Co. (A.E.G.)

GENERAL ELECTRIC CO. (A.E.G.)

Thus, *two* "Great Powers" in the electrical industry were formed. "There are no other electric companies in the world *completely* independent of them," wrote Heinig in his article "The Path of the Electric Trust." An idea, although far from complete, of the turnover and the size of the enterprises of the two "trusts" can be obtained from the following figures:

		TURNOVER (*mill. marks*)	NO. OF EMPLOYEES	NET PROFITS (*mill. marks*)
AMERICA:				
General Electric Co.	1907	252	28,000	35.4
	1910	298	32,000	45.6
GERMANY: A.E.G.	1907	216	30,700	14.5
	1911	362	60,800	21.7

In 1907, the German and American trusts concluded an agreement by which they divided the world between themselves. Competition between them ceased. The American General Electric Company "got" the United States and Canada. The A.E.G. "got" Germany, Austria, Russia, Holland, Denmark, Switzerland, Turkey and the Balkans. Special agreements, naturally secret, were concluded regarding the penetration of "subsidiary" companies into new branches of industry, into "new" countries formally not yet allotted. The two trusts were to exchange inventions and experiments.[2]

It is easy to understand how difficult competition has become against this trust, which is practically world-wide, which controls a capital of several billion, and has its "branches," agencies, representatives, connections, etc., in every corner of the world. But the division of the world between two powerful trusts does not remove the possibility of *redivision,* if the relation of forces changes as a result of uneven development, war, bankruptcy, etc.

The oil industry provides an instructive example of attempts at such a redivision, or rather of a struggle for redivision.

"The world oil market," wrote Jeidels in 1905, "is even today divided in the main between two great financial groups—Rockefeller's American Standard Oil Co., and the controlling interests of the Russian oil-fields in Baku, Rothschild and Nobel. The two groups are in close alliance. But for several years, five enemies have been threatening their monopoly:"[3]

[2] Riesser, *op. cit.;* Diouritch, *op. cit.,* p. 239; Kurt Heinig, *op. cit.*

[3] Jeidels, *op. cit.,* pp. 192-93.

1) The exhaustion of the American oil wells;[4] 2) the competition of the firm of Mantashev of Baku; 3) the Austrian wells; 4) the Rumanian wells; 5) the overseas oilfields, particularly in the Dutch colonies (the extremely rich firms, Samuel and Shell, also connected with British capital). The three last groups are connected with the great German banks, principally, the Deutsche Bank. These banks independently and systematically developed the oil industry in Rumania, in order to have a foothold of their "own." In 1907, 185,000,000 francs of foreign capital were invested in the Rumanian oil industry, of which 74,000,000 came from Germany.[5]

A struggle began, which in economic literature is fittingly called "the struggle for the division of the world." On one side, the Rockefeller trust, wishing to conquer *everything,* formed a subsidiary company *right in* Holland, and bought up oil wells in the Dutch Indies, in order to strike at its principal enemy, the Anglo-Dutch Shell trust. On the other side, the Deutsche Bank and the other German banks aimed at "retaining" Rumania "for themselves" and at uniting it with Russia against Rockefeller. The latter controlled far more capital and an excellent system of oil transport and distribution. The struggle had to end, and did end in 1907, with the utter defeat of the Deutsche Bank, which was confronted with the alternative: either to liquidate its oil business and lose millions, or to submit. It chose to submit, and concluded a very disadvantageous agreement with the American trust. The Deutsche Bank agreed "not to attempt anything which might injure American interests." Provision was made, however, for the annulment of the agreement in the event of Germany establishing a state oil monopoly.

Then the "comedy of oil" began. One of the German finance kings, von Gwinner, a director of the Deutsche Bank, began through his private secretary, Strauss, a campaign *for* a state oil monopoly. The gigantic machine of the big German bank and all its wide "connections" were set in motion. The press bubbled over with "patriotic" indignation against the "yoke" of the American trust, and, on March 15, 1911, the Reichstag by an almost unanimous vote, adopted a motion asking the government to intro-

[4] In Pennsylvania, chief oil region in U. S. at time of Jeidel's study.—*Ed.*

[5] Diouritch, *op. cit.,* p. 245.

duce a bill for the establishment of an oil monopoly. The government seized upon this "popular" idea, and the game of the Deutsche Bank, which hoped to cheat its American partner and improve its business by a state monopoly, appeared to have been won. The German oil magnates saw visions of wonderful profits, which would not be less than those of the Russian sugar refiners. ... But, firstly, the big German banks quarrelled among themselves over the division of the spoils. The Disconto-Gesellschaft exposed the covetous aims of the Deutsche Bank; secondly, the government took fright at the prospect of a struggle with Rockefeller; it was doubtful whether Germany could be sure of obtaining oil from other sources. (The Rumanian output was small.) Thirdly, just at that time the 1913 credits of a billion marks were voted for Germany's war preparations. The project of the oil monopoly was postponed. The Rockefeller trust came out of the struggle, for the time being, victorious.

The Berlin review, *Die Bank,* said in this connection that Germany could only fight the oil trust by establishing an electricity monopoly and by converting water power into cheap electricity.

"But," the author added, "the electricity monopoly will come when the producers need it, that is to say, on the eve of the next great crash in the electrical industry, and when the powerful, expensive electric stations which are now being put up at great cost everywhere by private electrical concerns, which obtain partial monopolies from the state, from towns, etc., can no longer work at a profit. Water power will then have to be used. But it will be impossible to convert it into cheap electricity at state expense; it will have to be handed over to a 'private monopoly controlled by the state,' because of the immense compensation and damages that would have to be paid to private industry.... So it was with the nitrate monopoly, so it is with the oil monopoly; so it will be with the electric power monopoly. It is time for our state socialists, who allow themselves to be blinded by beautiful principles, to understand once and for all that in Germany monopolies have never pursued the aim, nor have they had the result, of benefiting the consumer, or of handing over to the state part of the *entrepreneurs'* profits; they have served only to facilitate, at the expense of the state, the recovery of private industries which were on the verge of bankruptcy." [6]

[6] *Die Bank,* 1912, p. 1036; *cf.* also *ibid.,* p. 629 *et seq.;* 1913, I, p. 388.

Such are the valuable admissions which the German bourgeois economists are forced to make. We see plainly here how private monopolies and state monopolies are bound up together in the age of finance capital; how both are but separate links in the imperialist struggle between the big monopolists for the division of the world.

In mercantile shipping, the tremendous development of concentration has ended also in the division of the world. In Germany two powerful companies have raised themselves to first rank, the Hamburg-Amerika and the Norddeutscher Lloyd, each having a capital of 200,000,000 marks (in stocks and bonds) and possessing 185 to 189 million marks worth of shipping tonnage. On the other side, in America, on January 1, 1903, the Morgan trust, the International Mercantile Marine Co., was formed which united nine British and American steamship companies, and which controlled a capital of 120,000,000 dollars (480,000,000 marks). As early as 1903, the German giants and the Anglo-American trust concluded an agreement and divided the world in accordance with the division of profits. The German companies undertook not to compete in the Anglo-American traffic. The ports were carefully "allotted" to each; a joint committee of control was set up, etc. This contract was concluded for twenty years, with the prudent provision for its annulment in the event of war.[7]

Extremely instructive also is the story of the creation of the International Rail Cartel. The first attempt of the British, Belgian and German rail manufacturers to create such a cartel was made as early as 1884, at the time of a severe industrial depression. The manufacturers agreed not to compete with one another for the home markets of the countries involved, and they divided the foreign markets in the following quotas: Great Britain 66 per cent; Germany 27 per cent; Belgium 7 per cent. India was reserved entirely for Great Britain. Joint war was declared against a British firm which remained outside the cartel. The cost of this economic war was met by a percentage levy on all sales. But in 1886 the cartel collapsed when two British firms retired from it. It is characteristic that agreement could not be achieved in the period of industrial prosperity which followed.

[7] Riesser, *op. cit.*, p. 125.

At the beginning of 1904, the German steel syndicate was formed. In November 1904, the International Rail Cartel was revived, with the following quotas for foreign trade: England 53.5 per cent; Germany 28.83 per cent; Belgium 17.67 per cent. France came in later with 4.8 per cent, 5.8 per cent and 6.4 per cent in the first, second and third years respectively, in excess of the 100 per cent limit, *i.e.*, when the total was 104.8 per cent, etc. In 1905, the United States Steel Corporation entered the cartel; then Austria; then Spain.

"At the present time," wrote Vogelstein in 1910, "the division of the world is completed, and the big consumers, primarily the state railways—since the world has been parcelled out without consideration for their interests—can now dwell like the poet in the heaven of Jupiter."[8]

We will mention also the International Zinc Syndicate, established in 1909, which carefully apportioned output among three groups of factories: German, Belgian, French, Spanish and British. Then there is the International Dynamite Trust, of which Liefmann says that it is

"quite a modern, close alliance of all the manufacturers of explosives who, with the French and American dynamite manufacturers who have organised in a similar manner, have divided the whole world among themselves, so to speak."[9]

Liefmann calculated that in 1897 there were altogether about forty international cartels in which Germany had a share, while in 1910 there were about a hundred.

Certain bourgeois writers (with whom K. Kautsky, who has completely abandoned the Marxist position he held, for example, in 1909, has now associated himself) express the opinion that international cartels are the most striking expressions of the internationalisation of capital, and, therefore, give the hope of peace among nations under capitalism. Theoretically, this opinion is absurd, while in practice it is sophistry and a dishonest defence of the worst opportunism. International cartels show to what point

[8] Th. Vogelstein, *Organisationsformen* (*Forms of Organisation*), p. 100.
[9] R. Liefmann, *Kartelle und Trusts*, second ed., p. 161.

capitalist monopolies have developed, and they *reveal the object* of the struggle between the various capitalist groups. This last circumstance is the most important; it alone shows us the historico-economic significance of events; for the *forms* of the struggle may and do constantly change in accordance with varying, relatively particular, and temporary causes, but the *essence* of the struggle, its class *content, cannot* change while classes exist. It is easy to understand, for example, that it is in the interests of the German bourgeoisie, whose theoretical arguments have now been adopted by Kautsky (we will deal with this later), to obscure the *content* of the present economic struggle (the division of the world) and to emphasise this or that *form* of the struggle. Kautsky makes the same mistake. Of course, we have in mind not only the German bourgeoisie, but the bourgeoisie all over the world. The capitalists divide the world, not out of any particular malice, but because the degree of concentration which has been reached forces them to adopt this method in order to get profits. And they divide it in proportion to "capital," in proportion to "strength," because there cannot be any other system of division under commodity production and capitalism. But strength varies with the degree of economic and political development. In order to understand what takes place, it is necessary to know what questions are settled by this change of forces. The question as to whether these changes are "purely" economic or *non*-economic (*e.g.*, military) is a secondary one, which does not in the least affect the fundamental view on the latest epoch of capitalism. To substitute for the question of the *content* of the struggle and agreements between capitalist combines the question of the *form* of these struggles and agreements (today peaceful, tomorrow war-like, the next day war-like again) is to sink to the role of a sophist.

The epoch of modern capitalism shows us that certain relations are established between capitalist alliances, *based* on the economic division of the world; while parallel with this fact and in connection with it, certain relations are established between political alliances, between states, on the basis of the territorial division of the world, of the struggle for colonies, of the "struggle for economic territory."

CHAPTER VI

The Division of the World Among the Great Powers

In his book, *The Territorial Development of the European Colonies,* A. Supan,[1] the geographer, gives the following brief summary of this development at the end of the nineteenth century:

PERCENTAGE OF TERRITORIES BELONGING TO THE EUROPEAN COLONIAL POWERS (*Including United States*)

	1876	1900	INCREASE OR DECREASE
Africa	10.8	90.4	+ 79.6
Polynesia	56.8	98.9	+ 42.1
Asia	51.5	56.6	+ 5.1
Australia	100.0	100.0	—
America	27.5	27.2	— 0.3

"The characteristic feature of this period," he concludes, "is therefore, the division of Africa and Polynesia."

As there are no unoccupied territories—that is, territories that do not belong to any state—in Asia and America, Mr. Supan's conclusion must be carried further, and we must say that the characteristic feature of this period is the final partition of the globe—not in the sense that a *new* partition is impossible—on the contrary, new partitions are possible and inevitable—but in the sense that the colonial policy of the capitalist countries has *completed* the seizure of the unoccupied territories on our planet. For the first time the world is completely divided up, so that in the future *only* redivision is possible; territories can only pass from one "owner" to another, instead of passing as unowned territory to an "owner."

Hence, we are passing through a peculiar period of world colonial

[1] A. Supan, *Die territoriale Entwicklung der europäischen Kolonien,* Gotha, 1906, p. 254.

policy, which is closely associated with the "latest stage in the development of capitalism," with finance capital. For this reason, it is essential first of all to deal in detail with the facts, in order to ascertain exactly what distinguishes this period from those preceding it, and what the present situation is. In the first place, two questions of fact arise here. Is an intensification of colonial policy, an intensification of the struggle for colonies, observed precisely in this period of finance capital? And how, in this respect, is the world divided at the present time?

The American writer, Morris, in his book on the history of colonisation,[2] has made an attempt to compile data on the colonial possessions of Great Britain, France and Germany during different periods of the nineteenth century. The following is a brief summary of the results he has obtained:

COLONIAL POSSESSIONS

(Million square miles and million inhabitants)

	GREAT BRITAIN		FRANCE		GERMANY	
	AREA	POP.	AREA	POP.	AREA	POP.
1815-30	?	126.4	0.02	0.5	—	—
1860	2.5	145.1	0.2	3.4	—	—
1880	7.7	267.9	0.7	7.5	—	—
1899	9.3	309.0	3.7	56.4	1.0	14.7

For Great Britain, the period of the enormous expansion of colonial conquests is that between 1860 and 1880, and it was also very considerable in the last twenty years of the nineteenth century. For France and Germany this period falls precisely in these last twenty years. We saw above that the apex of pre-monopoly capitalist development, of capitalism in which free competition was predominant, was reached in the 'sixties and 'seventies of the last century. We now see that it is *precisely after that period* that the "boom" in colonial annexations begins, and that the struggle for the territorial division of the world becomes extraordinarily keen. It is beyond doubt, therefore, that capitalism's transition to the

[2] Henry C. Morris, *The History of Colonisation*, New York, 1900, II, p. 88; I, pp. 304, 419.

stage of monopoly capitalism, to finance capital, is *bound up* with the intensification of the struggle for the partition of the world.

Hobson, in his work on imperialism, marks the years 1884-1900 as the period of the intensification of the colonial "expansion" of the chief European states. According to his estimate, Great Britain during these years acquired 3,700,000 square miles of territory with a population of 57,000,000; France acquired 3,600,000 square miles with a population of 36,500,000; Germany 1,000,000 square miles with a population of 16,700,000; Belgium 900,000 square miles with 30,000,000 inhabitants; Portugal 800,000 square miles with 9,000,000 inhabitants. The quest for colonies by all the capitalist states at the end of the nineteenth century and particularly since the 1880's is a commonly known fact in the history of diplomacy and of foreign affairs.

When free competition in Great Britain was at its zenith, *i.e.*, between 1840 and 1860, the leading British bourgeois politicians were opposed to colonial policy and were of the opinion that the liberation of the colonies and their complete separation from Britain was inevitable and desirable. M. Beer, in an article, "Modern British Imperialism,"[8] published in 1898, shows that in 1852, Disraeli, a statesman generally inclined towards imperialism, declared: "The colonies are millstones round our necks." But at the end of the nineteenth century the heroes of the hour in England were Cecil Rhodes and Joseph Chamberlain, open advocates of imperialism, who applied the imperialist policy in the most cynical manner.

It is not without interest to observe that even at that time these leading British bourgeois politicians fully appreciated the connection between what might be called the purely economic and the politico-social roots of modern imperialism. Chamberlain advocated imperialism by calling it a "true, wise and economical policy," and he pointed particularly to the German, American and Belgian competition which Great Britain was encountering in the world market. Salvation lies in monopolies, said the capitalists as they formed cartels, syndicates and trusts. Salvation lies in monopolies, echoed the political leaders of the bourgeoisie, hastening to appro-

[8] *Die Neue Zeit,* XVI, I, 1898, p. 302.

priate the parts of the world not yet shared out. The journalist, Stead, relates the following remarks uttered by his close friend Cecil Rhodes, in 1895, regarding his imperialist ideas:

"I was in the East End of London yesterday and attended a meeting of the unemployed. I listened to the wild speeches, which were just a cry for 'bread,' 'bread,' 'bread,' and on my way home I pondered over the scene and I became more than ever convinced of the importance of imperialism.... My cherished idea is a solution for the social problem, *i.e.,* in order to save the 40,000,000 inhabitants of the United Kingdom from a bloody civil war, we colonial statesmen must acquire new lands to settle the surplus population, to provide new markets for the goods produced by them in the factories and mines. The Empire, as I have always said, is a bread and butter question. If you want to avoid civil war, you must become imperialists."[4]

This is what Cecil Rhodes, millionaire, king of finance, the man who was mainly responsible for the Boer War, said in 1895. His defence of imperialism is just crude and cynical, but in substance it does not differ from the "theory" advocated by Messrs. Maslov, Südekum, Potresov, David, and the founder of Russian Marxism and others. Cecil Rhodes was a somewhat more honest social-chauvinist.

To tabulate as exactly as possible the territorial division of the world, and the changes which have occurred during the last decades, we will take the data furnished by Supan in the work already quoted on the colonial possessions of all the powers of the world. Supan examines the years 1876 and 1900; we will take the year 1876—a year aptly selected, for it is precisely at that time that the pre-monopolist stage of development of West European capitalism can be said to have been completed, in the main, and we will take the year 1914, and in place of Supan's figures we will quote the more recent statistics of Hübner's *Geographical and Statistical Tables*. Supan gives figures only for colonies: we think it useful in order to present a complete picture of the division of the world to add brief figures on non-colonial and semi-colonial countries like Persia, China and Turkey. Persia is already almost

[4] *Ibid.*, p. 304.

completely a colony; China and Turkey are on the way to becoming colonies. We thus get the following summary:

COLONIAL POSSESSIONS OF THE GREAT POWERS

(Million square kilometres and million inhabitants)

	COLONIES				HOME COUNTRIES		TOTAL	
	1876		1914		1914		1914	
	AREA	POP.	AREA	POP.	AREA	POP.	AREA	POP.
Great Britain	22.5	251.9	33.5	393.5	0.3	46.5	33.8	440.0
Russia	17.0	15.9	17.4	33.2	5.4	136.2	22.8	169.4
France	0.9	6.0	10.6	55.5	0.5	39.6	11.1	95.1
Germany	—	—	2.9	12.3	0.5	64.9	3.4	77.2
U.S.A.	—	—	0.3	9.7	9.4	97.0	9.7	106.7
Japan	—	—	0.3	19.2	0.4	53.0	0.7	72.2
Total	40.4	273.8	65.0	523.4	16.5	437.2	81.5	960.6
Colonies of other powers (Belgium, Holland, etc.)							9.9	45.3
Semi-colonial countries (Persia, China, Turkey)							14.5	361.2
Other countries							28.0	289.9
Total area and population of the world							133.9	1,657.0

We see from these figures how "complete" was the partition of the world at the end of the nineteenth and beginning of the twentieth centuries. After 1876 colonial possessions increased to an enormous degree, more than one and a half times, from 40,000,000 to 65,000,000 square kilometres in area for the six biggest powers, an increase of 25,000,000 square kilometres, that is, one and a half times greater than the area of the "home" countries, which have a total of 16,500,000 square kilometres. In 1876 three powers had no colonies, and a fourth, France, had scarcely any. In 1914 these four powers had 14,100,000 square kilometres of colonies, or an area one and a half times greater than that of Europe, with a population of nearly 100,000,000. The unevenness in the rate of expansion of colonial possessions is very marked. If, for instance, we compare France, Germany and Japan, which do not differ very much in area and population, we will see that the first has annexed almost three times as much colonial territory as the other two combined. In regard to finance capital, also, France, at the beginning of the period we are considering, was perhaps several times richer than Germany and Japan put together. In addition to, and on the basis of, purely economic causes, geographical conditions and other factors also affect the dimensions of colonial possessions. However strong the process of levelling the world, of levelling the economic and living conditions in different countries, may have been in the past decades as a result of the pressure of large-scale industry, exchange and finance capital, great differences still remain; and among the six powers, we see, firstly, young capitalist powers (America, Germany, Japan) which progressed very rapidly; secondly, countries with an old capitalist development (France and Great Britain), which, of late, have made much slower progress than the previously mentioned countries, and, thirdly, a country (Russia) which is economically most backward, in which modern capitalist imperialism is enmeshed, so to speak, in a particularly close network of pre-capitalist relations.

Alongside the colonial possessions of these great powers, we have placed the small colonies of the small states, which are, so to speak, the next possible and probable objects of a new colonial "share-out." Most of these little states are able to retain their colonies only because of the conflicting interests, frictions, etc., among the big powers, which prevent them from coming to an agreement in regard to the division of the spoils. The "semi-colonial states" provide an example of the transitional forms which are to be found in all spheres of nature and society. Finance capital is such a great, it may be said, such a decisive force in all economic and international relations, that it is capable of subordinating to itself, and actually does subordinate to itself, even states enjoying complete political independence. We shall shortly see examples of this. Naturally, however, finance capital finds it most "convenient," and is able to extract the greatest profit from a subordination which involves the loss of the political independence of the subjected countries and peoples. In this connection, the semi-colonial countries provide a typical example of the "middle stage." It is natural that the struggle for these semi-dependent countries should have become particularly bitter during the period of finance capital, when the rest of the world had already been divided up.

Colonial policy and imperialism existed before this latest stage of capitalism, and even before capitalism. Rome, founded on slavery, pursued a colonial policy and achieved imperialism. But "general" arguments about imperialism, which ignore, or put into the background the fundamental difference of social-economic systems, inevitably degenerate into absolutely empty banalities, or into grandiloquent comparisons like "Greater Rome and Greater Britain."[5] Even the colonial policy of capitalism in its *previous* stages is essentially different from the colonial policy of finance capital.

The principal feature of modern capitalism is the domination of monopolist combines of the big capitalists. These monopolies are most firmly established when *all* the sources of raw materials are controlled by the one group. And we have seen with what zeal the international capitalist combines exert every effort to make it impossible for their rivals to compete with them; for example, by buying up mineral lands, oil fields, etc. Colonial possession alone gives complete guarantee of success to the monopolies against all the risks of the struggle with competitors, including the risk that the latter will defend themselves by means of a law establishing a state monopoly. The more capitalism is developed, the more the need for raw materials is felt, the more bitter competition becomes, and the more feverishly the hunt for raw materials proceeds throughout the whole world, the more desperate becomes the struggle for the acquisition of colonies.

Schilder writes:

> "It may even be asserted, although it may sound paradoxical to some, that in the more or less discernible future the growth of the urban industrial population is more likely to be hindered by a shortage of raw materials for industry than by a shortage of food."

For example, there is a growing shortage of timber—the price of which is steadily rising—of leather, and raw materials for the textile industry.

[5] A reference to the book by C. P. Lucas, *Greater Rome and Greater Britain*, Oxford 1912, or the Earl of Cromer's *Ancient and Modern Imperialism*, London, 1910.

"As instances of the efforts of associations of manufacturers to create an equilibrium between industry and agriculture in world economy as a whole, we might mention the International Federation of Cotton Spinners' Associations in the most important industrial countries, founded in 1904, and the European Federation of Flax Spinners' Associations, founded on the same model in 1910."[6]

The bourgeois reformists, and among them particularly the present-day adherents of Kautsky, of course, try to belittle the importance of facts of this kind by arguing that it "would be possible" to obtain raw materials in the open market without a "costly and dangerous" colonial policy; and that it would be "possible" to increase the supply of raw materials to an enormous extent "simply" by improving agriculture. But these arguments are merely an apology for imperialism, an attempt to embellish it, because they ignore the principal feature of modern capitalism: monopoly. Free markets are becoming more and more a thing of the past; monopolist syndicates and trusts are restricting them more and more every day, and "simply" improving agriculture reduces itself to improving the conditions of the masses, to raising wages and reducing profits. Where, except in the imagination of the sentimental reformists, are there any trusts capable of interesting themselves in the condition of the masses instead of the conquest of colonies?

Finance capital is not only interested in the already known sources of raw materials; it is also interested in potential sources of raw materials, because present-day technical development is extremely rapid, and because land which is useless today may be made fertile tomorrow if new methods are applied (to devise these new methods a big bank can equip a whole expedition of engineers, agricultural experts, etc.), and large amounts of capital are invested. This also applies to prospecting for minerals, to new methods of working up and utilising raw materials, etc., etc. Hence, the inevitable striving of finance capital to extend its economic territory and even its territory in general. In the same way that the trusts capitalise their property by estimating it at two or three times its value, taking into account its "potential" (and

[6] Schilder, *op. cit.*, pp. 38 and 42.

not present) returns, and the further results of monopoly, so finance capital strives to seize the largest possible amount of land of all kinds and in any place it can, and by any means, counting on the possibilities of finding raw materials there, and fearing to be left behind in the insensate struggle for the last available scraps of undivided territory, or for the repartition of that which has been already divided.

The British capitalists are exerting every effort to develop cotton growing in *their* colony, Egypt (in 1904, out of 2,300,000 hectares of land under cultivation, 600,000, or more than one-fourth, were devoted to cotton growing); the Russians are doing the same in *their* colony, Turkestan; and they are doing so because in this way they will be in a better position to defeat their foreign competitors, to monopolise the sources of raw materials and form a more economical and profitable textile trust in which *all* the processes of cotton production and manufacturing will be "combined" and concentrated in the hands of a single owner.

The necessity of exporting capital also gives an impetus to the conquest of colonies, for in the colonial market it is easier to eliminate competition, to make sure of orders, to strengthen the necessary "connections," etc., by monoplist methods (and sometimes it is the only possible way).

The non-economic superstructure which grows up on the basis of finance capital, its politics and its ideology, stimulates the striving for colonial conquest. "Finance capital does not want liberty, it wants domination," as Hilferding very truly says. And a French bourgeois writer, developing and supplementing, as it were, the ideas of Cecil Rhodes, which we quoted above, writes that social causes should be added to the economic causes of modern colonial policy.

"Owing to the growing difficulties of life which weigh not only on the masses of the workers, but also on the middle classes, impatience, irritation and hatred are accumulating in all the countries of the old civilisation and are becoming a menace to public order; employment must be found for the energy which is being hurled out of the definite class channel; it must be given an outlet abroad in order to avert an explosion at home."[7]

Since we are speaking of colonial policy in the period of capitalist imperialism, it must be observed that finance capital and its corresponding foreign policy, which reduces itself to the struggle of the Great Powers for the economic and political division of the world, give rise to a number of *transitional* forms of national dependence. The division of the world into two main groups—of colony-owning countries on the one hand and colonies on the other—is not the only typical feature of this period; there is also a variety of forms of dependent countries; countries which, officially, are politically independent, but which are, in fact, enmeshed in the net of financial and diplomatic dependence. We have already referred to one form of dependence—the semi-colony. Another example is provided by Argentina.

"South America, and especially Argentina," writes Schulze-Gaevernitz in his work on British imperialism, "is so dependent financially on London that it ought to be described as almost a British commercial colony."[8]

Basing himself on the report of the Austro-Hungarian consul at Buenos Aires for 1909, Schilder estimates the amount of British capital invested in Argentina at 8,750,000,000 francs. It is not difficult to imagine the solid bonds that are thus created between British finance capital (and its faithful "friend," diplomacy) and the Argentine bourgeoisie, with the leading businessmen and politicians of that country.

A somewhat different form of financial and diplomatic dependence, accompanied by political independence, is presented by Portugal. Portugal is an independent sovereign state. In actual fact, however, for more than two hundred years, since the war of the

[7] Wahl, *La France aux colonies* (*France in the Colonies*), quoted by Henri Bussier, *Le partage de l'Océanie* (*The Partition of Oceania*), Paris, 1905, pp. 165-66.

[8] Schulze-Gaevernitz, *Britischer Imperialismus und englischer Freihandel zu Beginn des 20. Jahrhunderts* (*British Imperialism and English Free Trade at the Beginning of the Twentieth Century*), Leipzig, 1906, p. 318. Sartorius von Waltershausen says the same in *Das volkswirtschaftliche System der Kapitalanlage im Auslande* (*The National Economic System of Capital Investments Abroad*), Berlin, 1907, p. 46.

Spanish Succession (1700-14), it has been a British protectorate. Great Britain has protected Portugal and her colonies in order to fortify her own positions in the fight against her rivals, Spain and France. In return she has received commercial advantages, preferential import of goods, and, above all, of capital into Portugal and the Portuguese colonies, the right to use the ports and islands of Portugal, her telegraph cables, etc.[9] Relations of this kind have always existed between big and little states. But during the period of capitalist imperialism they become a general system, they form part of the process of "dividing the world"; they become a link in the chain of operations of world finance capital.

In order to complete our examination of the question of the division of the world, we must make the following observation. This question was raised quite openly and definitely not only in American literature after the Spanish-American War, and in English literature after the Boer War, at the very end of the nineteenth century and the beginning of the twentieth; not only has German literature, which always "jealously" watches "British imperialism," systematically given its appraisal of this fact, but it has also been raised in French bourgeois literature in terms as wide and clear as they can be made from the bourgeois point of view. We will quote Driault, the historian, who, in his book, *Political and Social Problems at the End of the Nineteenth Century,* in the chapter "The Great Powers and the Division of the World," wrote the following:

"During recent years, all the free territory of the globe, with the exception of China, has been occupied by the powers of Europe and North America. Several conflicts and displacements of influence have already occurred over this matter, which foreshadow more terrible outbreaks in the near future. For it is necessary to make haste. The nations which have not yet made provisions for themselves run the risk of never receiving their share and never participating in the tremendous exploitation of the globe which will be one of the essential features of the next century" (*i.e.,* the twentieth). "That is why all Europe and America has lately been afflicted with the fever of colonial

[9] Schilder, *op. cit.,* Vol. I, pp. 159-61.

expansion, of 'imperialism,' that most characteristic feature of the end of the nineteenth century."

And the author added:

"In this partition of the world, in this furious pursuit of the treasures and of the big markets of the globe, the relative power of the empires founded in this nineteenth century is totally out of proportion to the place occupied in Europe by the nations which founded them. The dominant powers in Europe, those which decide the destinies of the Continent, are *not* equally preponderant in the whole world. And, as colonial power, the hope of controlling hitherto unknown wealth, will obviously react to influence the relative strength of the European powers, the colonial question—'imperialism,' if you will—which has already modified the political conditions of Europe, will modify them more and more."[10]

[10] Ed. Driault, *Problèmes politiques et sociaux,* Paris, 1907, p. 289.

CHAPTER VII

Imperialism as a Special Stage of Capitalism

We must now try to sum up and put together what has been said above on the subject of imperialism. Imperialism emerged as the development and direct continuation of the fundamental attributes of capitalism in general. But capitalism only became capitalist imperialism at a definite and very high stage of its development, when certain of its fundamental attributes began to be transformed into their opposites, when the features of a period of transition from capitalism to a higher social and economic system began to take shape and reveal themselves all along the line. Economically, the main thing in this process is the substitution of capitalist monopolies for capitalist free competition. Free competition is the fundamental attribute of capitalism, and of commodity production generally. Monopoly is exactly the opposite of free competition; but we have seen the latter being transformed into monopoly before our very eyes, creating large-scale industry and eliminating small industry, replacing large-scale industry by still larger-scale industry, finally leading to such a concentration of production and capital that monopoly has been and is the result: cartels, syndicates and trusts, and merging with them, the capital of a dozen or so banks manipulating thousands of millions. At the same time monopoly, which has grown out of free competition, does not abolish the latter, but exists over it and alongside of it, and thereby gives rise to a number of very acute, intense antagonisms, friction and conflicts. Monopoly is the transition from capitalism to a higher system.

If it were necessary to give the briefest possible definition of imperialism we should have to say that imperialism is the monopoly stage of capitalism. Such a definition would include what is most important, for, on the one hand, finance capital is the bank capital of a few big monopolist banks, merged with the capital of the monopolist combines of manufacturers; and, on the other hand, the division of the world is the transition from a colonial policy which has extended without hindrance to territories unoccupied by any capitalist power, to a colonial policy of monopolistic possession of the territory of the world which has been completely divided up.

But very brief definitions, although convenient, for they sum up the main points, are nevertheless inadequate, because very important features of the phenomenon that has to be defined have to be especially deduced. And so, without forgetting the conditional and relative value of all definitions, which can never include all the concatenations of a phenomenon in its complete development, we must give a definition of imperialism that will embrace the following five essential features:

1) The concentration of production and capital developed to such a high stage that it created monopolies which play a decisive role in economic life.

2) The merging of bank capital with industrial capital, and the creation, on the basis of this "finance capital," of a "financial oligarchy.

3) The export of capital, which has become extremely important, as distinguished from the export of commodities.

4) The formation of international capitalist monopolies which share the world among themselves.

5) The territorial division of the whole world among the greatest capitalist powers is completed.

Imperialism is capitalism in that stage of development in which the dominance of monopolies and finance capital has established itself; in which the export of capital has acquired pronounced importance; in which the division of the world among the international trusts has begun; in which the division of all territories of the globe among the great capitalist powers has been completed.

We shall see later that imperialism can and must be defined differently if consideration is to be given, not only to the basic, purely economic factors—to which the above definition is limited—

but also to the historical place of this stage of capitalism in relation to capitalism in general, or to the relations between imperialism and the two main trends in the working class movement. The point to be noted just now is that imperialism, as interpreted above, undoubtedly represents a special stage in the development of capitalism. In order to enable the reader to obtain as well grounded an idea of imperialism as possible, we deliberately quoted largely from *bourgeois* economists who are obliged to admit the particularly incontrovertible facts regarding modern capitalist economy. With the same object in view, we have produced detailed statistics which reveal the extent to which bank capital, etc., has developed, showing how the transformation of quantity into quality, of developed capitalism into imperialism, has expressed itself. Needless to say, all boundaries in nature and in society are conditional and changeable, and, consequently, it would be absurd to discuss the exact year or the decade in which imperialism "definitely" became established.

In this matter of defining imperialism, however, we have to enter into controversy, primarily, with K. Kautsky, the principal Marxian theoretician of the epoch of the so-called Second International—that is, of the twenty-five years between 1889 and 1914.

Kautsky, in 1915 and even in November 1914, very emphatically attacked the fundamental ideas expressed in our definition of imperialism. Kautsky said that imperialism must not be regarded as a "phase" or stage of economy, but as a policy; a definite policy "preferred" by finance capital; that imperialism cannot be "identified" with "contemporary capitalism"; that if imperialism is to be understood to mean "all the phenomena of contemporary capitalism"—cartels, protection, the domination of the financiers and colonial policy—then the question as to whether imperialism is necessary to capitalism becomes reduced to the "flattest tautology"; because, in that case, "imperialism is naturally a vital necessity for capitalism," and so on. The best way to present Kautsky's ideas is to quote his own definition of imperialism, which is diametrically opposed to the substance of the ideas which we have set forth (for the objections coming from the camp of the German Marxists, who have been advocating such ideas for many years already, have been long known to Kautsky as the objections of a definite trend in Marxism).

Kautsky's definition is as follows:

"Imperialism is a product of highly developed industrial capitalism. It consists in the striving of every industrial capitalist nation to bring under its control and to annex increasingly big *agrarian*" (Kautsky's italics) "regions irrespective of what nations inhabit those regions."[1]

This definition is utterly worthless because it one-sidedly, *i.e.*, arbitrarily, brings out the national question alone (although this is extremely important in itself as well as in its relation to imperialism), it arbitrarily and *inaccurately* relates this question *only* to industrial capital in the countries which annex other nations, and in an equally arbitrary and inaccurate manner brings out the annexation of agrarian regions.

Imperialism is a striving for annexations—this is what the *political* part of Kautsky's definition amounts to. It is correct, but very incomplete, for politically, imperialism is, in general, a striving towards violence and reaction. For the moment, however, we are interested in the *economic* aspect of the question, which Kautsky *himself* introduced into *his* definition. The inaccuracy of Kautsky's definition is strikingly obvious. The characteristic feature of imperialism is *not* industrial capital, *but* finance capital. It is not an accident that in France it was precisely the extraordinarily rapid development of *finance* capital, and the weakening of industrial capital, that, from 1880 onwards, gave rise to the extreme extension of annexationist (colonial) policy. The characteristic feature of imperialism is precisely that it strives to annex *not only* agricultural regions, but even highly industrialised regions (German appetite for Belgium; French appetite for Lorraine), because 1) the fact that the world is already divided up obliges those contemplating a *new* division to reach out for *any kind* of territory, and 2) because an essential feature of imperialism is the rivalry between a number of great powers in the striving for hegemony, *i.e.*, for the conquest of territory, not so much directly

[1] *Die Neue Zeit*, 32nd year (1913-14), II, p. 909; *cf.* also 34th year (1915-16), II, p. 107 *et seq.*

for themselves as to weaken the adversary and undermine *his* hegemony. (Belgium is chiefly necessary to Germany as a base for operations against England; England needs Bagdad as a base for operations against Germany, etc.)

Kautsky refers especially—and repeatedly—to English writers who, he alleges, have given a purely political meaning to the word "imperialism" in the sense that Kautsky understands it. We take up the work by the Englishman Hobson, *Imperialism,* which appeared in 1902, and therein we read:

> "The new imperialism differs from the older, first, in substituting for the ambition of a single growing empire the theory and the practice of competing empires, each motivated by similar lusts of political aggrandisement and commercial gain; secondly, in the dominance of financial or investing over mercantile interests."[2]

We see, therefore, that Kautsky is absolutely wrong in referring to English writers generally (unless he meant the vulgar English imperialist writers, or the avowed apologists for imperialism). We see that Kautsky, while claiming that he continues to defend Marxism, as a matter of fact takes a step backward compared with the *social-liberal* Hobson, who *more correctly* takes into account two "historically concrete" (Kautsky's definition is a mockery of historical concreteness) features of modern imperialism: 1) the competition between *several* imperialisms, and 2) the predominance of the financier over the merchant. If it were chiefly a question of the annexation of agrarian countries by industrial countries, the role of the merchant would be predominant.

Kautsky's definition is not only wrong and un-Marxian. It serves as a basis for a whole system of views which run counter to Marxian theory and Marxian practice all along the line. We shall refer to this again later. The argument about words which Kautsky raises as to whether the modern stage of capitalism should be called "imperialism" or "the stage of finance capital" is of no importance. Call it what you will, it matters little. The fact of the matter is that Kautsky detaches the politics of imperialism from its economics, speaks of annexations as being a policy "preferred"

[2] J. A. Hobson, *Imperialism—a Study,* London, 1902, p. 324.

by finance capital, and opposes to it another bourgeois policy which, he alleges, is possible on this very basis of finance capital. According to his argument, monopolies in economics are compatible with non-monopolistic, non-violent, non-annexationist methods in politics. According to his argument, the territorial division of the world, which was completed precisely during the period of finance capital, and which constitutes the basis of the present peculiar forms of rivalry between the biggest capitalist states, is compatible with a non-imperialist policy. The result is a slurring-over and a blunting of the most profound contradictions of the latest stage of capitalism, instead of an exposure of their depth; the result is bourgeois reformism instead of Marxism.

Kautsky enters into controversy with the German apologist of imperialism and annexations, Cunow, who clumsily and cynically argues that: imperialism is modern capitalism, the development of capitalism is inevitable and progressive; therefore imperialism is progressive; therefore, we should cringe before and eulogise it. This is something like the caricature of Russian Marxism which the Narodniki drew in 1894-95. They used to argue as follows: if the Marxists believe that capitalism is inevitable in Russia, that it is progressive, then they ought to open a public-house and begin to implant capitalism! Kautsky's reply to Cunow is as follows: imperialism is not modern capitalism. It is only one of the forms of the policy of modern capitalism. This policy we can and should fight; we can and should fight against imperialism, annexations, etc.

The reply seems quite plausible, but in effect it is a more subtle and more disguised (and therefore more dangerous) propaganda of conciliation with imperialism; for unless it strikes at the economic basis of the trusts and banks, the "struggle" against the policy of the trusts and banks reduces itself to bourgeois reformism and pacifism, to an innocent and benevolent expression of pious hopes. Kautsky's theory means refraining from mentioning existing contradictions, forgetting the most important of them, instead of revealing them in their full depth; it is a theory that has nothing in common with Marxism. Naturally, such a "theory" can only serve the purpose of advocating unity with the Cunows.

Kautsky writes: "from the purely economic point of view it is not impossible that capitalism will yet go through a new phase, that of the extension of the policy of the cartels to foreign policy, the phase of ultra-imperialism,"[3] *i.e.,* of a super-imperialism, a union of world imperialisms and not struggles among imperialisms; a phase when wars shall cease under capitalism, a phase of "the joint exploitation of the world by internationally combined finance capital."[4]

We shall have to deal with this "theory of ultra-imperialism" later on in order to show in detail how definitely and utterly it departs from Marxism. In keeping with the plan of the present work, we shall examine the exact economic data on this question. Is "ultra-imperialism" possible "from the purely economic point of view" or is it ultra-nonsense?

If, by purely economic point of view a "pure" abstraction is meant, then all that can be said reduces itself to the following proposition: evolution is proceeding towards monopoly; therefore the trend is towards a single world monopoly, to a universal trust. This is indisputable, but it is also as completely meaningless as is the statement that "evolution is proceeding" towards the manufacture of foodstuffs in laboratories. In this sense the "theory" of ultra-imperialism is no less absurd than a "theory of ultra-agriculture" would be.

If, on the other hand, we are discussing the "purely economic" conditions of the epoch of finance capital as an historically concrete epoch which opened at the beginning of the twentieth century, then the best reply that one can make to the lifeless abstractions of "ultra-imperialism" (which serve an exclusively reactionary aim: that of diverting attention from the depth of *existing* antagonisms) is to contrast them with the concrete economic realities of present-day world economy. Kautsky's utterly meaningless talk about ultra-imperialism encourages, among other things, that profoundly mistaken idea which only brings grist to the mill of the apologists of imperialism, *viz.,* that the rule of finance capital *lessens* the

[3] *Die Neue Zeit,* 32nd year (1913-14), II, Sept. 11, 1914, p. 909; *cf.* also 34th year (1915-16), II, p. 107 *et seq.*

[4] *Die Neue Zeit,* 33rd year, II (April 30, 1915), p. 144.

unevenness and contradictions inherent in world economy, whereas in reality it *increases* them.

R. Calwer, in his little book, *An Introduction to World Economics,*[5] attempted to compile the main, purely economic, data required to understand in a concrete way the internal relations of world economy at the end of the nineteenth and beginning of the twentieth centuries. He divides the world into five "main economic areas," as follows: 1) Central Europe (the whole of Europe with the exception of Russia and Great Britain); 2) Great Britain; 3) Russia; 4) Eastern Asia; 5) America; he includes the colonies in the "areas" of the state to which they belong and "leaves out" a few countries not distributed according to areas, such as Persia, Afghanistan and Arabia in Asia; Morocco and Abyssinia in Africa, etc.

Here is a brief summary of the economic data he quotes on these regions:

	Area	*Pop.*	*Transport*		*Trade*	*Industry*		
PRINCIPAL ECONOMIC AREAS	MILLION SQ. KM.	MILLIONS	RAILWAYS (THOUS. KM.)	MERCANTILE FLEET (MILLION TONS)	IMPORTS AND EXPORTS (BILLION MARKS)	OUTPUT OF COAL (MILLION TONS)	OUTPUT OF PIG IRON (MILLION TONS)	NO. OF COTTON SPINDLES (MILLION)
1) Central European	27.6 (23.6)[6]	388 (146)	204	8	41	251	15	26
2) British	28.9 (28.6)[6]	398 (355)	140	11	25	249	9	51
3) Russian	22	131	63	1	3	16	3	7
4) East Asian	12	389	8	1	2	8	0.02	2
5) American	30	148	379	6	14	245	14	19

We notice three areas of highly developed capitalism with a high development of means of transport, of trade and of industry, the Central European, the British and the American areas. Among these are three states which dominate the world: Germany, Great Britain, the United States. Imperialist rivalry and the struggle between these countries have become very keen because Germany

[5] R. Calwer, *Einführung in die Weltwirtschaft*, Berlin, 1906.

[6] The figures in parentheses show the area and population of the colonies.

has only a restricted area and few colonies (the creation of "Central Europe" is still a matter for the future; it is being born in the midst of desperate struggles). For the moment the distinctive feature of Europe is political disintegration. In the British and American areas, on the other hand, political concentration is very highly developed, but there is a tremendous disparity between the immense colonies of the one and the insignificant colonies of the other. In the colonies, capitalism is only beginning to develop. The struggle for South America is becoming more and more acute.

There are two areas where capitalism is not strongly developed: Russia and Eastern Asia. In the former, the density of population is very low, in the latter it is very high; in the former political concentration is very high, in the latter it does not exist. The partition of China is only beginning, and the struggle between Japan, U.S.A., etc., in connection therewith is continually gaining in intensity.

Compare this reality, the vast diversity of economic and political conditions, the extreme disparity in the rate of development of the various countries, etc., and the violent struggles of the imperialist states, with Kautsky's silly little fable about "peaceful" ultra-imperialism. Is this not the reactionary attempt of a frightened philistine to hide from stern reality? Are not the international cartels which Kautsky imagines are the embryos of "ultra-imperialism" (with as much reason as one would have for describing the manufacture of tabloids in a laboratory as ultra-agriculture in embryo) an example of the division and the *redivision* of the world, the transition from peaceful division to non-peaceful division and *vice versa*? Is not American and other finance capital, which divided the whole world peacefully, with Germany's participation, for example, in the international rail syndicate, or in the international mercantile shipping trust, now engaged in *redividing* the world on the basis of a new relation of forces, which has been changed by methods *by no means* peaceful?

Finance capital and the trusts are increasing instead of diminishing the differences in the rate of development of the various parts of world economy. When the relation of forces is changed, how else, *under capitalism,* can the solution of contradictions be found, except by resorting to *violence?* Railway statistics[7] provide remarkably exact data on the different rates of development of capitalism and finance capital in world economy. In the last decades of imperialist development, the total length of railways has changed as follows:

RAILWAYS (*thousand kilometres*)

	1890		1913		INCREASE	
Europe	224		346		122	
U.S.A.	268		411		143	
Colonies (total)	82	125	210	347	128	222
Independent and semi-dependent states of Asia and America	43		137		94	
Total	617		1,104			

Thus, the development of railways has been more rapid in the colonies and in the independent (and semi-dependent) states of Asia and America. Here, as we know, the finance capital of the four or five biggest capitalist states reigns undisputed. Two hundred thousand kilometres of new railways in the colonies and in the other countries of Asia and America represent more than 40,000,000,000 marks in capital, newly invested on particularly advantageous terms, with special guarantees of a good return and with profitable orders for steel works, etc., etc.

Capitalism is growing with the greatest rapidity in the colonies and in overseas countries. Among the latter, *new* imperialist powers are emerging (*e.g.*, Japan). The struggle of world imperialism is becoming more acute. The tribute levied by finance capital on the most profitable colonial and overseas enterprises is increasing. In sharing out this "booty," an exceptionally large part goes to countries which, as far as the development of productive forces is concerned, do not always stand at the top of the list. In the case

[7] *Statistisches Jahrbuch für das Deutsche Reich* (*Statistical Yearbook for the German Empire*), 1915, Appendix pp. 46, 47, *Archiv für Eisenbahnwesen* (*Railroad Archive*), 1892. Minor detailed figures for the distribution of railways among the colonies of the various countries in 1890 had to be estimated approximately.

of the biggest countries, considered with their colonies, the total length of railways was as follows (in thousands of kilometres):

	1890	1913	INCREASE
U.S.A.	268	413	145
British Empire	107	208	101
Russia	32	78	46
Germany	43	68	25
France	41	63	22
Total	491	830	339

Thus, about 80 per cent of the total existing railways are concentrated in the hands of the five Great Powers. But the concentration of the *ownership* of these railways, of finance capital, is much greater still: French and English millionaires, for example, own an enormous amount of stocks and bonds in American, Russian and other railways.

Thanks to her colonies, Great Britain has increased the length of "her" railways by 100,000 kilometres, four times as much as Germany. And yet, it is well known that the development of productive forces in Germany, and especially the development of the coal and iron industries, has been much more rapid during this period than in England—not to mention France and Russia. In 1892, Germany produced 4,900,000 tons of pig iron and Great Britain produced 6,800,000 tons; in 1912, Germany produced 17,600,000 tons and Great Britain 9,000,000 tons. Germany, therefore, had an overwhelming superiority over England in this respect.[8] We ask, is there *under capitalism* any means of removing the disparity between the development of productive forces and the accumulation of capital on the one side, and the division of colonies and "spheres of influence" for finance capital on the other side—other than by resorting to war?

[8] *Cf.* also Edgar Crummond, "The Economic Relation of the British and German Empires," in *Journal of the Royal Statistical Society*, July 1914, p. 777, *et seq.*

CHAPTER VIII

The Parasitism and Decay of Capitalism

We have to examine yet another very important aspect of imperialism to which, usually, too little importance is attached in most of the arguments on this subject. One of the shortcomings of the Marxist Hilferding is that he takes a step backward compared with the non-Marxist Hobson. We refer to parasitism, which is a feature of imperialism.

As we have seen, the most deep-rooted economic foundation of imperialism is monopoly. This is capitalist monopoly, *i.e.,* monopoly which has grown out of capitalism and exists in the general environment of capitalism, commodity production and competition, and remains in permanent and insoluble contradiction to this general environment. Nevertheless, like all monopoly, this capitalist monopoly inevitably gives rise to a tendency to stagnation and decay. As monopoly prices become fixed, even temporarily, so the stimulus to technical and, consequently, to all progress, disappears to a certain extent, and to that extent, also, the *economic* possibility arises of deliberately retarding technical progress. For instance, in America, a certain Mr. Owens invented a machine which revolutionised the manufacture of bottles. The German bottle manufacturing cartel purchased Owens' patent, but pigeonholed it, refrained from utilising it. Certainly, monopoly under capitalism can never completely, and for a long period of time, eliminate competition in the world market (and this, by the by, is one of the reasons why the theory of ultra-imperialism is so absurd). Certainly the possibility of reducing cost of production and increasing profits by introducing technical improvements operates in the direction of change. Nevertheless, the *tendency* to stagnation and decay, which is the feature of monopoly, continues, and in certain branches of industry, in certain countries, for certain periods of time, it becomes predominant.

The monopoly of ownership of very extensive, rich or well-situated colonies, operates in the same direction.

Further, imperialism is an immense accumulation of money capital in a few countries, which, as we have seen, amounts to 100-150 billion francs in various securities. Hence the extraordinary growth of a class, or rather of a category, of *bondholders* (*rentiers*), *i.e.*, people who live by "clipping coupons," who take no part whatever in production, whose profession is idleness. The export of capital, one of the most essential economic bases of imperialism, still more completely isolates the *rentiers* from production and sets the seal of parasitism on the whole country that lives by the exploitation of the labour of several overseas countries and colonies.

> "In 1893," writes Hobson, "the British capital invested abroad represented about 15 per cent of the total wealth of the United Kingdom."[1]

Let us remember that by 1915 this capital had increased about two and a half times.

> "Aggressive imperialism," says Hobson further on, "which costs the taxpayer so dear, which is of so little value to the manufacturer and trader... is a source of great gain to the investor.... The annual income Great Britain derives from commissions in her whole foreign and colonial trade, import and export, is estimated by Sir R. Giffen at £18,000,000 for 1899, taken at 2½ per cent, upon a turnover of £800,000,000."[2]

Great as this sum is, it does not explain the aggressive imperialism of Great Britain. This is explained by the 90 to 100 million pounds sterling income from "invested" capital, the income of the rentiers.

The income of the bondholders is *five times greater* than the income obtained from the foreign trade of the greatest "trading" country in the world. This is the essence of imperialism and imperialist parisitism.

For that reason the term, "rentier state" (*Rentnerstaat*), or

[1] *Op cit.*, p. 59.—*Ed.*
[2] *Op. cit.*, pp. 62-3.—*Ed.*

usurer state, is passing into current use in the economic literature that deals with imperialism. The world has become divided into a handful of usurer states on the one side, and a vast majority of debtor states on the other.

"The premier place among foreign investments," says Schulze-Gaevernitz, "is held by those placed in politically dependent or closely allied countries. Great Britain grants loans to Egypt, Japan, China and South America. Her navy plays here the part of bailiff in case of necessity. Great Britain's political power protects her from the indignation of her debtors." [3]

Sartorius von Waltershausen in his book, *The National Economic System of Foreign Investments,* cites Holland as the model "rentier state" and points out that Great Britain and France have taken the same road.[4] Schilder believes that five industrial nations have become "pronounced creditor nations": Great Britain, France, Germany, Belgium and Switzerland. Holland does not appear on this list simply because she is "industrially less developed." [5] The United States is creditor only of the other American countries.

"Great Britain," says Schulze-Gaevernitz, "is gradually becoming transformed from an industrial state into a creditor state. Notwithstanding the absolute increase in industrial output and the export of manufactured goods, the relative importance of income from interest and dividends, issues of securities, commissions and speculation is on the increase in the whole of the national economy. In my opinion it is precisely this that forms the economic basis of imperialist ascendancy. The creditor is more permanently attached to the debtor than the seller is to the buyer." [6]

In regard to Germany, A. Lansburgh, the editor of *Die Bank,* in 1911, in an article entitled "Germany—a Rentier State," wrote the following:

[3] Schulze-Gaevernitz, *Britischer Imperialismus,* p. 320 *et seq.*

[4] Sartorius von Waltershausen, *Das volkswirtschaftliche System, etc.* (*The National Economic System, etc.*), Book IV, B. 1907.

[5] Schilder, *op. cit.,* pp. 392-93.

[6] Schulze-Gaevernitz, *op. cit.,* p. 122.—*Ed.*

"People in Germany are ready to sneer at the yearning to become rentiers that is observed among the people in France. But they forget that as far as the middle class is concerned the situation in Germany is becoming more and more like that in France."[7]

The rentier state is a state of parasitic, decaying capitalism, and this circumstance cannot fail to influence all the social-political conditions of the countries affected generally, and the two fundamental trends in the working closs movement, in particular. To demonstrate this in the clearest possible manner we will quote Hobson, who will be regarded as a more "reliable" witness, since he cannot be suspected of leanings towards "orthodox Marxism"; moreover, he is an Englishman who is very well acquainted with the situation in the country which is richest in colonies, in finance capital, and in imperialist experience.

With the Boer War fresh in his mind, Hobson describes the connection between imperialism and the interests of the "financiers," the growing profits from contracts, etc., and writes:

"While the directors of this definitely parasitic policy are capitalists, the same motives appeal to special classes of the workers. In many towns, most important trades are dependent upon government employment or contracts; the imperialism of the metal and shipbuilding centres is attributable in no small degree to this fact."[8]

In this writer's opinion there are two causes which weakened the older empires: 1) "economic parasitism," and 2) the formation of armies composed of subject races.

"There is first the habit of economic parasitism, by which the ruling state has used its provinces, colonies, and dependencies in order to enrich its ruling class and to bribe its lower classes into acquiescence."[9]

And we would add that the economic possibility of such corruption, whatever its form may be, requires high monopolist profits.

As for the second cause, Hobson writes:

[7] *Die Bank*, 1911, I, pp. 10-11.
[8] *Op. cit.*, p. 103.—*Ed.*
[9] *Op. cit.*, p. 205.

"One of the strangest symptoms of the blindness of imperialism is the reckless indifference with which Great Britain, France and other imperial nations are embarking on this perilous dependence. Great Britain has gone farthest. Most of the fighting by which we have won our Indian Empire has been done by natives; in India, as more recently in Egypt, great standing armies are placed under British commanders; almost all the fighting associated with our African dominions, except in the southern part, has been done for us by natives."[10]

Hobson gives the following economic appraisal of the prospect of the partition of China:

"The greater part of Western Europe might then assume the appearance and character already exhibited by tracts of country in the South of England, in the Riviera, and in the tourist-ridden or residential parts of Italy and Switzerland, little clusters of wealthy aristocrats drawing dividends and pensions from the Far East, with a somewhat larger group of professional retainers and tradesmen and a large body of personal servants and workers in the transport trade and in the final stages of production of the more perishable goods; all the main arterial industries would have disappeared, the staple foods and manufactures flowing in as tribute from Asia and Africa."[11]

"We have foreshadowed the possibility of even a larger alliance of Western States, a European federation of great powers which, so far from forwarding the cause of world civilisation, might introduce the gigantic peril of a Western parasitism, a group of advanced industrial nations, whose upper classes drew vast tribute from Asia and Africa, with which they supported great, tame masses of retainers, no longer engaged in the staple industries of agriculture and manufacture, but kept in the performance of personal or minor industrial services under the control of a new financial aristocracy. Let those who would scout such a theory as undeserving of consideration examine the economic and social condition of districts in Southern England today which are already reduced to this condition, and reflect upon the vast extension of such a system which might be rendered feasible by the subjection of China to the economic control of similar groups of financiers, investors, and political and business officials, draining the greatest potential reser-

[10] *Op. cit.*, p. 144.
[11] *Op. cit.*, p. 335.

voir of profit the world has ever known, in order to consume it in Europe. The situation is far too complex, the play of world forces far too incalculable, to render this or any other single interpretation of the future very probable: but the influences which govern the imperialism of Western Europe today are moving in this direction, and, unless counteracted or diverted, make towards some such consummation."[12]

Hobson is quite right. *Unless* the forces of imperialism are counteracted they will lead precisely to what he has described. He correctly appraises the significance of a "United States of Europe" in the present conditions of imperialism. He should have added, however, that, *even within* the working class movement, the opportunists, who are for the moment predominant in most countries, are "working" systematically and undeviatingly in this very direction. Imperialism, which means the partition of the world, and the exploitation of other countries besides China, which means high monopoly profits for a handful of very rich countries, creates the economic possibility of corrupting the upper strata of the proletariat, and thereby fosters, gives form to, and strengthens opportunism. However, we must not lose sight of the forces which counteract imperialism in general, and opportunism in particular, which, naturally, the social-liberal Hobson is unable to perceive.

The German opportunist, Gerhard Hildebrand, who was expelled from the Party for defending imperialism, and who would today make a leader of the so-called "Social-Democratic" Party of Germany, serves as a good supplement to Hobson by his advocacy of a "United States of Western Europe" (without Russia) for the purpose of "joint" action ... against the African Negroes, against the "great Islamic movement," for the upkeep of a "powerful army and navy," against a "Sino-Japanese coalition," etc.[13]

The description of "British imperialism" in Schulze-Gaevernitz's book reveals the same parasitical traits. The national income of Great Britain approximately doubled from 1865 to 1898, while the income "from abroad" increased *ninefold* in the same period. While the "merit" of imperialism is that it "trains the Negro to

[12] *Op. cit.*, pp. 385-86.

[13] Gerhard Hildebrand, *Die Erschütterung der Industrieherrschaft und des Industriesozialismus*, Jena, 1910, p. 229 *et seq.*

habits of industry" (not without coercion of course...), the "danger" of imperialism is that:

"Europe...will shift the burden of physical toil—first agricultural and mining, then the more arduous toil in industry—on to the coloured races, and itself be content with the role of rentier, and in this way, perhaps, pave the way for the economic, and later, the political emancipation of the coloured races."

An increasing proportion of land in Great Britain is being taken out of cultivation and used for sport, for the diversion of the rich.

"Scotland," says Schulze-Gaevernitz, "is the most aristocratic playground in the world—it lives...on its past and on Mr. Carnegie."

On horse-racing and fox-hunting alone Britain annually spends £14,000,000. The number of rentiers in England is about one million. The percentage of the productively employed population to the total population is becoming smaller.

Year	POPULATION (*millions*)	NO. OF WORKERS IN BASIC INDUSTRIES (*millions*)	PER CENT OF TOTAL POPULATION
1851	17.9	4.1	23
1901	32.5	4.9	15

And in speaking of the British working class the bourgeois student of "British imperialism at the beginning of the twentieth century" is obliged to distinguish systematically between the *"upper stratum"* of the workers and the *"lower stratum of the proletariat proper."* The upper stratum furnishes the main body of members of co-operatives, of trade unions, of sporting clubs and of numerous religious sects. The electoral system, which in Great Britain is still *"sufficiently restricted to exclude the lower stratum of the proletariat proper,"* is adapted to their level!! In order to present the condition of the British working class in the best possible light, only this upper stratum—which constitutes only a *minority* of the proletariat—is generally spoken of. For instance, "the problem of unemployment is mainly a London problem and that of the lower proletarian stratum, *which is of little political moment* for politicians."[14] It would be better to say: which is of little political moment for the bourgeois politicians and the "socialist" opportunists.

Another special feature of imperialism, which is connected with the facts we are describing, is the decline in emigration from imperialist countries, and the increase in immigration into these countries from the backward countries where lower wages are paid. As Hobson observes, emigration from Great Britain has been declining since 1884. In that year the number of emigrants was 242,000, while in 1900, the number was only 169,000. German emigration reached the highest point between 1880 and 1890, with a total of 1,453,000 emigrants. In the course of the following two decades, it fell to 544,000 and even to 341,000. On the other hand, there was an increase in the number of workers entering Germany from Austria, Italy, Russia and other countries. According to the 1907 census, there were 1,342,294 foreigners in Germany, of whom 440,800 were industrial workers and 257,329 were agricultural workers.[15] In France, the workers employed in the mining industry are, "in great part," foreigners: Polish, Italian and Spanish.[16] In the United States, immigrants from Eastern and Southern Europe are engaged in the most poorly paid occupations, while American workers provide the highest percentage of overseers or of the better paid workers.[17] Imperialism has the tendency to create privileged sections even among the workers, and to detach them from the main proletarian masses.

It must be observed that in Great Britain the tendency of imperialism to divide the workers, to encourage opportunism among them and to cause temporary decay in the working class movement, revealed itself much earlier than the end of the nineteenth and the beginning of the twentieth centuries; for two important distinguishing features of imperialism were observed in Great Britain in the

[14] Schulze-Gaevernitz, *Britischer Imperialismus*, pp. 246, 301, 317, 323, 324, 361.

[15] *Statistik des Deutschen Reichs* (*Statistics of the German Empire*), Vol. 211.

[16] Henger, *Die Kapitalsanlage der Franzosen* (*French Investments*), Stuttgart, 1913.

[17] Hourwich, *Immigration and Labour*, New York, 1913.

middle of the nineteenth century, *viz.*, vast colonial possessions and a monopolist position in the world market. Marx and Engels systematically traced this relation between opportunism in the labour movement and the imperialist features of British capitalism for several decades. For example, on October 7, 1858, Engels wrote to Marx:

"The English proletariat is becoming more and more bourgeois, so that this most bourgeois of all nations is apparently aiming ultimately at the possession of a bourgeois aristocracy, and a bourgeois proletariat *as well as* a bourgeoisie. For a nation which exploits the whole world this is, of course, to a certain extent justifiable."

Almost a quarter of a century later, in a letter dated August 11, 1881, Engels speaks of "...the worst type of English trade unions which allow themselves to be led by men sold to, or at least, paid by the bourgeoisie."[18] In a letter to Kautsky, dated September 12, 1882, Engels wrote:

"You ask me what the English workers think about colonial policy? Well, exactly the same as they think about politics in general. There is no workers' party here, there are only Conservatives and Liberal-Radicals, and the workers merrily share the feast of England's monopoly of the colonies and the world market...."[19] (Engels expressed similar ideas in the press in his preface to the second edition of *The Condition of the Working Class in England,* which appeared in 1892.)

We thus see clearly the causes and effects. The causes are: 1) Exploitation of the whole world by this country. 2) Its monopolistic position in the world market. 3) Its colonial monopoly. The effects are: 1) A section of the British proletariat becomes bourgeois. 2) A section of the proletariat permits itself to be led by men sold to, or at least, paid by the bourgeoisie. The imperialism of the beginning of the twentieth century completed the division of the world among a handful of states, each of which today exploits (*i.e.,* draws super-profits from) a part of the world only a little

[18] Marx and Engels, *Selected Correspondence, 1846–1895,* International Publishers, New York, 1942, pp. 115–16, 399.—*Ed.*

[19] *Cf. Karl Kautsky, Sozialismus und Kolonialpolitik,* Berlin, 1907, p. 79; this pamphlet was written by Kautsky in those infinitely distant days when he was still a Marxist.

smaller than that which England exploited in 1858. Each of them, by means of trusts, cartels, finance capital, and debtor and creditor relations, occupies a monopoly position in the world market. Each of them enjoys to some degree a colonial monopoly. (We have seen that out of the total of 75,000,000 sq. km. which comprise the *whole* colonial world, *65,000,000* sq. km., or 86 per cent, belong to six great powers; *61,000,000* sq. km., or 81 per cent, belong to three powers.)

The distinctive feature of the present situation is the prevalence of economic and political conditions which could not but increase the irreconcilability between opportunism and the general and vital interests of the working class movement. Embryonic imperialism has grown into a dominant system; capitalist monopolies occupy first place in economics and politics; the division of the world has been completed. On the other hand, instead of an undisputed monopoly by Great Britain, we see a few imperialist powers contending for the right to share in this monopoly, and this struggle is characteristic of the whole period of the beginning of the twentieth century. Opportunism, therefore, cannot now triumph in the working class movement of any country for decades as it did in England in the second half of the nineteenth century. But, in a number of countries it has grown ripe, over-ripe, and rotten, and has become completely merged with bourgeois policy in the form of "social-chauvinism." [20]

[20] Russian social-chauvinism represented by Messrs. Potresov, Chkhenkeli, Maslov, etc., in its avowed form as well as in its tacit form, as represented by Messrs. Chkheidze, Skobelev, Axelrod, Martov, etc., also emerged from the Russian variety of opportunism, namely liquidationism.

CHAPTER IX

The Critique of Imperialism

By the critique of imperialism, in the broad sense of the term, we mean the attiude towards imperialist policy of the different classes of society as part of their general ideology.

The enormous dimensions of finance capital concentrated in a few hands and creating an extremely extensive and close network of ties and relationships which subordinate not only the small and medium, but also even the very small capitalists and small masters, on the one hand, and the intense struggle waged against other national state groups of financiers for the division of the world and domination over other countries, on the other hand, cause the wholesale transition of the possessing classes to the side of imperialism. The signs of the times are a "general" enthusiasm regarding its prospects, a passionate defence of imperialism, and every possible embellishment of its real nature. The imperialist ideology also penetrates the working class. There is no Chinese Wall between it and the other classes. The leaders of the so-called "Social-Democratic" Party of Germany are today justly called "social-imperialists," that is, socialists in words and imperialists in deeds; but as early as 1902, Hobson noted the existence of "Fabian imperialists" who belonged to the opportunist Fabian Society in England.

Bourgeois scholars and publicists usually come out in defence of imperialism in a somewhat veiled form, and obscure its complete domination and its profound roots; they strive to concentrate attention on partial and secondary details and do their very best to distract attention from the main issue by means of ridiculous schemes for "reform," such as police supervision of the trusts and banks, etc. Less frequently, cynical and frank imperialists speak out and are bold enough to admit the absurdity of the idea of reforming the fundamental features of imperialism.

We will give an example. The German imperialists attempt, in the magazine *Archives of World Economy,* to follow the movements for national emancipation in the colonies, particularly, of course, in colonies other than those belonging to Germany. They note the ferment and protest movements in India, the movement in Natal (South Africa), the movement in the Dutch East Indies, etc. One of them, commenting on an English report of the speeches delivered at a conference of subject peoples and races, held on June 28-30, 1910, at which representatives of various peoples subject to foreign domination in Africa, Asia and Europe were present, writes as follows in appraising the speeches delivered at this conference:

"We are told that we must fight against imperialism; that the dominant states should recognise the right of subject peoples to home rule; that an international tribunal should supervise the fulfilment of treaties concluded between the great powers and weak peoples. One does not get any further than the expression of these pious wishes. We see no trace of understanding of the fact that imperialism is indissolubly bound up with capitalism in its present form" (!!) "and therefore also no trace of the realisation that an open struggle against imperialism would be hopeless, unless, perhaps, the fight is confined to protests against certain of its especially abhorrent excesses."[1]

Since the reform of the basis of imperialism is a deception, a "pious wish," since the bourgeois representatives of the oppressed nations go no "further" forward, the bourgeois representatives of the oppressing nation go "further" *backward,* to servility, towards imperialism, concealed by the cloak of "science." "Logic," indeed!

The question as to whether it is possible to reform the basis of imperialism, whether to go forward to the accentuation and deepening of the antagonisms which it engenders, or backwards, towards allaying these antagonisms, is a fundamental question in the critique of imperialism. As a consequence of the fact that the political features of imperialism are reaction all along the line, and increased national oppression, resulting from the oppression of the financial oligarchy and the elimination of free competition, a petty-bourgeois—democratic opposition has been rising against imperialism in almost all imperialist countries since the beginning

[1] *Weltwirtschaftliches Archiv* (*Archives of World Economy*), Vol. II, pp. 194-95.

of the twentieth century. And the desertion of Kautsky and of the broad international Kautskyan trend from Marxism is displayed in the very fact that Kautsky not only did not trouble to oppose, not only was unable to oppose this petty-bourgeois reformist opposition, which is really reactionary in its economic basis, but in practice actually became merged with it.

In the United States, the imperialist war waged against Spain in 1898 stirred up the opposition of the "anti-imperialists," the last of the Mohicans of bourgeois democracy. They declared this war to be "criminal"; they denounced the annexation of foreign territories as being a violation of the Constitution, and denounced the "Jingo treachery" by means of which Aguinaldo, leader of the native Filipinos, was deceived (the Americans promised him the independence of his country, but later they landed troops and annexed it). They quoted the words of Lincoln:

> "When the white man governs himself, that is self-government; but when he governs himself and also governs another man, that is more than self-government—that is despotism."[2]

But while all this criticism shrank from recognising the indissoluble bond between imperialism and the trusts, and, therefore, between imperialism and the very foundations of capitalism; while it shrank from joining up with the forces engendered by large-scale capitalism and its development—it remained a "pious wish."

This is also, in the main, the attitude of Hobson in his criticism of imperialism. Hobson anticipated Kautsky in protesting against the "inevitability of imperialism" argument, and in urging the need to raise the consuming capacity of the "people" (under capitalism!). The petty-bourgeois point of view in the critique of imperialism, the domination of the banks, the financial oligarchy, etc., is that adopted by the authors we have often quoted, such as Agahd, A. Lansburgh, L. Eschwege; and among French writers, Victor Bérard, author of a superficial book entitled *England and Imperialism* which appeared in 1900. All these authors, who make

[2] Quoted by Patouillet, *L'impérialisme américain*, Dijon, 1904, p. 272. (From speech "On the Repeal of the Missouri Compromise," at Peoria, Illinois, October 16, 1854.—*Ed.*)

no claim to be Marxists, contrast imperialism with free competition and democracy; they condemn the Bagdad railway scheme as leading to disputes and war, utter "pious wishes" for peace, etc. This applies also to the compiler of international stock and share issue statistics, A. Neymarck, who, after calculating the hundreds of billions of francs representing "international" securities, exclaimed in 1912: "Is it possible to believe that peace may be disturbed... that, in the face of these enormous figures, anyone would risk starting a war?"[3]

Such simplicity of mind on the part of the bourgeois economists is not surprising. Besides, *it is in their interest* to pretend to be so naive and to talk "seriously" about peace under imperialism. But what remains of Kautsky's Marxism, when, in 1914-15-16, he takes up the same attitude as the bourgeois reformists and affirms that "everybody is agreed" (imperialists, pseudo-socialists and social-pacifists) as regards peace? Instead of an analysis of imperialism and an exposure of the depths of its contradictions, we have nothing but a reformist "pious wish" to wave it aside, to evade it.

Here is an example of Kautsky's economic criticism of imperialism. He takes the statistics of the British export and import trade with Egypt for 1872 and 1912. These statistics show that this export and import trade has developed more slowly than British foreign trade as a whole. From this Kautsky concludes that:

> "We have no reason to suppose that British trade with Egypt would have been less developed simply as a result of the mere operation of economic factors, without military occupation.... The urge of the present-day states to expand...can be best promoted, not by the violent methods of imperialism, but by peaceful democracy."[4]

This argument, which is repeated in every key by Kautsky's Russian armour-bearer (and Russian protector of the social-chauvinists), Mr. Spectator, represents the basis of Kautskyan criticism of imperialism and that is why we must deal with it in greater detail. We will begin with a quotation from Hilferding, whose

[3] *Bulletin de l'Institut International de Statistique*, Vol. XIX, Book II, p. 225.

[4] Karl Kautsky, *Nationalstaat, imperialistischer Staat und Staatenbund* (*National State, Imperialist State and Union of States*), Nuremberg, 1915, pp. 72, 70.

conclusions, as Kautsky on many occasions, and notably in April 1915, declared, have been "unanimously adopted by all socialist theoreticians."

> "It is not the business of the proletariat," writes Hilferding, "to contrast the more progressive capitalist policy with that of the now by-gone era of free trade and of hostility towards the state. The reply of the proletariat to the economic policy of finance capital, to imperialism, cannot be free trade, but socialism. The aim of proletarian policy cannot now be the ideal of restoring free competition—which has now become a reactionary ideal—but the complete abolition of competition by the vanquishment of capitalism."[5]

Kautsky departed from Marxism by advocating what is, in the period of finance capital, a "reactionary ideal," "peaceful democracy," "the mere operation of economic factors," for *objectively* this ideal drags us back from monopoly capitalism to the non-monopolist stage, and is a reformist swindle.

Trade with Egypt (or with any other colony or semi-colony) "would have grown more" *without* military occupation, without imperialism, and without finance capital. What does this mean? That capitalism would develop more rapidly if free competition were not restricted by monopolies in general, by the "connections" or the yoke (*i.e.,* also the monopoly) of finance capital, or by the monopolist possession of colonies by certain countries?

Kautsky's argument can have no other meaning; and *this* "meaning" is meaningless. But suppose, for the sake of argument, free competition, without any sort of monopoly, *would* develop capitalism and trade more rapidly. Is it not a fact that the more rapidly trade and capitalism develop, the greater is the concentration of production and capital which *gives rise* to monopoly? And monopolies have *already* come into being—precisely *out of* free competition! Even if monopolies have now begun to retard progress, it is not an argument in favour of free competition, which has become impossible since it gave rise to monopoly.

Whichever way one turns Kautsky's argument, one will find nothing in it except reaction and bourgeois reformism.

[5] Hilferding, *op. cit.,* pp. 471-72.

Even if we modify this argument and say, as Spectator says, that the trade of the British colonies with the mother country is now developing more slowly than their trade with other countries, it does not save Kautsky; for it is *also* monopoly and imperialism that is beating Great Britain, only it is the monopoly and imperialism of another country (America, Germany). It is known that the cartels have given rise to a new and peculiar form of protective tariffs, *i.e.*, goods suitable for export are protected (Engels noted this in Vol. III of *Capital*). It is known, too, that the cartels and finance capital have a system peculiar to themselves, that of "exporting goods at cut-rate prices," or "dumping," as the English call it: within a given country the cartel sells its goods at a high price fixed by monopoly; abroad it sells them at a much lower price to undercut the competitor, to enlarge its own production to the utmost, etc. If Germany's trade with the British colonies is developing more rapidly than that of Great Britain with the same colonies, it only proves that German imperialism is younger, stronger and better organised than British imperialism, is superior to it. But this by no means proves the "superiority" of free trade, for it is not free trade fighting against protection and colonial dependence, but two rival imperialisms, two monopolies, two groups of finance capital that are fighting. The superiority of German imperialism over British imperialism is stronger than the wall of colonial frontiers or of protective tariffs. To use this as an argument *in favour* of free trade and "peaceful democracy" is banal, is to forget the essential features and qualities of imperialism, to substitute petty-bourgeois reformism for Marxism.

It is interesting to note that even the bourgeois economist, A. Lansburgh, whose criticism of imperialism is as petty-bourgeois as Kautsky's, nevertheless got closer to a more scientific study of trade statistics. He did not compare merely one country, chosen at random, and a colony, with the other countries; he examined the export trade of an imperialist country: 1) with countries which are financially dependent upon it, which borrow money from it; and 2) with countries which are financially independent. He obtained the following results:

EXPORT TRADE OF GERMANY (*million marks*)

COUNTRIES FINANCIALLY DEPENDENT ON GERMANY	1889	1908	PER CENT INCREASE
Rumania	48.2	70.8	47
Portugal	19.0	32.8	73
Argentina	60.7	147.0	143
Brazil	48.7	84.5	73
Chile	28.3	52.4	85
Turkey	29.9	64.0	114
Total	234.8	451.5	92
COUNTRIES FINANCIALLY INDEPENDENT OF GERMANY			
Great Britain	651.8	997.4	53
France	210.2	437.9	108
Belgium	137.2	322.8	135
Switzerland	177.4	401.1	127
Australia	21.2	64.5	205
Dutch East Indies	8.8	40.7	363
Total	1,206.6	2,264.4	87

Lansburgh did not draw *conclusions* and therefore, strangely enough, failed to observe that *if* the figures prove anything at all, they prove that *he is wrong,* for the exports to countries financially dependent on Germany have grown *more rapidly,* if only slightly, than those to the countries which are financially independent. (We emphasise the "if," for Lansburgh's figures are far from complete.)

Tracing the connection between export trade and loans, Lansburgh writes:

"In 1890-91, a Rumanian loan was floated through the German banks, which had already in previous years made advances on this loan. The loan was used chiefly for purchases of railway materials in Germany. In 1891 German exports to Rumania amounted to 55,000,000 marks. The following year they fell to 39,400,000 marks; then with fluctuations, to 25,400,000 in 1900. Only in very recent years have they regained the level of 1891, thanks to several new loans.

"German exports to Portugal rose, following the loans of 1888-89, to

21,100,000 (1890); then fell, in the two following years, to 16,200,000 and 7,400,000; and only regained their former level in 1903.

"German trade with the Argentine is still more striking. Following the loans floated in 1888 and 1890, German exports to the Argentine reached, in 1889, 60,700,000 marks. Two years later they only reached 18,600,000 marks, that is to say, less than one-third of the previous figure. It was not until 1901 that they regained and surpassed the level of 1889, and then only as a result of new loans floated by the state and by municipalities, with advances to build power stations, and with other credit operations.

"Exports to Chile rose to 45,200,000 marks in 1892, after the loan negotiated in 1889. The following year they fell to 22,500,000 marks. A new Chilean loan floated by the German banks in 1906 was followed by a rise of exports in 1907 to 84,700,000 marks, only to fall again to 52,400,000 marks in 1908."[6]

From all these facts Lansburgh draws the amusing petty-bourgeois moral of how unstable and irregular export trade is when it is bound up with loans, how bad it is to invest capital abroad instead of "naturally" and "harmoniously" developing home industry, how "costly" is the *backsheesh* that Krupp has to pay in floating foreign loans, etc.! But the facts are clear. The increase in exports is *closely* connected with the swindling tricks of finance capital, which is not concerned with bourgeois morality, but with skinning the ox twice—first, it pockets the profits from the loan; then it pockets other profits from the *same* loan which the borrower uses to make purchases from Krupp, or to purchase railway material from the Steel Syndicate, etc.

We repeat that we do not by any means consider Lansburgh's figures to be perfect. But we had to quote them because they are more scientific than Kautsky's and Spectator's, and because Lansburgh showed the correct way of approaching the question. In discussing the significance of finance capital in regard to exports, etc., one must be able to single out the connection of exports especially and solely with the tricks of the financiers, especially and solely with the sale of goods by cartels, etc. Simply to compare colonies with non-colonies, one imperialism with another imperialism,

[6] *Die Bank*, 1909, Vol. II, pp. 826-27.

one semi-colony or colony (Egypt) with all other countries, is to evade and to tone down the very *essence* of the question.

Kautsky's theoretical critique of imperialism has nothing in common with Marxism and serves no other purpose than as a preamble to propaganda for peace and unity with the opportunists and the social-chauvinists, precisely for the reason that it evades and obscures the very profound and radical contradictions of imperialism: the contradictions between monopoly and free competition that exists side by side with it, betwen the gigantic "operations" (and gigantic profits) of finance capital and "honest" trade in the free market, the contradictions between cartels and trusts, on the one hand, and non-cartelised industry, on the other, etc.

The notorious theory of "ultra-imperialism," invented by Kautsky, is equally reactionary. Compare his arguments on this subject in 1915, with Hobson's arguments in 1902.

Kautsky:

"Cannot the present imperialist policy be supplanted by a new, ultra-imperialist policy, which will introduce the common exploitation of the world by internationally united finance capital in place of the mutual rivalries of national finance capital? Such a new phase of capitalism is at any rate conceivable. Can it be achieved? Sufficient premises are still lacking to enable us to answer this question." [7]

Hobson:

"Christendom thus laid out in a few great federal empires, each with a retinue of uncivilised dependencies, seems to many the most legitimate development of present tendencies, and one which would offer the best hope of permanent peace on an assured basis of inter-imperialism." [8]

Kautsky called ultra-imperialism or super-imperialism what Hobson, thirteen years earlier, described as inter-imperialism. Except for coining a new and clever word, by replacing one Latin prefix by another, the only progress Kautsky has made in the sphere of "scientific" thought is that he has labelled as Marxism what Hobson, in effect, described as the cant of English parsons. After the Anglo-Boer War it was quite natural for this worthy caste

[7] *Die Neue Zeit,* April 30, 1915, p. 144.

[8] Hobson, *op. cit.*, p. 351.

to exert every effort to *console* the British middle class and the workers who had lost many of their relatives on the battlefields of South Africa and who were obliged to pay higher taxes in order to guarantee still higher profits for the British financiers. And what better consolation could there be than the theory that imperialism is not so bad; that it stands close to inter- (or ultra-) imperialism, which can ensure permanent peace? No matter what the good intentions of the English parsons, or of sentimental Kautsky, may have been, the only objective, *i.e.*, real, social significance Kautsky's "theory" can have, is that of a most reactionary method of consoling the masses with hopes of permanent peace being possible under capitalism, distracting their attention from the sharp antagonisms and acute problems of the present era, and directing it towards illusory prospects of an imaginary "ultra-imperialism" of the future. Deception of the masses—there is nothing but this in Kautsky's "Marxian" theory.

Indeed, it is enough to compare well-known and indisputable facts to become convinced of the utter falsity of the prospects which Kautsky tries to conjure up before the German workers (and the workers of all lands). Let us consider India, Indo-China and China. It is known that these three colonial and semi-colonial countries, inhabited by six to seven hundred million human beings, are subjected to the exploitation of the finance capital of several imperialist states: Great Britain, France, Japan, the U.S.A., etc. We will asume that these imperialist countries form alliances against one another in order to protect and extend their possessions, their interests and their "spheres of influence" in these Asiatic states; these alliances will be "inter-imperialist," or "ultra-imperialist" alliances. We will assume that *all* the imperialist countries conclude an alliance for the "peaceful" division of these parts of Asia; this alliance would be an alliance of "internationally united finance capital." As a matter of fact, alliances of this kind have been made in the twentieth century, notably with regard to China. We ask, is it "conceivable," assuming that the capitalist system remains intact—and this is precisely the assumption that Kautsky does make—that such alliances would be more than temporary, that they would eliminate friction, conflicts and struggle in all and every possible form?

This question need only be stated clearly enough to make it impossible for any other reply to be given than that in the negative, for there can be *no* other conceivable basis under capitalism for the division of spheres of influence, of interests, of colonies, etc., than a calculation of the *strength* of the participants in the division, their general economic, financial, military strength, etc. And the strength of these participants in the division does not change to an equal degree, for under capitalism the development of different undertakings, trusts, branches of industry, or countries cannot be *even*. Half a century ago, Germany was a miserable, insignificant country, as far as its capitalist strength was concerned, compared with the strength of England at that time. Japan was similarly insignificant compared with Russia. Is it "conceivable" that in ten or twenty years' time the relative strength of the imperialist powers will have remained *un*changed? Absolutely inconceivable.

Therefore, in the realities of the capitalist system, and not in the banal philistine fantasies of English parsons, or of the German "Marxist," Kautsky, "inter-imperialist" or "ultra-imperialist" alliances, no matter what form they may assume, whether of one imperialist coalition against another, or of a general alliance embracing *all* the imperialist powers, are *inevitably* nothing more than a "truce" in periods between wars. Peaceful alliances prepare the ground for wars, and in their turn grow out of wars; the one is the condition for the other, giving rise to alternating forms of peaceful and non-peaceful struggle out of *one and the same* basis of imperialist connections and the relations between world economics and world politics. But in order to pacify the workers and to reconcile them with the social-chauvinists who have deserted to the side of the bourgeoisie, wise Kautsky *separates* one link of a single chain from the other, separates the present peaceful (and ultra-imperialist, nay, ultra-ultra-imperialist) alliance of *all* the powers for the "pacification" of China (remember the suppression of the Boxer Rebellion) from the non-peaceful conflict of tomorrow, which will prepare the ground for another "peaceful" general alliance for the partition, say, of Turkey, on the day after tomorrow, etc., etc. Instead of showing the vital connection between periods of imperialist peace and periods of imperialist war, Kautsky puts before the workers a lifeless abstraction solely in order to reconcile them to their lifeless leaders.

An American writer, Hill, in his *History of Diplomacy in the International Development of Europe*,[9] points out in his preface the following periods of contemporary diplomatic history: 1) The era of revolution; 2) The constitutional movement; 3) The present era of "commercial imperialism." Another writer divides the history of Great Britain's foreign policy since 1870 into four periods: 1) The first Asiatic period (that of the struggle against Russia's advance in Central Asia towards India); 2) The African period (approximately 1885-1902): that of struggles against France for the partition of Africa (the Fashoda incident of 1898 which brought France within a hair's breadth of war with Great Britain); 3) The second Asiatic period (alliance with Japan against Russia), and 4) The European period, chiefly anti-German.[10] "The political skirmishes of outposts take place on the financial field," wrote Riesser, the banker, in 1905, in showing how French finance capital operating in Italy was preparing the way for a political alliance of these countries, and how a conflict was developing between Great Britain and Germany over Persia, between all the European capitalists over Chinese loans, etc. Behold, the living reality of peaceful "ultra-imperialist" alliances in their indissoluble connection with ordinary imperialist conflicts!

Kautsky's toning down of the deepest contradictions of imperialism, which inevitably becomes the embellishment of imperialism, leaves its traces in this writer's criticism of the political features of imperialism. Imperialism is the epoch of finance capital and of monopolies, which introduce everywhere the striving for domination, not for freedom. The result of these tendencies is reaction all along the line, whatever the political system, and an extreme intensification of existing antagonisms in this domain also. Par-

[9] David Jayne Hill, *A History of Diplomacy in the International Development of Europe*, Vol. I, p. x.

[10] Schilder, *op. cit.*, Vol. I, p. 178.

ticularly acute becomes the yoke of national oppression and the striving for annexations, *i.e.*, the violation of national independence (for annexation is nothing but the violation of the right of nations to self-determination). Hilferding justly draws attention to the connection between imperialism and the growth of national oppression.

"In the newly opened up countries themselves," he writes, "the capitalism imported into them intensifies contradictions and excites the constantly growing resistance against the intruders of the peoples who are awakening to national consciousness. This resistance can easily become transformed into dangerous measures directed against foreign capital. The old social relations become completely revolutionised. The age-long agrarian incrustation of 'nations without a history' is blasted away, and they are drawn into the capitalist whirlpool. Capitalism itself gradually procures for the vanquished the means and resources for their emancipation and they set out to achieve the same goal which once seemed highest to the European nations: the creation of a united national state as a means to economic and cultural freedom. This movement for national independence threatens European capital just in its most valuable and most promising fields of exploitation, and European capital can maintain its domination only by continually increasing its means of exerting violence."[11]

To this must be added that it is not only in newly opened up countries, but also in the old, that imperialism is leading to annexation, to increased national oppression, and, consequently, also to increasing resistance. While opposing the intensification of political reaction caused by imperialism, Kautsky obscures the question, which has become very serious, of the impossibility of unity with the opportunists in the epoch of imperialism. While objecting to annexations, he presents his objections in a form that will be most acceptable and least offensive to the opportunists. He addresses himself to a German audience, yet he obscures the most topical and important point, for instance, the annexation by Germany of Alsace-Lorraine. In order to appraise this "lapse of mind" of Kautsky's we will take the following example. Let us suppose that a Japanese

[11] Hilferding, *op. cit.*, p. 406.

is condemning the annexation of the Philippine Islands by the Americans. Will many believe that he is doing so because he has a horror of annexations as such, and not because he himself has a desire to annex the Philippines? And shall we not be constrained to admit that the "fight" the Japanese are waging against annexations can be regarded as being sincere and politically honest only if he fights against the annexation of Korea by Japan, and urges freedom for Korea to secede from Japan?

Kautsky's theoretical analysis of imperialism, as well as his economic and political criticism of imperialism, are permeated *through and through* with a spirit, absolutely irreconcilable with Marxism, of obscuring and glossing over the most profound contradictions of imperialism and with a striving to preserve the crumbling unity with opportunism in the European labour movement at all costs.

CHAPTER X

The Place of Imperialism in History

We have seen that the economic quintessence of imperialism is monopoly capitalism. This very fact determines its place in history, for monopoly that grew up on the basis of free competition, and precisely out of free competition, is the transition from the capitalist system to a higher social-economic order. We must take special note of the four principal forms of monopoly, or the four principal manifestations of monopoly capitalism, which are characteristic of the epoch under review.

Firstly, monopoly arose out of the concentration of production at a very advanced stage of development. This refers to the monopolist capitalist combines, cartels, syndicates and trusts. We have seen the important part that these play in modern economic life. At the beginning of the twentieth century, monopolies acquired complete supremacy in the advanced countries. And although the first steps towards the formation of the cartels were first taken by countries enjoying the protection of high tariffs (Germany, America), Great Britain, with her system of free trade, was not far behind in revealing the same basic phenomenon, namely, the birth of monopoly out of the concentration of production.

Secondly, monopolies have accelerated the capture of the most important sources of raw materials, especially for the coal and iron industries, which are the basic and most highly cartelised industries in capitalist society. The monopoly of the most important sources of raw materials has enormously increased the power of big capital, and has sharpened the antagonism between cartelised and non-cartelised industry.

Thirdly, monopoly has sprung from the banks. The banks have developed from modest intermediary enterprises into the monopolists of finance capital. Some three or five of the biggest banks in each of the foremost capitalist countries have achieved the "personal union" of industrial and bank capital, and have concentrated in their hands the disposal of thousands upon thousands of millions which form the greater part of the capital and income of entire countries. A financial oligarchy, which throws a close net of relations of dependence over all the economic and political institutions of contemporary bourgeois society without exception—such is the most striking manifestation of this monopoly.

Fourthly, monopoly has grown out of colonial policy. To the numerous "old" motives of colonial policy, finance capital has added the struggle for the sources of raw materials, for the export of capital, for "spheres of influence," *i.e.*, for spheres for profitable deals, concessions, monopolist profits and so on; in fine, for economic territory in general. When the colonies of the European powers in Africa, for instance, comprised only one-tenth of that territory (as was the case in 1876), colonial policy was able to develop by methods other than those of monopoly—by the "free grabbing" of territories, so to speak. But when nine-tenths of Africa had been seized (approximately by 1900), when the whole world had been divided up, there was inevitably ushered in a period of colonial monopoly and, consequently, a period of particularly intense struggle for the division and the redivision of the world.

The extent to which monopolist capital has intensified all the contradictions of capitalism is generally known. It is sufficient to mention the high cost of living and the oppression of the cartels. This intensification of contradictions constitutes the most powerful driving force of the transitional period of history, which began from the time of the definite victory of world finance capital.

Monopolies, oligarchy, the striving for domination instead of the striving for liberty, the exploitation of an increasing number of small or weak nations by an extremely small group of the richest or most powerful nations—all these have given birth to those distinctive characteristics of imperialism which compel us to define it as parasitic or decaying capitalism. More and more prominently there emerges, as one of the tendencies of imperialism, the creation of the "bondholding" (rentier) state, the usurer state, in which the bourgeoisie lives on the proceeds of capital exports and by "clipping coupons." It would be a mistake to believe that this tendency to decay precludes the possibility of the rapid growth of capitalism. It does not. In the epoch of imperialism, certain branches of industry, certain strata of the bourgeoisie and certain countries betray, to a more or less degree, one or other of these tendencies. On the whole, capitalism is growing far more rapidly than before. But this growth is not only becoming more and more uneven in general; its unevenness also manifests itself, in particular, in the decay of the countries which are richest in capital (such as England).

In regard to the rapidity of Germany's economic development, Riesser, the author of the book on the big German banks, states:

> "The progress of the preceding period (1848-70), which had not been exactly slow, stood in about the same ratio to the rapidity with which the whole of Germany's national economy, and with it German banking, progressed during this period (1870-1905) as the mail coach of the Holy Roman Empire of the German nation stood to the speed of the present-day automobile ... which in whizzing past, it must be said, often endangers not only innocent pedestrians in its path, but also the occupants of the car." [1]

In its turn, this finance capital which has grown so rapidly is not unwilling (precisely because it has grown so quickly) to pass on to a more "tranquil" possession of colonies which have to be seized—and not only by peaceful methods—from richer nations. In the United States, economic development in the last decades has been even more rapid than in Germany, and *for this very reason* the parasitic character of modern American capitalism has stood out with particular prominence. On the other hand, a comparison of, say, the republican American bourgeoisie with the monarchist Japanese or German bourgeoisie shows that the most pronounced political distinctions diminish to an extreme degree in the epoch of imperialism—not because they are unimportant in general, but because in all these cases we are discussing a bourgeoisie which has definite features of parasitism.

[1] Riesser, *op. cit.*, third ed., p. 354.—*Ed.*

The receipt of high monopoly profits by the capitalists in one of the numerous branches of industry, in one of numerous countries, etc., makes it economically possible for them to corrupt certain sections of the working class, and for a time a fairly considerable minority, and win them to the side of the bourgeoisie of a given industry or nation against all the others. The intensification of antagonisms between imperialist nations for the division of the world increases this striving. And so there is created that bond between imperialism and opportunism, which revealed itself first and most clearly in England, owing to the fact that certain features of imperialist development were observable there much earlier than in other countries.

Some writers, L. Martov, for example, try to evade the fact that there is a connection between imperialism and opportunism in the labour movement—which is particularly striking at the present time—by resorting to "official optimistic" arguments (*à la* Kautsky and Huysmans) like the following: the cause of the opponents of capitalism would be hopeless if it were precisely progressive capitalism that led to the increase of opportunism, or, if it were precisely the best paid workers who were inclined towards opportunism, etc. We must have no illusion regarding "optimism" of this kind. It is optimism in regard to opportunism; it is optimism which serves to conceal opportunism. As a matter of fact the extraordinary rapidity and the particularly revolting character of the development of opportunism is by no means a guarantee that its victory will be durable: the rapid growth of a malignant abscess on a healthy body only causes it to burst more quickly and thus to relieve the body of it. The most dangerous people of all in this respect are those who do not wish to understand that the fight against imperialism is a sham and humbug unless it is inseparably bound up with the fight against opportunism.

From all that has been said in this book on the economic nature of imperialism, it follows that we must define it as capitalism in transition, or, more precisely, as moribund capitalism. It is very instructive in this respect to note that the bourgeois economists, in describing modern capitalism, frequently employ terms like "interlocking," "absence of isolation," etc.; "in conformity with their functions and course of development," banks are "not purely private business enterprises; they are more and more outgrowing the sphere of purely private business regulation." And this very Riesser, who uttered the words just quoted, declares with all seriousness that the "prophecy" of the Marxists concerning "socialisation" has "not come true"!

What then does this word "interlocking" express? It merely expresses the most striking feature of the process going on before our eyes. It shows that the observer counts the separate trees, but cannot see the wood. It slavishly copies the superficial, the fortuitous, the chaotic. It reveals the observer as one who is overwhelmed by the mass of raw material and is utterly incapable of appreciating its meaning and importance. Ownership of shares and relations between owners of private property "interlock in a haphazard way." But the underlying factor of this interlocking, its very base, is the changing social relations of production. When a big enterprise assumes gigantic proportions, and, on the basis of exact computation of mass data, organises according to plan the supply of primary raw materials to the extent of two-thirds, or three-fourths of all that is necessary for tens of millions of people; when the raw materials are transported to the most suitable place of production, sometimes hundreds or thousands of miles away, in a systematic and organised manner; when a single centre directs all the successive stages of work right up to the manufacture of numerous varieties of finished articles; when these products are distributed according to a single plan among tens and hundreds of millions of consumers (as in the case of the distribution of oil in America and Germany by the American "oil trust")—then it becomes evident that we have socialisation of production, and not mere "interlocking"; that private economic relations and private property relations constitute a shell which is no longer suitable for its contents, a shell which must inevitably begin to decay if its destruction be delayed by artificial means; a shell which may continue in a state of decay for a fairly long period (particularly if the cure of the opportunist abscess is protracted), but which will inevitably be removed.

The enthusiastic admirer of German imperialism, Schulze-Gaevernitz, exclaims:

"Once the supreme management of the German banks has been entrusted to the hands of a dozen persons, their activity is even today more significant for the public good than that of the majority of the Ministers of State." (The "interlocking" of bankers, ministers, magnates of industry and rentiers is here conveniently forgotten.)... "If we conceive of the tendencies of development which we have noted as realised to the utmost: the money capital of the nation united in the banks; the banks themselves combined into cartels; the investment capital of the nation cast in the shape of securities, then the brilliant forecast of Saint-Simon will be fulfilled: 'The present anarchy of production caused by the fact that economic relations are developing without uniform regulation must make way for organisation in production. Production will no longer be shaped by isolated manufacturers, independent of each other and ignorant of man's economic needs, but by a social institution. A central body of management, being able to survey the large fields of social economy from a more elevated point of view, will regulate it for the benefit of the whole of society, will be able to put the means of production into suitable hands, and above all will take care that there be constant harmony between production and consumption. Institutions already exist which have assumed as part of their task a certain organisation of economic labour: the banks.' The fulfilment of the forecasts of Saint-Simon still lies in the future, but we are on the way to its fulfilment—Marxism, different from what Marx imagined, but different only in form." [2]

A crushing "refutation" of Marx, indeed! It is a retreat from Marx's precise, scientific analysis to Saint-Simon's guesswork, the guesswork of a genius, but guesswork all the same.

January-July, 1916.

[2] Schulze-Gaevernitz, in *Grundriss der Socialökonomik*, pp. 145-46.

OTHER BOOKS BY FREDERICK ELLIS

(Buy Direct at 35% off – Contact frederick659@yahoo.com)

Author - Jack London

MARTIN EDEN

WAR OF THE CLASSES

JOHN BARLEYCORN

THE PEOPLE OF THE ABYSS

JACK LONDON ON THE ROAD

THE ASSASSINATION BUREAU, LTD.

THE IRON HEEL

Author – B. Traven

GENERAL FROM THE JUNGLE

THE DEATH SHIP

THE REBELLION OF THE HANGED

THE WHITE ROSE

THE BRIDGE IN THE JUNGLE

MARCH TO THE MONTERIA

THE TREASURE OF THE SIERRA MADRE

Author - Carl Frederick

est PLAYING THE GAME THE NEW WAY

Authors - Frederick Ellis & Carl Frederick

THE OAKLAND STATEMENT

Author – Mao Tsetung

QUOTATIONS FROM CHAIRMAN MAO TSETUNG

Author – Upton Sinclair

OUR LADY

THE FLIVVER KING: THE STORY OF FORD-AMERICA

ONE HUNDRED PERCENT: THE STORY OF A PATRIOT

WORLD'S END I

WORLD'S END II

THE SECRET LIFE OF JESUS

THE MONEYCHANGERS

MENTAL RADIO

THE MILLENNIUM

A PERSONAL JESUS

PROFITS OF RELIGION

THEY CALL ME CARPENTER: A TALE OF THE SECOND COMING

Author – Thomas Paine

COMMON SENSE, THE RIGHTS OF MAN & THE AGE OF REASON

THE AMERICAN CRISIS

Author – Karl Marx

DAS KAPITAL

THE COMMUNIST MANIFESTO & WAGES, PRICE AND PROFIT

WAGE-LABOUR AND CAPITAL & VALUE. PRICE AND PROFIT

Author – Eugene Debs

WALLS AND BARS

Author – Jean-Jacques Rousseau

THE SOCIAL CONTRACT

Author – John Reed

TEN DAYS THAT SHOOK THE WORLD

INSURGENT MEXICO

Author – Antonio Gramsci

THE MODERN PRINCE AND SELECTED WRITINGS

Author – V. I. Lenin

THE STATE AND REVOLUTION

FIGHT AGAINST STALINISM & IMPERIALISM: THE HIGHEST STAGE OF CAPITALISM

Author – David Ricardo

PRINCIPLES OF POLITICAL ECONOMY AND TAXATION

Author – Thomas Jefferson

BIOGRAPHY OF THOMAS JEFFERSON & THE LIFE AND MORALS OF JESUS OF NAZARETH

Author – Emma Goldman

ANARCHISM AND OTHER WRITINGS

Author – Rosa Luxemburg

REFORM OR REVOLUTION & THE MASS STRIKE

Author – John Stuart Mill

ON SOCIALISM & THE SUBJECTION OF WOMEN

Author – THE HOLY SPIRIT

THE GOOD NEWS: AS TOLD BY MATTHEW, MARK, LUKE AND JOHN

Author – John Quincy Adams

THE AMISTAD ARGUMENT & THE STATE OF THE UNION ADDRESSES

www.ingramcontent.com/pod-product-compliance
Lightning Source LLC
Chambersburg PA
CBHW021535260326
41914CB00001B/25

* 9 7 8 0 9 7 9 3 3 6 3 7 9 *